POLITICAL VIEWS AND THOUGHTS OF NEHRU

POLITICAL VIEWS AND THOUGHTS OF NEHRU

H.K. Gusain

CYBER TECH PUBLICATIONS
4264/3, Ansari Road, Daryaganj, New Delhi-110002 (India)
Ph.: 011-23244078. Fax: 011-23280028
E-Mail: cyberpublicationsdelhi@yahoo.com

POLITICAL VIEWS AND THOUGHTS OF NEHRU

H.K. Gusain

First Edition 2009

Published by :

G.S. Rawat for **Cyber Tech Publications**
4264/3, Ansari Road, Daryaganj, New Delhi-110002 (India)
Ph.: 011-23244078. Fax: 011-23280028
E-Mail: cyberpublicationsdelhi@yahoo.com

Printed at : Asian Offset Printers

Preface

Nehru was a political leader, a politician, one who has devoted most of his life to the practice rather than the theory of politics. However, we must note the fact that through- out his career Nehru has maintained a more than casual interest in theory as well. His considerable reading and philosophical bent of mind have enabled him to interpret day-to-day political problems with broad theoretical perspective.

This book is an attempt to draw together Nehru's ideas regarding democracy, and to present them in logical arrange-ment — a task which Nehru himself has never undertaken. It is the author's earnest hope that this work may contribute to a better understanding of Nehru and what he stands for. The future of Asia is very much in the balance. It may well hinge on the ultimate success or failure of India's democratic experi-ment under the leadership of Jawaharlal Nehru. The facts certainly point to the need for a clearer understanding of the man upon whom so much depends.

The study is basically an exposition of Nehru's *ideas*. But it is not thereby implied that political theories are or should be speculative and somehow divorced from the realities of political life. As the author has so clearly pointed out, theories of politics are themselves a part of politics. In other words, they do not refer to an.external reality but are produced as a normal art of the social *milieu* in which politics itself has its being. The attempt has been made to present Nehru's ideas against the background of the situation in modern India — for it is in this context that his ideas have developed. However, it would obviously be impossible to include within the scope of this book a detailed description of all of the social, economic, and political factors which impinge on Nehru's thought. The reader's general orientation with regard to these facts must to a certain extent be presupposed.

— *Author*

CONTENTS

1

Birth and Early Life

Pandit Jawaharlal Nehru (November 14,1889–May 27, 1964) was a major political leader of the Congress Party, a pivotal figure in the Indian independence movement and the first Prime Minister of independent India. He was also a key figure in international politics in the post-war period (in which he was considered the leader of third world interests) and patriarch of the Nehru-Gandhi family, one of the most influential forces in Indian politics. He is popularly referred to as Panditji (*Scholar*) and Pandit Nehru.

The son of the wealthy Indian barrister and politician Motilal Nehru, Nehru became a leader of the left-wing of the Indian National Congress at a remarkably young age. Rising to Congress President under the mentorship of Mahatma Gandhi, Nehru was a charismatic, radical leader, advocating complete independence from the British Empire, and was eventually recognised as Gandhi's political heir. A life-long liberal intellectually, Nehru was also an advocate for Fabian socialism and the public sector as the means by which long-standing challenges of economic development could be addressed.

Serving as Congress President, Nehru raised the flag of independent India in New Delhi on August 15, 1947, and served as Prime Minister. His daughter Indira and grandson Rajiv would both also serve as Prime Minister and President of the Indian National Congress, as would Rajiv's wife Sonia. His long tenure was instrumental in shaping the traditions and structures of independent India.

EARLY LIFE

Jawaharlal Nehru was born in the city of Allahabad, situated along the banks of the Ganges River (now in the state of Uttar Pradesh). He was the eldest child of Swarup Rani, the wife of wealthy barrister Motilal Nehru. The Nehru family descended from Kashmiri heritage and belonged to the Saraswat Brahmin caste of Hindus. Training as a lawyer, Motilal had moved to Allahabad and developed a successful practise and had become active in India's largest political party, the Indian National Congress. Nehru and his sisters — Vijaya Lakshmi and Krishna — lived in a large mansion called Anand Bhavan and were raised with English customs, mannerisms and dress. While learning Hindi and Sanskrit, the Nehru children would be trained to converse fluently and regularly in English.

After being tutored at home and attending some of the most modern schools in India, Nehru travelled to England at the age of 15 to attend Harrow. Nicknamed "Joe" while there, he proceeded to study natural sciences at Trinity College, Cambridge before choosing to train as a barrister at the Inner Temple in London. Frequenting the theatres, museums and opera houses of London, he would spend his vacations travelling across Europe. Observers later described him as an elegant, charming young intellectual and socialite. Nehru also actively participated in the political activities of the Indian student community, growing increasingly attracted to socialism and liberalism, which were beginning to influence the politics and economies of Europe.

Upon his return to India, Nehru's marriage was arranged with Kamala Kaul. Married on February 8, 1916, Nehru was 27 and his bride was 17 years old, at the time. The first few years of their marriage were hampered by the cultural gulf between the anglicized Nehru and Kamala, who observed Hindu traditions and focused on family affairs. The following year Kamala gave birth to their only child, their daughter Indira Priyadarshini. Having made few attempts to establish himself in a legal practise, Nehru was immediately attracted to Indian political life, which at the time was emerging from divisions over World War I. The moderate and extremist factions of the

Congress had reunited in its 1916 session in Lucknow, and Indian politicians had demanded *Home Rule* and dominion status for India. Joining the Congress under the patronage of his father, Nehru grew increasingly disillusioned with the liberal and anglicized nature of Congress politicians, which included his father. Although frequently hailed as a future leader of the Congress and India, Nehru's political rise did not begin until the arrival of Mahatma Gandhi on India's political arena.

Young Leader

Nehru was very strongly attracted to Gandhi's philosophy and leadership. Gandhi had led a successful rebellion on behalf of indentured Indian workers while a lawyer in South Africa. Upon his return to India, Gandhi organised the peasants and farmers of Champaran and Kheda in successful rebellions against oppressive tax policies levied by the British. Gandhi espoused what he termed as *satyagraha* — mass civil disobedience governed by *ahimsa*, or complete non-violence. A forceful exponent of Indian self-reliance, Gandhi's success electrified Indians, who had been divided in their approach to contesting British rule. Having met Gandhi and learning his ideas, Nehru assisted him during the Champaran agitation.

Following Gandhi's example, Nehru and his family abandoned their Western-style clothes, possessions and wealthy lifestyle. Wearing clothes spun out of *khadi*, Nehru emerged as one of the most energetic supporters of Gandhi. Under Gandhi's influence, Nehru began studying the *Bhagavad Gita* and practiced yoga throughout his life.

He would increasingly look to Gandhi for advice and guidance in his personal life, and would spend a lot of time travelling and living with Gandhi. Nehru travelled across India delivering political speeches aimed at recruiting India's masses, especially its youth into the agitation launched in 1919 against the Rowlatt Acts and the Khilafat struggle. He spoke passionately and forcefully to encourage Hindu-Muslim unity, spread education and self-reliance and the need to eradicate social evils such as untouchability, poverty, ignorance and unemployment.

Emerging as a key orator and prominent organiser, Nehru became one of the most popular political leaders in northern India, especially with the people of the United Provinces, Bihar and the Central Provinces. His youth and passion for social justice and equality attracted India's Muslims, women and other minorities. Nehru's role grew especially important following the arrest of senior leaders such as Gandhi and his father, and he was also imprisoned along with his mother and sisters for many months. Alarmed by growing violence in the conduct of mass agitations, Gandhi suspended the struggle after the killing of 22 state policemen by a mob at Chauri Chaura on February 4, 1922. This sudden move disillusioned some, including Nehru's father Motilal, who joined the newly formed Swaraj Party in 1923. However, Nehru remained loyal to Gandhi and publicly supported him.

A lull in nationalist activities enabled Nehru to turn his attention to social causes and local government. In 1924, he was elected president of the municipal corporation of Allahabad, serving as the city's chief executive for two years. Nehru launched ambitious schemes to promote education, sanitation, expand water and electricity supply and reduce unemployment — his ideas and experience proved valuable to him when he would assume charge of India's government in 1947. Achieving some success, Nehru was dissatisfied and angered by the obstruction of British officials and corruption amongst civil servants. He resigned from his position within two years.

In the early part of the decade, his marriage and family life had suffered owing to the constant activity on his part and that of his father. Although facing domestic pressures and tensions in the absence of her husband, Kamala would increasingly travel with Nehru, address public meetings and seek to sponsor and encourage nationalist activities in her hometown. In the late 1920s, the initial marital gulf between the two disappeared and the couple grew closer to each other and their daughter. In 1926 Nehru took his wife and daughter to Europe so that Kamala could receive special medical care. The family travelled and lived in England, Switzerland, France and Germany. Continuing his political work, Nehru was deeply impressed by the rising currents of radical socialism in Europe, and delivered fervent speeches in condemnation of imperialism. On a visit to the Soviet Union, Nehru was favourably impressed by the command economy, but grew critical of Stalin's totalitarianism.

Congress President

In the 1920s, Nehru was elected president of the All India Trade Unions Congress. He and Subhash Chandra Bose had become the most prominent youth leaders, and both demanded outright political independence of India. In 1927, he became a member of the League against Imperialism created in Brussels. Nehru criticised the Nehru Report prepared by his father in 1928, which called for dominion status for India within the British Empire. The radicalism of Nehru and Bose would provoke intense debates during the 1928 Congress session in Guwahati. Arguing that India would deliver an ultimatum to the British and prepare for mass struggle, Nehru and Bose won the hearts of many young Indians. To resolve the issue, Gandhi said that the British would be given two years to grant India dominion status. If they did not, the Indian National Congress (INC) would launch a national struggle for full political independence. Nehru and Bose succeeded in reducing the statutory deadline to one year.

The failure of talks with the British caused the December 1929 session in Lahore to be held in an atmosphere charged with anti-Empire sentiment. Preparing for the declaration of independence, the AICC elected Jawaharlal Nehru as Congress President at the encouragement of Gandhi. Nehru himself recalled that he was sensible of the fact that it was considered somewhat surprising:

> *"I have seldom felt quite so annoyed and humiliated... It is not that I was not sensible of the honour... But I did not come to it by the main entrance or even the side entrance: I appeared suddenly from a trap door and bewildered the audience into acceptance."*

On December 31, 1929 President Nehru hoisted the flag of independence before a massive public gathering along the banks of the Ravi River. The Congress would promulgate the *Purna Swaraj* (*Complete Independence*) declaration on January 26, 1930. With the launching of the Salt Satyagraha in 1930, Nehru travelled across Gujarat and other parts of the country participating and encouraging in the mass rebellion against the salt tax. Despite his father's death in 1931, Nehru and his family remained at the forefront of the struggle. Arrested with his wife and sisters, Nehru was imprisoned for all but four months between 1931 and 1935. During that same period, however, his popularity grew enormously. According to John Gunther, Nehru was both "distrustful of it, while simultaneously unable to control being somewhat " exhilarated and impressed".

His family quickly chastened him with raillery; his wife and sisters, and even his small daughter, began to call him in the home the names he was given by the crowd. They would say, "Oh Jewel of India, what time is it?" or "Oh Embodiment of Sacrifice, please pass the bread."

Nehru was released by the British and he traveled with his family once again to Europe in 1935, where his ailing wife Kamala would remain bed-ridden. Torn between the freedom struggle and tending to his wife, Nehru would travel back and forth between India and Europe. Kamala Nehru died on February 28, 1936. Deeply saddened, Nehru nevertheless continued to maintain a hectic schedule. In her memory, he wore a fresh rose on his coat for the rest of his life.

His popularity continued to grow, and his personal discomfort with that popularity rose with it. In the November, 1937 issue of the Calcutta-based journal *Modern Review*, an article entitled 'The Rashtrapati' severely criticized him. The anonymous author acknowledged Nehru's initiative and innate drive but also pointed out glaring streaks of autocracy, saying that his character was marked by "intolerance of others and a certain contempt for the weak and inefficient". The author, who signed himself "*Chanakya*", added that Nehru's conceit was "already formidable", and worried that soon "Jawaharlal might fancy himself as a Caesar". It was not suspected at the time that *Chanakya* was Nehru himself. This publication is a significantly important example of autocritique.

Nehru had been re-elected Indian National Congress(INC) President in 1936, and had presided over its session in Lucknow. Here he participated in a fierce debate with Gandhi, Patel and other Congress leaders over the adoption of socialism as the official goal of the party. Younger socialists such as Jaya Prakash Narayan, Mridula Sarabhai, Narendra Dev and Asoka Mehta began to see Nehru as leader of Congress socialists. Under their pressure, the Congress passed the *Avadi Resolution* proclaiming socialism as the model for India's future government. Nehru was re-elected the following year, and oversaw the Congress national campaign for the 1937 elections. Largely leaving political organisation work to others, Nehru travelled the length and breadth of the country, exhorting the masses on behalf of the Congress, which would win an outright majority in the central and most of the provincial legislatures. Although he did not contest elections himself, Nehru was seen by the national media as the leader of the Congress.

Maulana Azad and Nehru

At the outbreak of World War II, the Assemblies were informed that the Viceroy had unilaterally declared war on the Axis on behalf of India, without consulting the people's representatives. Outraged at the viceroy's arbitrary decision, all elected Congressmen resigned from their offices at the instigation of Subhash Bose and Nehru. But even as Bose would call for an outright revolt and would proceed to seek the aid of Nazi Germany and Japan, Nehru remained sympathetic to the British cause. He joined Maulana Azad, Chakravarthi Rajagopalachari and Patel in offering Congress support for the war effort in return for a commitment from the British to grant independence after the war.

In doing so, Nehru broke ranks with Gandhi, who had resisted in supporting war and remained suspicious of the British. The failure of negotiations and Britain's refusal to concede independence outraged the nationalist movement. Gandhi and Patel called for an all-out rebellion, a demand that was opposed by Rajagopalachari and resisted by Nehru and Azad. After intensive debates and heated discussions, the Congress leaders called for the British to *Quit India* — to transfer power to Indian hands immediately or face a mass rebellion.

Despite his skepticism, Nehru travelled the country to exhort India's masses into rebellion. He was arrested with the entire Congress Working Committee on August 9, 1942 and transported to a maximum security prison at a fort in Ahmednagar. Here he remained incarcerated with his colleagues till June 1945. His daughter Indira and her husband Feroze Gandhi were also imprisoned for a few months. Nehru's first grandchild, Rajiv Gandhi was born in 1944.

After his release from prison at the end of the Second World War, Nehru immediately resumed his political work and toured through India preparing grounds for the elections that had been promised for 1946. In October 1945, with the decisions to carry on with the INA trials announced, Nehru was instrumental in announcing the formation of the INA Defence Committee for the defence of the officers of the Indian National Army who faced court Martial in Delhi. Nehru chaired the INA Defence Committee and the legal defence team, while at the same time carrying on with his political work.

India's First Prime Minister

Nehru and his colleagues had been released as the British Cabinet Mission arrived to propose plans for transfer of power. The Congress held a presidential election in the knowledge that its chosen leader would become India's head of government.

Once elected, Nehru headed an interim government, which was impaired by outbreaks of communal violence and political disorder, and the opposition of the Muslim League led by Muhammad Ali Jinnah, who were demanding a separate Muslim state of Pakistan. After failed bids to form coalitions, Nehru reluctantly supported the partition of India as per a plan released by the British on June 3, 1947. He would take office as the Prime Minister of India on August 15, and delivered his inaugural address titled "A Tryst With Destiny:"

"Long years ago we made a tryst with destiny, and now the time comes when we shall redeem our pledge, not wholly or in full measure, but very substantially. At the stroke of the midnight hour, when the world sleeps, India will awake to life and freedom. A moment comes, which comes but rarely in history, when we step out from the old to the new, when an age ends, and when the soul of a nation, long suppressed, finds utterance. It is fitting that at this solemn moment we take the pledge of dedication to the service of India and her people and to the still larger cause of humanity."

However, this period was marked with intense communal violence. This violence swept across the Punjab region, Delhi, Bengal and other parts of India. Nehru conducted joint tours with Pakistani leaders to encourage peace and calm angry and disillusioned refugees. Nehru would work with Maulana Azad and other Muslim leaders to safeguard and encourage Muslims to remain in India.

The violence of the time deeply affected Nehru, who called for a ceasefire and UN intervention to stop the Indo-Pakistani War of 1947. Fearing communal reprisals, Nehru also hesitated in supporting the annexation of Hyderabad State, and clashed with Patel on the Kashmir dispute and relations with Pakistan. Nehru asserted his own control over Kashmir policy while Patel objected to Nehru sidelining his Home Ministry's officials. Nehru felt offended by Patel's decision-making regarding the states' integration without consulting either him or the Cabinet. Patel asked Gandhi to relieve him of his obligation to serve. He knew that he lacked Nehru's youth and popularity, and believed that an open political battle would hurt India. After much personal deliberation and contrary to Patel's prediction, Gandhi on January 30, 1948 told Patel not to leave the Government, and to stay by Nehru's side in joint leadership. A free India, according to Gandhi, desperately needed both Patel and Nehru's joint leadership.

Nehru climbs atop the gate at Birla House to announce the death of Gandhi to the crowd outside. This photograph by Henri Cartier-Bresson is one of the most famous images of the 1940s.

Gandhi was assassinated on January 30, 1948. At Gandhi's wake, Nehru and Patel embraced each other and addressed the nation together. Despite working together, the two leaders would clash on various issues. Nehru declined Patel's counsel on sending assistance to Tibet in 1950 with the disputed entrance of the People's Republic of China and ejecting the Portuguese from Goa by military force. When Nehru pressured Dr. Rajendra Prasad to decline a nomination to become the first President of India in 1950 in favour of Rajagopalachari, he thus angered the party, which felt Nehru was attempting to impose his will. Nehru sought Patel's help in winning the party over, but Patel declined, and Prasad was duly elected. When Nehru opposed the 1950 Congress presidential candidacy of Purushottam Das Tandon, a conservative Hindu leader, he endorsed Jivatram Kripalani and threatened to resign if Tandon was elected. Patel rejected Nehru's views and endorsed Tandon in Gujarat, in a disputed election where Kripalani received not one vote despite hailing from that state himself.

In the years following independence, Nehru frequently turned to his daughter Indira to look after him and manage his personal affairs. Following Patel's death in 1950, Nehru became the most popular and powerful Indian politician. Under his leadership, the Congress won an overwhelming majority in the elections of 1952, in which his son-in-law Feroze Gandhi was also elected. Indira moved into Nehru's official residence to attend to him, inadvertently estranging her husband, who would become a critic of Nehru's government. Nevertheless, Indira would virtually become Nehru's chief of staff and constant companion in his travels across India and the world.

ECONOMIC POLICIES

Nehru's Study in Teen Murti Bhavan

Nehru presided over the introduction of a modified, "Indian" version of state planning and control over the economy. Creating the Planning commission of India, Nehru drew up the first Five-Year Plan in 1951, which charted the government's investments in industries and agriculture. Increasing business and income taxes, Nehru envisaged a mixed economy in which the government would manage strategic industries such as mining, electricity and heavy industries, serving public interest and a check to private enterprise. Nehru pursued land redistribution and launched programmes to build irrigation canals, dams and spread the use of fertilizers to increase agricultural production. He also pioneered a series of *community development programs* aimed at spreading diverse cottage industries and increasing efficiency into rural India. While encouraging the construction of large dams, irrigation works and the generation of hydroelectricity, Nehru also launched India's programme to harness nuclear energy.

For most of Nehru's term as prime minister, India would continue to face serious food shortages despite progress and increases in agricultural production. Nehru's industrial policies encouraged the growth of diverse manufacturing and heavy industries, yet state planning, controls and regulations began to impair productivity, quality and profitability. Although the Indian economy enjoyed a steady rate of growth, chronic unemployment amidst entrenched poverty continued to plague the population. Nehru's popularity remained unaffected, and his government succeeded to an extent in extending water and electricity supply, health care, roads and infrastructure for India's vast rural population.

Education and Social Reform

Jawaharlal Nehru was a passionate advocate of education for India's children and youth, believing it essential for India's future progress. His government oversaw the establishment of many institutions of higher learning, including the All India Institute of Medical Sciences, the Indian Institutes of Technology and the Indian Institutes of Management. Nehru also outlined a commitment in his five-year plans to guarantee free and compulsory primary education to all of India's children. For this purpose, Nehru oversaw the creation of mass village enrollment programmes and the construction of thousands of schools. Nehru also launched initiatives such as the provision of free milk and meals to children in order to fight malnutrition. Adult education centres, vocational and technical schools were also organised for adults, especially in the rural areas.

Under Nehru, the Indian Parliament enacted many changes to Hindu law to criminalize caste discrimination and increase the legal rights and social freedoms of women. A system of reservations in government services and educational institutions was created to eradicate the social inequalities and disadvantages faced by peoples of the scheduled castes and scheduled tribes. Nehru also championed secularism and religious harmony, increasing the representation of minorities in government. The founding leaders of the Non-Aligned states meet in New York in October 1960. From left: Nehru, representing India; Kwame Nkrumah (Ghana); Gamal Abdel Nasser (Egypt); Sukarno (Indonesia); and Josip Broz Tito (Yugoslavia).

National Security and Foreign Policy

Although having promised in 1948 to hold a plebiscite in Kashmir under the auspices of the U.N., Nehru grew increasingly wary of the U.N. and declined to hold a plebiscite in 1953. He ordered the arrest of the Kashmiri politician Sheikh Abdullah, whom he had previously supported but now suspected of harbouring separatist ambitions; Bakshi Ghulam Mohammad replaced him.

On the international scene, Nehru was a champion of pacifism and a strong supporter of the United Nations. He pioneered the policy of non-alignment and co-founded the Non-Aligned Movement of nations professing neutrality between the rival blocs of nations led by the U.S. and the U.S.S.R. Recognising the People's Republic of China soon after its founding (while most of the Western bloc continued relations with the Republic of China), Nehru sought to establish warm and friendly relations with it despite the invasion of Tibet in 1950, and hoped to act as an intermediary to bridge the gulf and tensions between the communist states and the Western bloc. This policy of pacifism and appeasement with respect to China soon came unraveled when China annexed Aksai Chin, the region of Kashmir adjoining Tibet in 1962 that led to the Sino-Indian war. Jawaharlal Nehru declined a United States offer for India to occupy a permanent seat on the United Nations Security Council around 1953. Nehru instead suggested that the seat be given to China. Jawaharlal Nehru talks to Pakistan prime minister Muhammad Ali Bogra during his 1953 visit to

Karachi. Nehru was hailed by many for working to defuse global tensions and the threat of nuclear weapons. He commissioned the first study of the human effects of nuclear explosions, and campaigned ceaselessly for the abolition of what he called "these frightful engines of destruction." He also had pragmatic reasons for promoting de-nuclearisation, fearing that a nuclear arms race would lead to over-militarisation that would be unaffordable for developing countries such as his own. In 1956 he had criticised the joint invasion of the Suez Canal by the British, French and Israelis. Suspicion and distrust cooled relations between India and the U.S., which suspected Nehru of tactily supporting the Soviet Union. Accepting the arbitration of the UK and World Bank, Nehru signed the Indus Water Treaty in 1960 with Pakistani ruler Ayub Khan to resolve long-standing disputes about sharing the resources of the major rivers of the Punjab region.

LAST YEARS

Mr. Nehru had led the Congress to a major victory in the 1957 elections, but his government was facing rising problems and criticism. Disillusioned by intra-party corruption and bickering, Nehru contemplated resigning but continued to serve. The election of his daughter Indira as Congress President in 1959 aroused criticism for alleged nepotism, although Nehru disapproved of her election, partly because he considered it smacked of "dynastism"; he said, indeed it was "wholly undemocratic and an undesirable thing", and refused her a position in his cabinet. Indira herself was at loggerheads with her father over policy; most notably, she used his oft-stated personal deference to the Congress Working Committee to push through the dismissal of the Communist Party of India government in the state of Kerala, over his own objections. Nehru began to be frequently embarrassed by her ruthlessness and disregard for parliamentary tradition, and was "hurt" by what he saw as an assertiveness with no purpose other than to stake out an identity independent of her father.

Although the Pancha Sila (Five Principles of Peaceful Coexistence) was the basis of the 1954 Sino-Indian treaty over

Tibet, in later years, Nehru's foreign policy suffered through increasing Chinese antagonism over border disputes and Nehru's decision to grant asylum to the Dalai Lama. After years of failed negotiations, Nehru authorized the Indian Army to annex Goa from Portugal in 1961. While increasing his popularity, Nehru received criticism for opting for military action. In the 1962 elections, Nehru led the Congress to victory yet with a diminished majority. Opposition parties ranging from the right-wing Bharatiya Jana Sangh and Swatantra Party, socialists and the Communist Party of India performed well.

In a matter of months, the border disputes with China turned into open conflict. Nehru assumed that as former victims of imperialism (India being a colony itself) they shared a sense of solidarity, as expressed in the phrase "Hindi-Chini bhai bhai" (Indians and Chinese are brothers). He was dedicated to the ideals of brotherhood and solidarity among developing nations. Nehru, naively, did not believe that one fellow Socialist country would attack another; and in any event, he felt secure behind the impregnable wall of ice that is the Himalayas. Both proved to be severe miscalculations of China's intentions and military capabilities. Following reports of his intention to confront Chinese occupation of the disputed areas-summarised in a memorable statement that he had asked the Army to "throw them (Chinese) out"-China launched a pre-emptive attack.

In a matter of months, a Chinese invasion of northeastern India exposed the weaknesses of India's military as Chinese forces came as far as Assam. Widely criticised for his government's insufficient attention to defence, Nehru was forced to sack the defence minister Krishna Menon and accept U.S. military aid. Nehru's health began declining steadily, and he was forced to spend months recuperating in Kashmir through 1963. Upon his return from Kashmir in May 1964, Nehru suffered a stroke and later a heart attack. He died in the early hours of May 27, 1964. Nehru was cremated in accordance with Hindu rites at the Shantivana on the banks of the Yamuna River, witnessed by hundreds of thousands of mourners who had flocked into the streets of Delhi and the cremation grounds.

2

Nehru's Works in Politics

Nehru came from a family of Kashmiri Brahmins, who had migrated to the plains early in the eighteenth century. He was the son of Motilal Nehru, a renowned lawyer and one of Mahatma Gandhi's prominent lieutenants. Jawaharlal was the eldest of four children, two of whom were daughters. His sister, Vijaya Lakshmi Pandit, later became the first woman president of the UN General Assembly. Until the age of 16, Nehru was educated at home by a series of English governesses and tutors. Only one of these, a part-Irish, part-Belgian theosophist, Ferdinand T. Brooks, appears to have made any impression on him. Gradually, he developed a taste for writers such as Walter Scott, Charles Dickens, Thackery, H.G. Wells, and Mark Twain, as well as for John Stuart Mill, Gladstone, John Morley, Bertrand Russell, and Bernard Shaw. Jawaharlal also had an Indian tutor who taught him Hindi and Sanskrit. In 1905 he went to Harrow, a leading English school, where he stayed for two years. Nehru's academic career was in no way outstanding.

From Harrow he went to Trinity College, Cambridge, where he spent three years earning an honours degree in natural science. On leaving Cambridge, Nehru joined the Inner Temple in 1910 to read law, where in his own words he passed his examinations "with neither glory nor ignominy". It was here that he also confessed: "In my likes and dislikes, I was perhaps more an Englishman than an Indian." In London he was drawn to the Fabian socialists, also known as the Bloomsbury group. He returned home in 1912 after seven years of education in England. Four years after his return to India, in March 1916,

Nehru married Kamala Kaul, who came from a Kashmiri family settled in Delhi. Their only child, Indira Priyadarshini, was born in 1917; she would later (under her married name of Indira Gandhi) also serve as prime minister of India.

POLITICAL APPRENTICESHIP

On his return to India, Nehru at first tried to settle down as a lawyer. But, unlike his father, he had only a desultory interest in his profession and did not relish either the practice of law or the company of lawyers. At this time he might be described, like many of his generation, as an instinctive nationalist who yearned for his country's freedom, but, like most of his contemporaries, he had not formulated any precise ideas on how it could be achieved.

Nehru's autobiography discloses his lively interest in politics. His letters to his father over the same period reveal their common interest in India's freedom. But not until father and son met Gandhi and were persuaded to follow in his political footsteps did either of them develop any definite ideas on how freedom was to be attained. The quality in Gandhi that impressed the two Nehrus was his insistence on action. A wrong, the Mahatma argued, should not only be condemned, it should be resisted. Earlier, Nehru and his father had been contemptuous of the run of contemporary Indian politicians, whose nationalism, with a few notable exceptions, consisted of interminable speeches and long-winded resolutions. Jawaharlal was also attracted by Gandhi's insistence on fighting Great Britain without fear or hate. Nehru met Gandhi for the first time in 1916 at the annual meeting of the Indian National Congress in Lucknow. Gandhi was 20 years his senior. Neither seems to have made any initially strong impression on the other. Nehru did not assume a leadership role in Indian politics, however, until his election as Congress president in 1929, when he presided over the historic Lahore session that proclaimed complete independence as India's political goal. Until then the objective had been dominion status.

Nehru had joined the Allahabad High Court Bar in 1916, practising till 1920. But the legal profession did not hold him for long, and he found a meaningful vocation in politics. The year 1917 had seen the Russian Revolution, and it was also the year of agitation for Home Rule, under the leadership of Annie Besant (1847-1933). Expelled from Bombay and then from the Central Provinces, she was finally interned. Jawaharlal signed up as one of the joint secretaries of the Home Rule League in the United Provinces with Motilal Nehru as president. "Home Rule has come and we have to take it if we stand up like men and falter not", so wrote Jawaharlal in a letter to *The Leader*. Nehru's close association with the Congress party dates from 1919 in the immediate aftermath of World War I. This period saw a wave of nationalist activity and governmental repression.

According to his testimony and that of his contemporaries, three events during 1919 and 1920 had a profound influence on Nehru's political career. The first was the Jallianwala Bagh massacre (April 1919), when General Reginald E.H. Dyer, a British officer, ordered his troops to fire on an unarmed crowd of Indians gathered for an anti-British political meeting. By the time the ammunition ran out, nearly 400 civilians were dead and 1,200 wounded. The massacre shook Nehru's faith in the beneficence of British rule. The second experience was Nehru's first-hand encounter with India's poverty in the countryside in the 1920s, and lastly, Gandhi's emergence during 1919-20, and his call for civil disobedience struck Nehru deeply. In fact, the Non-cooperation Movement (1920-22) of the Congress under Gandhi's leadership seemed to him to answer some of the major challenges of the time. Jawaharlal accepted the non-violent method as the only practical strategy that was then available.

Beginning his political career in the United Provinces (now Uttar Pradesh), during the Non-cooperation Movement, Jawaharlal came in contact with the impoverished peasants whose indomitable spirit defied the crushing economic burden, which an oppressive imperial regime imposed upon them. Nehru left a graphic account of the India which his sojourn in the rural areas opened up before him: "I went (to the rural districts near Allahabad) with some colleagues and we spent three days in the villages far from the railways and even the *pucca* (paved) road. The visit was a revelation to me. We found the whole countryside afire with enthusiasm and full of strange excitement...(The) people would come streaming out or even running as fast as they could.

They were in miserable rags, men and women, but their faces were full of excitement and their eyes glistened and seemed to expect strange happenings which would, as if by a miracle, put an end to their long misery....(A) new picture of India seemed to arise before me." He was, as he records, "filled with shame and sorrow....at the degradation and overpowering poverty of India", and this experience was to shape his later political thinking. The Non-cooperation Movement helped him emerge as a popular leader: "I took to the crowd and the crowd took to me." The movement also widened his political and social perspective. When, late in 1921, the prominent leaders and workers of the Congress party were outlawed in some provinces, Nehru went to prison for the first time. Over the next 24 years he was to serve another eight periods of detention, the last and longest ending in June 1945, after an imprisonment of almost three years. In all, Nehru spent more than nine years in jail. Characteristically, he described his terms of incarceration as normal interludes in a life of abnormal political activity.

His political apprenticeship with the Congress lasted from 1919 to 1929. In 1923 he became general secretary of the party for two years and again, in 1927, for another two years. His interests and duties took him on journeys over wide areas of India, particularly in his native United Provinces, where his first exposure to the overwhelming poverty and degradation of the peasantry had a profound influence on his basic ideas for solving these vital problems. Though vaguely inclined towards socialism, Nehru's radicalism had set in no definite mould. The watershed in his political and economic thinking was his tour of Europe and the erstwhile Soviet Union.

Nehru's explorations into the socialist theory after his visit to Europe in 1926-27, and his experiences with Nazi Germany marked a turning point in his social and political outlook. In 1927 he, as a representative of the Indian National Congress, attended the International Congress against colonial oppression and imperialism in Brussels. There he met some of the leading leftists of the world including George Lansbury, Ellen Wilkinson, Fenner Brockway, and Harry Pollitt, besides a large number of nationalists from Asia, Africa, and Latin America.

This was followed by his visit to Moscow where he was greeted by the newspaper *Pravda* as a "leader of the left wing of the Congress". There he had a first-hand glimpse of the reconstruction of a major society on the basis of socialism. His experience made him realise the need for an economic revolution, which would redeem India from the backwardness of its agrarian structure and, in fact, from its dependence on agriculture itself. He was convinced that the solution to India's socio-economic problems lay in socialism "not in a vague humanitarian way, but in the scientific economic sense." He thus involved himself with the Trade Union Movement and emerged as a champion of independence and socialism.

Nehru's radicalism came to the fore in 1927 over the debate on the extent and character of *swaraj* or self-government that the Congress was struggling for. In 1927, the British government sent an all-British commission (the Simon Commission), under the terms of the Government of India Act of 1919, to report as to "whether and to what extent it was desirable to establish the principle of responsible government, or to extend, modify, or restrict the degree of responsible government existing therein". The Congress gave a call for the boycott of the Simon Commission in its Madras (now Chennai) session (December 1927), with Nehru and his associates contributing to the success of the boycott.

The Simon Commission thus raised the issue of the type of constitution or the kind of independence that India should obtain for itself. So far *swaraj*, for the Congress leaders, had meant dominion status for India (similar to the position of self-governing Australia, New Zealand, and South Africa) within the ambit of the British Empire. But to Jawaharlal and his associates the acceptance of the dominion status implied recognizing the inevitability of British presence in India, as well as the perpetuation of imperialistic exploitation. In the Madras session in December 1927, Jawaharlal moved a resolution demanding real independence instead of dominion status. It was, however, at the Congress session at Calcutta (now Kolkata) in December 1928 that he, joined by Subhash Chandra Bose, pressed claim for complete independence as the Congress objective. The actual success of this demand came in the following year when as the newly elected president of the Indian National Congress at the Lahore session, Nehru gave the call for a new goal: *purna swaraj* (complete independence). When the clock struck at midnight on the night of December 31, 1929, Jawaharlal Nehru rose and led a solemn procession on the banks of the Ravi River. It was here that he raised India's national flag.

STRUGGLE FOR INDIAN INDEPENDENCE

After the Lahore session of 1929, Nehru emerged as the leader of the country's intellectuals and youth. Hoping that Nehru would draw India's youth, at that time gravitating towards extreme leftist causes, into the mainstream of the Congress movement, Gandhi had elevated him to the presidency of the Congress party over the heads of some of his seniors. The Mahatma also correctly calculated that, with added responsibility, Nehru himself would be inclined to keep to the middle way.

It was also in these years Nehru and Subhas Chandra Bose were communicating with the people in general and to the youth (through the Youth League, the Hindustani Seva Dal, the Naujawan Bharat Sabha and the Volunteers' Movement), the students (through the students' organizations and conferences), and the workers (mainly through the All India Trade Union Congress whose presidentship was taken over by Jawaharlal in 1929 and Subhas in 1931) in particular.

In 1931, Jawaharlal and his wife Kamala were arrested in connection with the salt *satyagraha*. Jawaharlal clearly defined the kind of independence the Congress must stand for. In his draft of the Fundamental Rights that was adopted in the Karachi session of the Congress (March 1931), he stated: "In order to end the exploitation of the masses, political freedom must include real economic freedom of the starving millions."

The Congress, he hoped, could be converted into a real anti-imperialist "joint popular front", and he suggested as a first step "corporate membership" of trade unions and *kisan sabhas*. This indeed was an important step in the march towards Congress socialism and Nehru's emergence as a champion of civil liberties.

After his father's death in 1931, Jawaharlal moved into the inner councils of the Congress party and became closer to the Mahatma. Although Gandhi did not officially designate him his political heir until 1942, the country as early as the mid-1930s saw in Nehru the natural successor to Gandhi. The Gandhi-Irwin Pact of March 1931, signed between Gandhi and the British viceroy, Lord Irwin (later Lord Halifax), signalized a truce between the two. It climaxed one of Gandhi's more effective civil-disobedience movements, launched the year before, in the course of which Nehru had been arrested.

As an ardent anti-imperialist, Nehru was unhappy at the enactment of the Gandhi-Irwin compromise (March 1931), as well at the prospect of the Round Table Conference (September-December 1931) in London to resolve the Indian political question. He also saw no point in the formal withdrawal of the Civil Disobedience Movement (May 1933). In the closing stage of the Civil Disobedience Movement, Nehru had renewed his interest in the agitation of the Uttar Pradesh peasantry His commitment to the youth, the students, and the underprivileged inspired him towards a radical political temper. This eventually facilitated the formation of the Congress Socialist Party (May 1934) within the framework of the Congress organization. Though Nehru did not formally join the party, he drew its support on vital issues. He continued to give importance to the principles of Democratic Socialism in India, as well as a vision of an independent, liberated, and secular India.

After he was elected the Congress president in the Lucknow and the Faizpur sessions in 1936, Nehru offered his socialist ideas with greater clarity. He made significant advances on the agrarian question (by contributing to the formulation of a liberal Faizpur Congress Agrarian Programme), on the issue of constitution, and on the question of civil liberties (by ordering the Congress provincial ministries to release all political prisoners), on responsible government (especially by championing the cause of the *Praja Mandal* (peoples group) movement in the Indian states against the tyranny of their rulers) and on the world-wide campaign against Fascism (by taking the side of "forces of progress" in the Spanish Civil War, by protesting against the Italian attack on Ethiopia, and by organizing relief for China when it was attacked by Japan).

Hopes that the Gandhi-Irwin pact would be the prelude to a more relaxed period of Indo-British relations were not borne out; Lord Willingdon (who replaced Irwin as viceroy in 1931) jailed Gandhi in January 1932, shortly after his return from the Second Round Table Conference in London. He was charged with attempting to mount another civil-disobedience movement; Nehru was also arrested and sentenced to two years' imprisonment.

The Round Table Conferences in London, held to advance India's progress to self-government, eventually resulted in the Government of India Act of 1935, giving the Indian provinces a system of popular autonomous government. Ultimately, it provided for a federal system composed of the autonomous provinces and princely states. Although federation never came into being, provincial autonomy was implemented. During the mid-1930s Nehru was much concerned with developments in Europe, which seemed to be drifting towards another world war. He was in Europe early in 1936, visiting his ailing wife, shortly before she died in a sanitarium in Switzerland. Even at this time he emphasized that in the event of war India's place was alongside the democracies, though he insisted that India could only fight in support of Great Britain and France as a free country.

In the 1936-37 election campaign for the provincial legislatures under the Government of India Act of 1935, Nehru was the principal vote-getter for the Congress and came to occupy a powerful position in the ranks of the Congress party. When the elections following the introduction of provincial autonomy brought the Congress party to power in a majority of the provinces, Nehru was faced with a dilemma. The Muslim League under Mohammed Ali Jinnah (who was to become the creator of Pakistan) had fared badly at the polls. Congress, therefore, unwisely rejected Jinnah's plea for the formation of coalition Congress-Muslim League governments in some of the provinces, a decision on which Nehru had significant influence. The subsequent clash between the Congress and the League hardened into a conflict between Hindus and Muslims that was ultimately to lead to the partition of India and the creation of Pakistan.

IMPRISONMENT DURING WORLD WAR II

When, at the outbreak of World War II in September 1939, the viceroy, Lord Linlithgow, committed India to war without consulting the autonomous provincial ministries, the Congress party's High Command withdrew its provincial ministries as a protest. Congress's action left the political field virtually open to Jinnah and the Muslim League. Nehru's views on the war differed from those of Gandhi. Initially, the Mahatma believed that whatever support was given to the British should be given unconditionally and that it should be of a non-violent character. Nehru held that non-violence had no place in defense against aggression and that India should support Great Britain in a war against Nazism, but only as a free nation. If it could not help, it should not hinder.

In October 1940, Gandhi, abandoning his original stand, decided to launch a limited civil-disobedience campaign in which leading advocates of Indian independence were selected to participate one by one. Nehru was arrested and sentenced to four years' imprisonment. After spending a little more than a year in jail, he was released, along with other Congress prisoners, three days before the bombing of Pearl Harbor in Hawaii. When the Japanese carried their attack through Burma to the borders of India in the spring of 1942, the British government, faced by this new military threat, decided to make some overtures to India.

Prime Minister Winston Churchill dispatched Sir Stafford Cripps, a member of the war Cabinet who was politically close to Nehru and also knew Jinnah, with proposals for a settlement of the constitutional problem. Cripps's mission failed, however, for Gandhi would accept nothing less than independence. Nehru played a significant role in negotiations with Sir Stafford Cripps as well as in the developments leading to the Quit India Movement (1942). Equally memorable is his role during the trial of the three officers of the Indian National Army in the Red Fort in November 1945, when he, along with Bhulabhai Desai and T.B. Sapru fought on behalf of the INA officers. He was also a chief negotiator during the Simla Conference (June 1945), Cabinet Mission (May 16, 1946), and June 3rd Plan (1947). The initiative in the Congress party now passed to Gandhi, who called on the British to leave India; Nehru, though reluctant to embarrass the war effort, had no alternative but to join Gandhi. Following the Quit India resolution passed by the Congress party in Bombay on August 8, 1942, the entire Congress working committee, including Gandhi and Nehru, was arrested and imprisoned. Nehru emerged from this — his ninth and last detention—only on June 15, 1945.

Though there were perceptible differences between Nehru and Gandhi, they were inseparable. Gandhi's verdict on him also points to Nehru's contribution to India's struggle for freedom: "Jawaharlal is as pure as crystal, he is truthful beyond suspicion. He is knight *sanspeur, sans reproche*. The nation is safe in his hands." The Mahatma regarded him as his political heir. Nehru adopted Gandhi's idea of non-violent struggle for liberating India from British rule, and believed that only the right means could produce right ends.

Within two years India was to be partitioned and free. A final attempt by the viceroy, Lord Wavell, to bring the Congress party and the Muslim League together failed. The Labour government that had meanwhile displaced Churchill's wartime administration dispatched, as one of its first acts, a Cabinet mission to India and later also replaced Lord Wavell with Lord Mountbatten. The question was no longer whether India was to be independent but whether it was to consist of one or more independent states. While Gandhi refused to accept partition, Nehru reluctantly but realistically acquiesced. On August 15,

1947, India and Pakistan emerged as two separate, independent countries. Nehru became independent India's first prime minister.

PRIME MINISTER

In the 35 years from 1929, when Gandhi chose Nehru as president of the Congress session at Lahore, until his death as prime minister in 1964, Nehru remained —despite the Chinese debacle of 1962—the idol of his people.

Nehru imported and imparted modern values and ways of thinking, which he adapted to Indian conditions. Apart from his stress on secularism and on the basic unity of India, despite its racial and religious diversities, Nehru was deeply concerned with carrying India forward into the modern age of scientific discovery and technological development. In addition, he aroused in his people an awareness of the necessity of social concern with the poor and the outcast and of respect for democratic values. One of the achievements of which he was particularly proud was the reform of the ancient Hindu civil code that finally enabled Hindu widows to enjoy equality with men in matters of inheritance and property.

Internationally, Nehru's star was in the ascendant until October 1956, when India's attitude on the Hungarian revolt against the Soviets brought his policy of nonalignment under sharp scrutiny. In the United Nations, India was the only non-aligned country to vote with the erstwhile Soviet Union on the invasion of Hungary, and thereafter it was difficult for Nehru to command credibility in his calls for non-alignment. In the early years after independence, anticolonialism had been the cornerstone of his foreign policy, but, by the time of the Belgrade conference of non-aligned countries in 1961, Nehru had substituted non-alignment for anticolonialism as his pressing concern. In 1962, however, the Chinese threatened to overrun the Brahmaputra River valley as a result of a long-standing border dispute. Nehru called for Western aid, exposing the weakness of his non-alignment policy, and China withdrew.

Kashmir—claimed by both India and Pakistan — remained a perennial problem throughout Nehru's term as prime minister.

His tentative efforts to settle the dispute by adjustments along the cease-fire lines having failed, Pakistan, in 1948, made an unsuccessful attempt to seize Kashmir by force. In solving the problem of the Portuguese colony of Goa — the last remaining colony in India—Nehru was more fortunate. Although its military occupation by Indian troops in December 1961 raised a furore in many Western countries, in the hindsight of history, Nehru's action is justifiable. With the withdrawal of the British and the French, the Portuguese colonial presence in India had become an anachronism.

Both the British and the French had withdrawn peacefully. If the Portuguese were not prepared to follow suit, Nehru had to find ways to dislodge them. After first trying persuasion, in August 1955 he had permitted a group of unarmed Indians to march into Portuguese territory in a non-violent demonstration. Even though the Portuguese opened fire on the demonstrators, killing nearly 30, Nehru stayed his hand for six years, appealing meanwhile to Portugal's Western friends to persuade its government to cede the colony. When India finally struck, Nehru could claim that neither he nor the government of India had ever been committed to non-violence as a policy.

Nehru's health showed signs of deteriorating not long after the clash with China. He suffered a slight stroke in 1963, followed by a more debilitating attack in January 1964. He died a few months later from a third and fatal stroke.

Assessment

While assertive in his Indianness, because of his modern political and economic outlook, he attracted the younger intelligentsia of India to Gandhi's movement of non-violent resistance against the British and later to rally them around him after independence. Nehru's Western upbringing and his visits to Europe before independence had acclimatized him to Western ways of thinking. Nehru has been held responsible for Wavell's recall, and his relationship with Mountbatten may have been responsible for smoothing things over during the transfer of power. In free India, Nehru as first prime minister laid the foundations of a democratic and secular India. If Gandhi was India's liberator, Nehru was its modernizer. Throughout his 17 years in office, he held up democratic socialism as the guiding star. With the help of the overwhelming majority that the Congress party maintained in Parliament during his term of office, he advanced towards that goal. The four pillars of his domestic policies were democracy, socialism, unity, and secularism. He succeeded to a large extent in maintaining the edifice supported by these four pillars during his lifetime.

Even during his lifetime, individual and collective perceptions of his leadership ranged from him being adored as a revolutionary and vibrant personification of the forward-looking spirit of India to being described as a pampered young man who accidentally acquired national leadership owing to the influence of his father and the favouritism of Mahatma Gandhi. Doubtless, Nehru was a leader of the freedom movement, as the founding father of institutional democracy in India and as the architect of India's policy in all its manifestations, and the longest serving prime minister of India (from 1946 to 1964). As an international statesman and as a popular leader, he was second only to Gandhi in this century.

Nehru came to such prominence in the freedom struggle primarily for two reasons. First, the Congressmen made him their leader because of their conviction that he was committed to the cause of freedom and to the service of the people of India. Second, Nehru worked his way up through municipal elections in Allahabad and through mass movements in Pratapgarh of Uttar Pradesh. After that there was no looking back from him.

Though Nehru accepted Gandhi as his mentor, they differed on many points. Gandhi's non-violence stemmed from his religious convictions, while Nehru believed in a liberal conception of ethics. Nehru believed in representative institutions, especially the dominance of the poorer classes in the elected institutions. In other words, he believed in the democratic empowerment of the poorer and lower castes. So if Gandhi was the father of India, Nehru was the principle architect of India's democracy and planning.

Nehru's only child, Indira Gandhi, served as India's prime minister from 1966 to 1977 and from 1980 to 1984. Her son,

Rajiv Gandhi, was prime minister from 1984 to 1989. Nehru wrote extensively, especially during his interminable jail detentions—*Glimpses of World History* (1934-35) in the form of letters to his daughter Indira; his *Autobiography* (1936), largely a story of the nationalist struggle for independence; *Discovery of India* (1946), a foray into India's historical and cultural past; and *Selected Works* that contain several useful materials pertaining to India's freedom struggle.

TRYST WITH DESTINY

Jawaharlal Nehru's Tryst with Destiny Speech

Tryst with Destiny was a speech made by Jawaharlal Nehru, the first Prime Minister of the Republic of India. The speech was made to the Indian Constituent Assembly, on the eve of India's independence, towards midnight on August 14, 1947. It focuses on the aspects that transcend India's history.

It is considered in modern India to be a landmark oration that captures the essence of the triumphant culmination of the hundred-year Indian freedom struggle against the British Empire in India.

Text

Long years ago we made a tryst with destiny, and now the time comes when we shall redeem our pledge, not wholly or in full measure, but very substantially. At the stroke of the midnight hour, when the world sleeps, India will awake to life and freedom. A moment comes, which comes but rarely in history, when we step out from the old to the new, when an age ends, and when the soul of a nation, long suppressed, finds utterance. It is fitting that at this solemn moment we take the pledge of dedication to the service of India and her people and to the still larger cause of humanity.

At the dawn of history India started on her unending quest, and trackless centuries are filled with her striving and the grandeur of her success and her failures. Through good and ill fortune alike she has never lost sight of that quest or forgotten the ideals which gave her strength. We end today a period of ill fortune and India discovers herself again. The achievement we celebrate today is but a step, an opening of opportunity, to the greater triumphs and achievements that await us. Are we brave enough and wise enough to grasp this opportunity and accept the challenge of the future?

That future is not one of ease or resting but of incessant striving so that we may fulfil the pledges we have so often taken and the one we shall take today. The service of India means the service of the millions who suffer. It means the ending of poverty and ignorance and disease and inequality of opportunity. The ambition of the greatest man of our generation has been to wipe every tear from every eye. That may be beyond us, but as long as there are tears and suffering, so long our work will not be over.

And so we have to labour and to work, and work hard, to give reality to our dreams. Those dreams are for India, but they are also for the world, for all the nations and peoples are too closely knit together today for any one of them to imagine that it can live apart Peace has been said to be indivisible; so is freedom, so is prosperity now, and so also is disaster in this One World that can no longer be split into isolated fragments.

We have to build the noble mansion of free India where all her children may dwell. The appointed day has come-the day appointed by destiny-and India stands forth again, after long slumber and struggle, awake, vital, free and independent. The past clings on to us still in some measure and we have to do much before we redeem the pledges we have so often taken. Yet the turning-point is past, and history begins anew for us, the history which we shall live and act and others will write about. It is a fateful moment for us in India, A new star rises, the star of freedom in the East, a new hope comes into being, a vision long cherished materializes. May the star never set and that hope never be betrayed! We rejoice in that freedom,

The future beckons to us. Whither do we go and what shall be our endeavour? To bring freedom and opportunity to the common man, to the peasants and workers of India; to fight and end poverty and ignorance and disease; to build up a prosperous, democratic and progressive nation, and to create social, economic and political institutions which will ensure justice and fullness of life to every man and woman. We have hard work ahead. There is no resting for any one of us till we redeem our pledge in full, till we make all the people of India what destiny intended them to be. We are citizens of a great country on the verge of bold advance, and we have to live up to that high standard. All of us, to whatever religion we may belong, are equally the children of India with equal rights, privileges and obligations. We cannot encourage communalism or narrow-mindedness, for no nation can be great whose people are narrow in thought or in action.

To the nations and peoples of the world we send greetings and pledge ourselves to cooperate with them in furthering peace, freedom and democracy. And to India, our much-loved motherland, the ancient, the eternal and the ever-new, we pay our reverent homage and we bind ourselves afresh to her service.

Jai Hind.

POPULAR CULTURE

The speech is referenced in the 1998 Hindi film *Earth* directed by Deepa Mehta. The film portrays the main characters listening to the speech on radio, against the backdrop of the Hindu-Muslim riots following the Partition of India. This provides an interesting juxtaposition between the realities of Partition and the optimism that followed Independence.

1947, First-hand between Karachi and Delhi

I shall skip past her delightful account of the Karachi ceremony—which took place on August 13 and 14 within eyeshot of a bronze statue of Mahatma Gandhi in a nearby circle—even though some of her irreverent comments are worth quoting even now ("Jinnah, whose smile muscles seem to be permanently out of order ..."). Karachi was still a Hindu-majority city, and large sections of the population were understandably subdued at the partition of the country.Delhi's mood was altogether more joyous. The Talbots arrived at the Constituent Assembly just in time after a hair-raising journey from Pakistan on the afternoon of August 14. Mildred describes Nehru's famous "tryst with destiny" speech, recounts the now-forgotten exuberance of a delegate who marred the decorum of the occasion by shouting a cheer for the Mahatma, and then tells a story I have not come across elsewhere: "At the moment when the clock was chiming the [midnight] hour there was a rude interruption which startled everyone. A conch shell was blown long and loudly from the rear of the hall. Involuntarily every head turned .... It was revealing to witness the [...] relief [...] when they saw that it was one of the most highly respected members of the Assembly, a devout Hindu, simply invoking the gods to witness this ceremony.... I happened to spot Nehru just as he was turning away, trying to hide a smile by covering his mouth with his hand." Mildred describes the pressure of the throngs outside the Assembly clamouring for a glimpse of their idol, Nehru, whom the police obliged "to slip out by a back entrance". As an American, she was struck by the fact that when the crowds got out of hand it was the VIP who changed his plans. There are numerous fascinating vignettes in her letter of the next morning's Independence Day events: of Nehru's horror at seeing a horse fall (he only turned his attention back to the ceremony when he saw the horse rise again and move); of the U.S.

Ambassador's irritation that President Truman's cable of congratulations had been omitted when other leaders' greetings were read (it turned out that it had been misplaced); of Mountbatten's demeanour of "sincere pleasure", a sharp contrast with his stiffness in Karachi ("Here he was relaxed and at home among friendly companions ... his good wishes were obviously heartfelt.") Mildred's harrowing account of the evening's ceremony, ruined by rain and by 5,00,000 people turning out for an event planned for 25,000, is too long to summarise here, but for one detail: amidst the chaos, Indira Gandhi "looking woebegone and bedraggled. Her sari was torn, her hair straggling, her fingernails ruined. And she was one of the dignitaries!"

The Flag Goes up

But the highlight of Mildred's account is of the morning of August 15, 1947, when the national flag was raised over the Council Hall: "the multitudes had gathered as far as the eye could see in the two-mile long parkway approach to the Secretariat, on tops of buildings, in windows, on cornices, in trees, perched everywhere like so many birds. The raising of that first flag was the single most thrilling experience of the entire celebration .... The first who spotted it pointed like eager childen; others ... looked up and tried to push their way to a vantage point so they too could see this miracle. For a few minutes there was almost a subdued hush over the whole crowd; then a soft bass undertone slowly swelled until, perhaps when the flag reached the top,... there was a breathtaking roar of cheering, shouting, and excited cries which others said penetrated to the hall inside and made their spines tingle. While I was being stirred by the sheer power and grandeur of the spectacle,... the Indians either stood mute, immersed in their own overwhelming thoughts, or were shouting almost uncontrollably. It was a grand emotional experience that left most of us with shaky voices or complete inability to speak."

These are the words not of an Indian nationalist but of a young American woman. Mildred Talbot wrote to her American friend two weeks after witnessing that first flag-raising: "The memory of the feelings that surged up within us as we watched their [i.e. the Indian masses'] excitement and awe still brings tears to my eyes." Fifty-seven years later, the memories of that first Independence Day have faded in all but a tiny percentage of our population. But the power of that magical moment when India became free, and the hopes raised of what we would make of that freedom, must never be forgotten. Today is the day to remember that moment, and to rededicate ourselves to its promise. It is a promise every Indian can do his or her own part to fulfil.

Gandhi & Nehru

They were opposite in nature, but they shared a passion for freedom and justice, and together created a giant of democracy.

The 20th century produced many remarkable leaders, but few nations were blessed with a pair quite like India's Mahatma Gandhi and his protégé Jawaharlal Nehru. Gandhi was idealistic, quirky, quixotic and determined, a cross between a saint and a ward politician; like the best crossbreeds, he managed to distill the qualities of both and yet transcend their contradictions. Nehru was a moody, idealistic intellectual who felt an almost mystical empathy for the toiling peasant masses; an aristocrat who had passionate socialist convictions; a product of Harrow and Cambridge who spent over 10 years in British jails; an agnostic radical who became an unlikely follower of the deeply spiritual Mahatma. Together they brought a nation to freedom and laid the underpinnings for the world's largest democracy.

Gandhi was the extraordinary leader of the world's first successful nonviolent movement for independence from colonial rule. To describe his method, he coined the expression *satyagraha*—literally, "holding on to truth" or, as he variously described it, truth force, love force or soul force. He disliked the English term passive resistance because *satyagraha* required activism, not passivity. If you believed in truth and cared enough to obtain it, Gandhi felt, you could not afford to be passive. You had to be prepared actively to suffer for truth. It was *satyagraha* that first bound Nehru to Gandhi, soon after the latter's return to India in 1915 from a long sojourn in South Africa, where his morally charged leadership of the Indian community against racial discrimination had earned him the sobriquet of Mahatma ("Great Soul," a term he detested).

Gandhi's unique method of resistance through civil disobedience, allied to a talent for organization, gave the Indian nationalist movement both a saint and a strategist. His singular insight was that self-government would never be achieved by the resolutions passed by a self-regarding and unelected élite pursuing the politics of the drawing room. To him, self-government had to involve the empowerment of India's suffering multitudes in whose name the upper classes were clamoring for Home Rule. This position did not go over well with India's political class, which consisted largely of maharajahs and lawyers—men of means who discoursed in English and demanded the rights of Englishmen. To put his principles into practice, Gandhi lived in near-absolute poverty in an ashram and traveled across the land in third-class railway compartments, campaigning against untouchability, poor sanitation and child marriage, while also preaching an eclectic set of virtues from sexual abstinence and frequent enemas to the weaving of hand-spun cotton cloth. That he was an eccentric was beyond doubt. That he had touched a chord amongst the masses was equally apparent. That he was a potent political force soon became clear. He captured the imagination of the nation by publicly breaking English law in the name of a higher law ("the voice of conscience") and challenging the British to jail him.

Despite differences over both tactics (Nehru wanted independence immediately whereas Gandhi believed Indians had to be made ready for their own freedom) and philosophy (the agnostic Nehru had little patience for the Mahatma's spirituality), the two men proved a formidable combination. Gandhi guided Nehru to the political pinnacle; Nehru in turn proved an inspirational campaigner as President of the Indian National Congress, electrifying the nation with his speeches and tireless travel. Gandhi took the issue of freedom to the masses as one of simple right and wrong and gave them a technique to which the British had no response.

By abstaining from violence Gandhi wrested the moral advantage. By breaking the law nonviolently he demonstrated the injustice of the law. By accepting the punishments imposed on him he confronted his captors with their own brutalization. By voluntarily imposing suffering upon himself in his hunger strikes he demonstrated the lengths to which he was prepared to go in defense of what he considered right. Gandhi's moral rectitude and Nehru's political passion made the perpetuation of British rule an impossibility.

Of course there was much more to Gandhism—physical self-denial, self-reliance, a belief in the human capacity for selfless love, religious ecumenism, idealistic internationalism, and a passionate commitment to equality and social justice. The improvement of his fellow human beings was arguably more important to him than the political goal of ridding India of the British. But it is his central tenet of nonviolence in the pursuit of these ends that represents his most significant original contribution to the world. Martin Luther King in the U.S., Adolfo Pérez Esquivel in Argentina, Nelson Mandela in South Africa and Aung San Suu Kyi in Burma all sought inspiration from the Mahatma's teachings.

Upon Gandhi's assassination in 1948, a year after independence, Nehru, the country's first Prime Minister, became the keeper of the national flame, the most visible embodiment of India's struggle for freedom. Gandhi's death could have led Nehru to assume untrammeled power. Instead, he spent a lifetime trying to instill the habits of democracy in his people—a disdain for dictators, a respect for parliamentary procedures, an abiding faith in the constitutional system. He himself was such a convinced democrat that, at the crest of his rise, he authored an anonymous article warning Indians of the dangers of giving dictatorial temptations to Jawaharlal Nehru. "He must be checked," he wrote of himself. "We want no Caesars." During Nehru's 17 years as Prime Minister, democratic values became so entrenched that when his daughter Indira suspended India's freedoms with a State of Emergency for 21 months, she felt compelled to return to the Indian people for vindication, held an election, and comprehensively lost it.

While the world was disintegrating into fascism, violence and war in the 20th century, Gandhi taught the virtues of truth, nonviolence and peace. The principal pillars of Nehru's legacy—democratic institution-building, staunch pan-Indian secularism, socialist economics at home and a foreign policy of nonalignment—were all integral to a vision of Indianness that sustained the nation for decades. Today, both legacies are fundamentally contested, and many Indians have strayed from the ideals bequeathed to them by Gandhi and Nehru. Yet they, in their very different ways, each represented that rare kind of leader who is not diminished by the inadequacies of his followers.

The American editor Norman Cousins once asked Nehru what he hoped his legacy to India would be. "Four hundred million people capable of governing themselves," Nehru replied. The numbers have grown, but the very fact that each day over a billion Indians govern themselves in a pluralist democracy is testimony to the deeds and words of these two men.

Nehru Declined offer of Permanent U.N. Seat'

Jawaharlal Nehru "declined a United States offer" to India to "take the permanent seat on the United Nations Security Council" around 1953 and suggested that it be given to China, according to the United Nations Under-Secretary General, Sashi Tharoor.

In his latest book, "Nehru — The Invention of India," Mr. Tharoor writes that Indian diplomats who have seen files swear that Nehru declined the offer about the same time as he turned down "with scorn" John Foster Dulles' support for an Indian Monroe Doctrine.

Nehru had suggested that the seat, till then held by Taiwan, be offered to Beijing instead. He wrote that "the seat was held with scant credibility by Taiwan."

Rafiq Zakaria, historian and scholar, and Murli Deora, MP, highlighted the disclosure at a function organised here to release the book. Manmohan Singh, Leader of Opposition in the Rajya Sabha, handed over the first copy to the Maharashtra Chief Minister, Sushilkumar Shinde.

Later, talking of the book, brought out by Penguin Viking, Mr.Tharoor spoke of Nehru's legacy which included four elements — democratic institution building, socialism, a non-aligned foreign policy and secularism, and said the legacy was far too important not to be re-looked at from the point of view of the 21st century.

In Nehru's time, India had no foreign policy and it was correct to say "Nehru had a foreign policy."

Often, other politicians and the foreign office mandarins came to know about the policy when they heard Nehru speak on the issue, Mr. Tharoor said.

He had been alive, Jawaharlal Nehru would have been 110 years and one month old at the turn of the century. It is 36 years since his moving away from the centrestage of Indian and world politics. With death and with the passage of time, great leaders undergo a process of demystification. Distances in terms of time and the elimination of the physical presence of these larger-than-life figures enable succeeding generations to a assess their lives more objectively, without being afflicted by their charisma and power, whatever the ingredients of that power might have been.

Nehru even during his life-time went through the spectrum of individual and collective reactions to his leadership, from being adored as a revolutionary and vibrant personification of the forward-looking spirit of India to being described as a pampered young man who accidentally acquired national leadership due to the influence of his father and the favouritism of Mahatma Gandhi. He has been admired as a leader of the freedom movements, as the founding father of institutional democracy in India and as the architect of India's policy in all its manifestations, being the longest serving prime minister of India (from 1946 to 1964).

It would be pertinent to evaluate Nehru as a leader and a statesman because of the decisive and over-arching role that he played in Indian history in the 20th century. Regardless of criticisms, he was one of the most influential leaders of our freedom struggle. He was a pioneering articulator of Asian resurgence and was an unusually idealistic advocate of conscience in international politics. India's parliamentary democracy, free judiciary and media, the apolitical civil servants and armed forces, the commitment to secularism, social justice and equality before law, all originated in the blue print for free India which he worked out.

Nehru had a profound belief in India's destiny as a moral and stabilizing force in inter-state relations. He had faith in the Indian people and an equally strong hope that their maturity and civilisational wisdom would ensure for India an important role in the world. His education in the West, and his exposure to the political movements of Europe in the first three decades of this century, combined with his eclectic sense of history, made him realise that science, technology and economic modernisation and development were essential pre-requisites to fulfill the vision of a free India that he had in mind and to which he devoted three-fourths of his life. These ingredients and influences, cannot be denied in generic terms but in is necessary to assess Nehru through the prism of India's realities today, and to judge him in the context of criticisms leveled against him as an individual and as a public figure.

This exercise should necessarily be an assessment of him as a leader of the freedom struggle, as a founding ideologue of the Indian Republic, as the prime minister, as an international statesman and as a leader beloved of the people of India, second only to Gandhi in this century. I can do no better than to recall two remarks made by senior members of the Congress over his role as leader of the freedom struggle. Acharya Kripalani, speaking at a seminar of the Gandhi Vichar Parishad in Wardha in 1954, said Nehru became a prominent leader of the freedom struggle basically because of the colonial mindset of the Indians. "He is an Englishman in Indian clothing." So the respect for him. I was one of the audience to which this remark was made. Though we were very young, we did not accept this assessment. We attributed it to the breaking away of Jayaprakash Narayan and Kriplani from the Congress at the point of time.

The second view was expressed years later by former prime minister P.V. Narasimha Rao when I asked him how Nehru came to such prominence in the freedom struggle. He said Congressmen made him their leader because of their conviction that he was committed to the cause of freedom and to the service of the people of India. But he also reminded me that Nehru had worked his way up through municipal elections in Allahabad and through mass movements in Pratapgarh of Uttar Pradesh.

As the ideologue of the Indian Constitution and the Indian polity, Nehru's contributions cannot be denied. It is his implementation of the doctrine of secularism and his approach to harmonizing the diversities of India which seem flawed in retrospect. The basic reasoning of secularism which he put forward was valid—that a plural, multi-religious, civil society like that of India's could remain harmonious and united only if it is underpinned by religious tolerance and separation of religion from politics. The flaw, however, was that he did not underline the fact that the secular ethos of Indian society was rooted in two factors. That Hindus constituted the majority of the people of the country and that Hindu ethos at the profoundest intellectual and spiritual levels believed deeply in religious tolerance and respect for other religions.

If the majority of people in India were not Hindus, India would not have been a secular country. Instead of emphasising this, Nehru put the Hindu majority somewhat on the defensive, predicating Indian secularism on certification by the minorities, that the majority is secular. This resulted in a certain defensiveness and self-conscious denial of their religious and cultural identity by the Hindu community, which has perhaps made secularism a surface phenomenon in India's socio-political processes.

Similarly, Nehru's decision to reorganise the states on the basis of languages, while being good-intentioned, perhaps germinated the seeds of the present centrifugal territorial demands, affecting the unity of our country. While he was the builder of democratic institutions and conventions, one has to acknowledge that he did not groom a second generation of leadership in the party or the country, nor did he show any awareness of the need for anchoring the Congress in a trained cadre of party workers. He presumed that the commitment and organisational cohesion of the Congress during the freedom struggle would continue which was not to be because the party in a freedom movement is always different from a party in power in terms of ethos and motivations.

It is fashionable now to criticise Nehru's economic policies. He is castigated for making the public sector occupy the commanding heights of Indian economy. He is criticised for not linking up with western market economies.

It has to be remembered that the Indian private sector did not have the resources and motivation to invest in infrastructural sectors of the economy which required long-term investments and gestation periods. More importantly, between 1947 and 1955, all his efforts to get the major western powers involved in infrastructural development did not get a positive response. It was in consequence of this predicament that he entrusted the responsibility of mobilising resources and channelling them to fundamental sectors of the Indian economy to the government and the public sector.

While the decisions that he took seem logical and relevant to those times, the question to be answered is whether he would have continued the same policies had he lived into the '80s. Whatever his faults, he was alert and sensitive to changing domestic and international situations. Who knows, he might have been an equally active participant in the process of economic liberalisation and modernisation?

As an international statesman and foreign minister, there is a questioning of his founding the Non-Aligned Movement and its relevance today. It is true that the movement has not been very effective in safeguarding the interests of its member countries, particularly India. Two facts have to be kept in mind while evaluating Nehru's adherence to the movement. First, he made a distinction between being "non-aligned" and being part of "the Non-Aligned Movement".

He believed in non-alignment as a guiding principle of India's foreign policy so that India is assured of having the freedom of choice in making decisions responsive to its national interests without being subject to external influences. He articulated apprehensions about being part of a movement which in itself could become a bloc of countries. It was Krishna Menon who ultimately persuaded him to make India join the movement, arguing that the parallel interests of the countries of the movement would increase their influence in international transactions.

He did not believe in the non-aligned movement as a dogma. He rightly believed in non-alignment (as distinct from neutrality) as a guiding principle of India's foreign and security policies. Nehru can certainly be faulted for his idealism and belief in the sanctity of international law and agreements, in the light of his decision to go to the United Nations on the Kashmir issue and his faith in morality and goodwill as effective principles in inter-state relations. It was only at the end of 1962 after the military debacle against China that he acknowledged this reality, but it was too late. He can be blamed with

Vallabhbhai Patel for the impatience which led to Partition about which Maulana Azad has written. In retrospect, Partition was good. It is preferable to India facing more profound centrifugal alienations than it is facing now.

Nehru was the beloved leader of his people. But when one intermeshes his individual persona with his public persona, one cannot but come to the conclusion that he was for the people, was committed to India's destiny being governed by the people but to a great extent was not "of the people". He was essentially a remote, aristocratic, glamorous and private person. Gandhi, Patel and Ambedkar were perhaps more immersed in the mass identity of Indians. Regardless of the fault lines, Nehru remains the most important architect of free India. The words of Justice Oliver Wendell Holmes come to mind here. "A great man represents a great ganglion in the nerves of society, or to vary the figure, at a strategic point in the campaign of history and his greatness consists in seizing that opportunity and being there at that particular strategic point."

Interim Prime Minister

Nanda was the interim Prime Minister of India twice for thirteen days each: the first time after the death of Prime Minister Jawaharlal Nehru in 1964, and the second time after the death of Prime Minister Lal Bahadur Shastri in 1966. His both terms were uneventful, yet they were important because of potential danger to the country following Nehru's death soon after a war with China in 1962, and Shastri's death after a war with Pakistan in 1965.

THE PRE-INDEPENDENCE ERA

Founded in 1885 with the objective of obtaining a greater share in government for educated Indians, the Indian National Congress was initially not opposed to British rule. The Congress met once a year during December. Indeed, it was a Scotsman, Allan Octavian Hume, who brought about its first meeting in Bombay, with the approval of Lord Dufferin, the then-Viceroy.

Womesh Chandra Bonerjee was the first President of the INC. The first meeting was scheduled to be held in Pune, but due to a plague outbreak there, the meeting was later shifted to Bombay. The first Session of INC was held from 28-31 December 1885, and was attended by 72 delegates.

A few years down the line, the demands of INC became more radical in the face of constant opposition from the government, and the party became very active in the independence movement. By 1907 the party was split into two halves: the *Garam Dal* of Bal Gangadhar Tilak, or Extremists (literally "hot faction"), and the *Naram Dal* of Gopal Krishna Gokhale, or Moderates (literally "soft faction"), distinguished by their attitude towards the British. Under the influence of Bal Gangadhar Tilak, the Congress became the first integrated mass organization in the country, bringing together millions of people against the British.

In its time as the nation's leader in the freedom struggle, it produced the nation's greatest leaders. Before the Gandhi Era came leaders like Bal Gangadhar Tilak, Bipin Chandra Pal, Lala Lajpat Rai, Gopal Krishna Gokhale, Mohammed Ali Jinnah (later leader of the Muslim League and instrumental in the creation of Pakistan), all starting with the first legendary icon of Indians: Dadabhai Naoroji, the president of the sister Indian National Association and later the first Indian Member of Parliament in the British House of Commons.

With the rise of Mahatma Gandhi's popularity and his Satyagraha art of revolution came Sardar Vallabhbhai Patel, Pandit Jawaharlal Nehru (the nation's first Prime Minister), Dr. Rajendra Prasad (the nation's first President), Khan Mohammad Abbas Khan, Khan Abdul Ghaffar Khan, Chakravarti Rajgopalachari, Jivatram Kripalani and Maulana Abul Kalam Azad.

With the already existing nationalistic feeling combinded with Gandhi's popularity the Congress became a forceful mass organization in the country, bringing together millions of people by specifically working against caste differences, untouchability, poverty, and religious and ethnic boundaries. Although predominantly Hindu, it had members from virtually every religion, ethnic group, economic class and linguistic group. At the time of the Quit India movement, the Congress was undoubtedly the strongest political and revolutionary organization in India. The Indian National Congress could claim to be the true representative of the Indian people.

The 1929 Lahore session under the presidency of Jawaharlal Nehru holds special significance as in this session "Poorna Swaraj" (complete independence) was declared as the goal of INC. The 26th January 1930 was declared as "Poorna Swaraj Diwas," Independence Day although the British remained in India a number of years longer. It was to commemorate this date particularly that The Indian Constitution was formally adopted on 26 January 1950 (even though it was passed on 26 November 1949). After the First World War the party became associated with Mahatma Gandhi, who remained its unofficial, spiritual leader and mass icon even as younger men and women became party president. The party was in many ways an umbrella organization, sheltering within itself radical socialists, traditionalists and even Hindu and Muslim conservatives.

The Post-independence Era

The party remained in power for thirty *continuous* years between independence in 1947 and its first taste of electoral defeat (at the national level) in 1977.

History of the Republic of India

The History of the Republic of India began on August 15, 1947 when India became an independent Dominion within the British Commonwealth. Concurrently the Muslim-majority northwest and east of British India was separated into the Dominion of Pakistan. Lord Louis Mountbatten, and later Chakravarti Rajagopalachari served in the office of the Governor General of India. Jawaharlal Nehru became the first Prime Minister of India and Sardar Vallabhbhai Patel became the Deputy Prime Minister of India and its Minister of Home Affairs.

1947–1950

Independent India's first years were marked with turbulent events — a massive exchange of population with Pakistan, the

Indo-Pakistani War of 1947 and the integration of over 500 princely states to form a united nation.

AFTERMATH OF PARTITION

An estimated 3.5 million Hindus and Sikhs living in West Punjab, NWFP, Baluchistan, East Bengal and Sind migrated to India in fear of domination and suppression in Muslim Pakistan. Communal violence killed an estimated 1 million Hindus, Muslims and Sikhs, and gravely destabilized both Dominions along their Punjab and Bengal boundaries, and the cities of Calcutta, Delhi and Lahore. The violence was stopped by early September owing to the cooperative efforts of both Indian and Pakistani leaders, and especially due the efforts of Mohandas Gandhi, the leader of the Indian freedom struggle, who undertook a *fast-unto-death* in Calcutta and later in Delhi to calm people and emphasize peace despite the threat to his life. Both Governments constructed large relief camps for incoming and leaving refugees, and the Indian Army was mobilized to provide humanitarian assistance on a massive scale.

The assassination of Mahatma Gandhi on January 30, 1948 was a major setback to the young nation. Gandhi was murdered by Nathuram Vinayak Godse, allegedly affiliated with the Hindu nationalist movement, who held him responsible for partition and charged that Gandhi was appeasing Muslims. More than one million people flooded the streets of Delhi to follow the procession to cremation grounds and pay their last respects.

In 1949, India recorded close to 1 million Hindu refugees flooded into West Bengal and other states from East Pakistan, owing to communal violence, intimidation and repression from Muslim authorities. The plight of the refugees outraged Hindus and Indian nationalists, and the refugee population drained the resources of Indian states, who were unable to absorb them. While not ruling out war, Prime Minister Nehru and Sardar Patel invited Liaquat Ali Khan for talks in Delhi.

Although many Indians termed this appeasement, Nehru signed a pact with Liaquat Ali Khan that pledged both nations to the protection of minorities and creation of minority commissions. Although opposed to the principle, Patel decided to back this Pact for the sake of peace, and played a critical role in garnering support from West Bengal and across India, and enforcing the provisions of the Pact. Khan and Nehru also signed a trade agreement, and committed to resolving bilateral disputes through peaceful means. Steadily, hundreds of thousands of Hindus returned to East Pakistan, but the thaw in relations did not last long, primarily owing to the Kashmir dispute.

Union's Integration

British India consisted of 17 provinces and a few hundred princely states. The provinces were given to India or Pakistan, in some cases in particular — Punjab and Bengal — after being partitioned. The princes of the princely states, however, won the right to either remain independent or join either nation. Thus India's leaders faced the prospect of inheriting a nation fragmented between medieval-era kingdoms and provinces organized by colonial powers. Under the leadership of Sardar Vallabhbhai Patel, the new Government of India employed political negotiations backed with the option (and, on several occasions, the use) of military action to ensure the primacy of the Central government and of the Constitution then being drafted.

There were three States that proved more difficult to integrate than others:

1. Junagadh – a December 1947 plebiscite resulted in a 99% vote to merge with India, annulling the controversial accession to Pakistan, which was made despite the people of the state being overwhelmingly Hindu.
2. Hyderabad – Patel ordered the Indian army to depose the government of the Nizam after the failure of negotiations, which was done between September 13 – September 17, 1948. It was incorporated as a state of India the next year.
3. The area of Kashmir in the far north of the subcontinent quickly became a source of controversy that erupted

into the First Indo-Pakistani War which lasted from 1947 to 1949. Eventually a United Nations-overseen ceasefire was agreed that left India in control of two thirds of the contested region.

The Constituent Assembly adopted the Constitution of India, drafted by a committee headed by B. R. Ambedkar, on November 26, 1949. India became a federal, democratic republic after its Constitution came into effect on January 26, 1950. Rajendra Prasad became the first President of India.

1950s and 1960s

India held its first national elections under the Constitution in 1952, where a turnout of over 60% was recorded. The Congress Party won an overwhelming majority, and Jawaharlal Nehru began a second term as Prime Minister. President Prasad was also elected to a second term by the electoral college of the first Parliament of India.

NEHRU ADMINISTRATION (1952–1964)

Prime Minister Nehru led the Congress to major election victories in 1957 and 1962. The Parliament passed extensive reforms that increased the legal rights of women in Hindu society, and further legislated against caste discrimination and untouchability. Nehru advocated a strong initiative to enroll India's children to complete primary education, and thousands of schools, colleges and institutions of advanced learning, such as the Indian Institutes of Technology were founded across the nation. Nehru advocated a socialist model for the economy of India—no taxation for Indian farmers, minimum wage and benefits for blue-collar workers, and the nationalization of heavy industries such as steel, aviation, shipping, electricity and mining. An extensive public works and industrialization campaign resulted in the construction of major dams, irrigation canals, roads, thermal and hydroelectric power stations.

States Reorganization

Potti Sreeramulu's *fast-unto-death*, and consequent death for the demand of an Andhra State in 1953 sparked a major re-shaping of the Indian Union. Nehru appointed the *States*

Reorganization Commission, upon whose recommendations, the States Reorganization Act was passed in 1956. Old states were dissolved and new states created on the lines of shared linguistic and ethnic demographics. The separation of Kerala and the Telugu-speaking regions of Madras State enabled the creation of an exclusively Tamil-speaking state of Tamil Nadu. On May 1, 1960, the states of Maharashtra and Gujarat were created out of the Bombay state. The creation of Punjabi Suba on November 1, 1966, an exclusively Punjabi speaking state of Punjab (India), occurred after a long struggle.

Foreign Policy and Military Conflicts

Nehru's foreign policy was the inspiration of the Non-Aligned Movement, of which India was a co-founder. Nehru maintained friendly relations with both the United States and the Soviet Union, and encouraged the People's Republic of China to join the global community of nations. In 1956, when the Suez Canal Company was seized by the Egyptian government, an international conference voted 18-4 to take action against Egypt. India was one of the 4 backers of Egypt, along with Indonesia, Sri Lanka, and the USSR.

India had controversially opposed the partition of Palestine and the 1956 invasion of the Sinai by Israel, Britain and France, but did not oppose the Chinese occupation of Tibet and the suppression of a pro-democracy movement in Hungary by the Soviet Union. Although Nehru disavowed nuclear ambitions for India, Canada and France aided India in the development of nuclear power stations for electricity. India also negotiated an agreement in 1960 with Pakistan on the just use of the waters of seven rivers shared by the countries. Nehru had visited Pakistan in 1953, but owing to political turmoil in Pakistan, no headway was made on the Kashmir dispute.

1. India has fought a total of four wars/military conflicts with its rival nation Pakistan, two in this period.In the Indo-Pakistani War of 1947 fought over Kashmir, Pakistan occupied one third of Kashmir (which India claims as its territory), and India occupied three fifths (which Pakistan claims as its territory). In the Indo-

Pakistani War of 1965 India attacked Pakistan on all fronts after attempts by Pakistani troops to infiltrate into Indian controlled Kashmir. #In 1961, after continual petitions for a peaceful handover, India invaded and annexed the Portuguese colony of Goa on the west coast of India.

2. In 1962 China and India engaged in the brief Sino-Indian War over the border in the Himalayas. The war was a complete rout for the Indians and led to a refocusing on arms build-up and an improvement in relations with the United States. While China withdrew from occupied lands in the northeast, it continues to occupy Aksai Chin in Kashmir. China disputes India's sovereignty over Arunachal Pradesh and until recently, Sikkim.

POST-NEHRU INDIA

Jawaharlal Nehru died on May 27, 1964. Lal Bahadur Shastri succeeded him as Prime Minister. In 1965 in the Second Kashmir War India and Pakistan again went to war, but without any definitive outcome or alteration of the Kashmir boundary. The Tashkent Agreement was signed under the mediation of the Soviet government, but Shastri died on the night after the signing ceremony. A leadership election resulted in the elevation of Indira Gandhi, Nehru's daughter who had been serving as Minister for Information and Broadcasting, as the third Prime Minister. She defeated right-wing leader Morarji Desai.

The Congress Party won a reduced majority in the 1967 elections owing to widespread disenchantment over rising prices of commodities, unemployment, economic stagnation and a food crisis. Indira Gandhi had started on a rocky note after agreeing to a devaluation of the Indian rupee, which created much hardship for Indian businesses and consumers, and the import of wheat from the U.S. fell through due to political disputes.

Morarji Desai entered Indira's government as Deputy Prime Minister and Finance Minister, and with senior Congress politicians attempted to constrain Indira's authority. But following the counsel of her political advisor P. N. Haksar, Indira resuscitated her popular appeal by a major shift towards socialist policies. She successfully ended the privy purse guarantee for former Indian royalty, and waged a major offensive against party hierarchy over the nationalization of India's banks. Although resisted by Desai and India's business community, the policy was popular with the masses.

When Congress politicians attempted to oust Indira by suspending her Congress membership, Indira was empowered with a large exodus of MPs to her own Congress (R). The bastion of the freedom struggle, the Indian National Congress had split in 1969. Indira continued to govern with a slim majority.

Nehru and States Reorganisation Act

The States Reorganization Act of 1956 was a major reform of the boundaries and governance of India's states and territories. The act reorganized the boundaries of India's states along linguistic lines, and amended the Indian Constitution to replace the three types of states, known as Parts A, B, and C states, with a single type of state. Although additional changes to India's state boundaries have been made since 1956, the States Reorganisation Act of 1956 remains the single most extensive change in state boundaries since the independence of India in 1947.

Political Integration after Independence and the Constitution of 1950

British India, which included most of present-day India as well as Pakistan and Bangladesh, was divided into two types of territories: provinces, which were governed directly by British officials, responsible to the Governor-General of India; and princely states, under the rule of local hereditary rulers who recognised British sovereignty in return for local autonomy, as established by treaty.

As a result of the reforms of the early 20th century, most of the provinces had elected legislatures and governors, although some of the smaller provinces were governed by a chief commissioner appointed by the Governor-General. The 20th century reforms of British India also established the principle of federalism, also known in British India as "dyarchy", which was carried forward into the governance of independent India.

On August 15, 1947, British India was granted independence as the separate dominions of India and Pakistan. The British dissolved their treaty relations with the over 600 princely states, who were encouraged to accede to either India or Pakistan. Most of the states acceded to India, and a few to Pakistan. Bhutan and Hyderabad opted for independence, although the armed intervention of India brought Hyderabad into the Indian Union.

During the 1947-1950 period, the territories of the princely states were politically integrated into the Indian Union. Most were merged into the existing provinces; others were organised into new provinces, like Rajputana, Himachal Pradesh, Madhya Bharat, and Vindhya Pradesh made up of multiple princely states; a few, including Mysore, Hyderabad, Bhopal, and Bilaspur, became separate provinces. The Government of India Act 1935 remained the constitutional law of India pending adoption of a new Constitution. The Constitution of India, which went into effect on January 26, 1950, made India a sovereign, democratic republic, and a union of states (replacing provinces) and territories. The states would have extensive autonomy and complete democracy in the Union, while the Union territories would be administered by the Government of India. The constitution of 1950 distinguished between three types of states.

Part A states, which were the former governors' provinces of British India, were ruled by an elected governor and state legislature. The nine Part A states were Assam, West Bengal, Bihar, Bombay, Madhya Pradesh (formerly Central Provinces and Berar), Madras, Orissa, Punjab, and Uttar Pradesh (formerly United Provinces). The eight Part B states were former princely states or groups of princely states, governed by a rajpramukh, who was often a former prince, along with an elected legislature. The rajpramukh was appointed by the President of India. The Part B states were Hyderabad,

Saurashtra, Mysore, Travancore-Cochin, Madhya Bharat, Vindhya Pradesh, Patiala and East Punjab States Union (PEPSU), and Rajasthan. The ten Part C states included both the former chief commissioners' provinces and princely states, and were governed by a chief commissioner. The chief commissioner was appointed by the President of India. The Part C states included Delhi, Kutch, Himachal Pradesh, Bilaspur, Coorg, Bhopal, Manipur, Ajmer-Merwara, and Tripura. Jammu and Kashmir had special status until 1957. The Andaman and Nicobar Islands was established as a union territory, ruled by a lieutenant governor appointed by the central government.

The Movement for Linguistic States

Political movements for the creation of new, linguistic-based states developed around India in the years after independence. The movement to create a Telugu-speaking state out of the northern portion of Madras State gathered strength in the years after independence, and in 1953, the 16 northern, Telugu-speaking districts of Madras State became the new State of Andhra. Other small changes were made to state boundaries during the 1950-1956 period. The small state of Bilaspur was merged with Himachal Pradesh on July 1, 1954, and Chandernagore, a former enclave of French India, was incorporated into West Bengal in 1955.

The States Reorganisation Commission

In December 1953, Prime Minister Jawaharlal Nehru appointed the States Reorganisation Commission to prepare for the creation of states on linguistic lines. This was headed by Justice Fazal Ali and the commission itself was also known as the *Fazal Ali Commission*. The efforts of this commission was overseen by Govind Ballabh Pant, who served as Home Minister from December 1954. The commission created a report in 1955 recommending the reorganisation of India's states.

The States Reorganisation Act

The States Reorganisation Act of 1956, which went into effect on November 1, eliminated the distinction between part

A, B, and C states. It also reorganised the state boundaries and created or dissolved states and union territories.

India and the Non-Aligned Movement

India played an important role in the multilateral movements of colonies and newly independent countries that developed into the Non-Aligned Movement.

Origin of Non Alignment Movement

The founding leaders of the Non-Aligned states meet in New York in October 1960. From left: Nehru of India, Nkrumah of Ghana, Nasser of Egypt, Sukarno of Indonesia and Tito of Yugoslavia.

Nonalignment had its origins in India's colonial experience and the nonviolent Indian independence struggle led by the Congress, which left India determined to be the master of its fate in an international system dominated politically by Cold War alliances and economically by Western capitalism.

The principles of nonalignment, as articulated by Nehru and his successors, were preservation of India's freedom of action internationally through refusal to align India with any bloc or alliance, particularly those led by the United States or the Soviet Union; nonviolence and international cooperation as a means of settling international disputes. Nonalignment was a consistent feature of Indian foreign policy by the late 1940s and enjoyed strong, almost unquestioning support among the Indian elite.

The term "Non-Alignment" itself was coined by Indian Prime Minister Jawaharlal Nehru during his speech in 1954 in Colombo, Sri Lanka. In this speech, Nehru described the five pillars to be used as a guide for Sino-Indian relations, which were first put forth by Chinese Premier Zhou Enlai. Called Panchsheel (five restraints), these principles would later serve as the basis of the Non-Aligned Movement. The five principles were:

1. Mutual respect for each other's territorial integrity and sovereignty
2. Mutual non-aggression

3. Mutual non-interference in domestic affairs
4. Equality and mutual benefit
5. Peaceful co-existence

Jawaharlal Nehru's concept of nonalignment brought India considerable international prestige among newly independent states that shared India's concerns about the military confrontation between the superpowers and the influence of the former colonial powers. New Delhi used nonalignment to establish a significant role for itself as a leader of the Third World in such multilateral organizations as the United Nations (UN) and the Nonaligned Movement.

The signing of the Treaty of Peace, Friendship, and Cooperation between India and the Soviet Union in 1971 and India's involvement in the internal affairs of its smaller neighbors in the 1970s and 1980s tarnished New Delhi's image as a nonaligned nation and led some observers to note that in practice, nonalignment applied only to India's relations with countries outside South Asia.

EARLY DEVELOPMENTS

The movement had its origins in the 1947 Asian Relations Meeting in New Delhi and the 1955 Asian-African Conference in Bandung, Indonesia. India also participated in the 1961 Belgrade Conference that officially established the Nonaligned Movement, but Jawaharlal Nehru's declining prestige limited his influence. In the 1960s and 1970s, New Delhi concentrated on internal problems and bilateral relations, yet retained membership in an increasingly factionalized and radicalized movement. During the contentious 1979 Havana summit, India worked with moderate nations to reject Cuban president Fidel Castro's proposition that "socialism" (that is, the Soviet Union) was the "natural ally" of nonalignment.

3

Political Thinking

Even before the formation of the Indian National Congress on December 28, 1885 in Bombay, the leaders of the national movement (a number of whom came to play a very important role in the Congress) had devoted a great deal of their time and energy to a deep study and understanding of India's deteriorating economic situation.

Going through the records, there is mention of discontent among the people and their resorting to some sort of passive resistance as early as 1824-25. Bishop Reginald Heber who undertook a tour of Northern Provinces during this period found the existence of a small middle class (he called it "middling classes") which was somewhat articulate. He talked of the agitation of the people of Varanasi against the imposition of house tax. "The whole population of Benaras and its neighbourhood determined to sit on dhurna till their grievances were redressed." Further, "above 300,000 persons deserted their houses, shut up their shops, suspended the labour of their farms, forbore to light fires, dress victuals, many of them even to eat and sat down with folded arms and drooping heads." "This ... strange method of remonstrance against oppression" made the government withdraw the tax.' Raja Rammohun Roy was perhaps th c earliest Indian leader to talk of modernisation of the economy and he was of the opinion that there was in existence an enterprising class or group of people but without "sufficient capital to enter business."

He attacked fiercely both the Permanent Settlement and Ryotwari Settlement introduced by the British. He held: "Under both systems the condition of the cultivators is very miserable; in one they are placed at the mercy of the zamindar's avarice and ambition, in the other they are subjected to the extortion and intrigues of the surveyors and other government revenue officers: I deeply compassionate both, with this difference, in regard to agricultural peasantry of Bengal, that there the landlords have met with indulgence from government in the assessment of their revenue, while no part of this indulgence is extended towards the poor cultivators. In an abundant season, when the price of corn is low, the sale of their whole crops is required to meet the demands of the landholder, leaving little or nothing for seed or subsistence to the labourer or his family.'

Proceeding from the assumption that modernisation of the economy was necessary and this modernisation depended on accumulation of capital, which was not possible so long as the existing agrarian system, introduced by the British lasted. The mass of the population remained poor and deprived and had no capacity to invest in agriculture. What was needed was a rational altering of the agrarian relations in favour of tillers of the land. He was of the view that "Indian workers had the same capacity of improvement as any other civilized people."

According to Prof. B.N. Ganguli, Rammohun Roy was "in search of a *modernised, butIndian,* economy and polity with a viable rural base. For one thing, without such a base, *modern* industrialisation was bound to peter out in a predominantly agricultural country. For another thing, any' hot-house growth' that did not take account of the distinctiveness of India's rural civilisation was also not likely to bear fruit."

He was of the opinion that much depended on the acquisition of modern scientific knowledge and he wanted the spread of Western education throughout the country and the "diffusion of knowledge of European arts and sciences in the interest of *national improvement."* It must be noted here that Rammohun Roy was the earliest Indian leader to use the term "national" and thought of the nation as a whole. It must not be forgotten that the concept of India as a nation was extremely rare or non-existent. During the period when Rammohun Roy lived and worked, the exploitative mechanism of the British had neither fully unfolded itself nor had it become so intensive and merciless as it became after 1857. The British officials had not distanced themselves as they did later. That is why, he could talk of British settlers coming to India as agents of modernisation.

Dadabhai Naoroji was the first Indian leader to provide an insight into the mechanism of colonial exploitation and its intricacies and made it clear that the Indians were in a miserable condition not because of any inherent disability in them but because they were deprived of a large part of wealth produced by them. In 1876, on the basis of his study, "Poverty of India", he asserted that "India is suffering seriously in several ways and is sinking in poverty," and the people were so poor that they did not get enough even to meet the bare necessities of life. In 1881 he talked of "the wretched, heart-rending, blood-boiling condition of India". In 1900, he asserted: "The fact was that Indian Natives were mere helots. They were worse than American slaves, for the latter were at least taken care of by their masters whose property they were."

This was substantiated by him on the basis of his calculation of per capita average income for the year 1867-68 which came to just rupees 20. This amount fell short of even the expenditure on the upkeep of a prisoner. He calculated, on the basis of government reports, the main-tenance expenditure for a prisoner in Indian jails varied from rupees 21 and annas 13 in North-West Province to rupees 53 and annas 2 in Madras. In Bombay, it came to rupees 47 and annas 7 and in Bengal rupees 31 and annas 11. Thus, a person outside the jail was worse off than an inmate of the jail."

To explain the abysmal misery of the Indian people, he brought in his famous Drain Theory which was the result of his painstaking study in the British Museum and meticulous care for data and calculations. In fact, the idea of Drain was present even in the thinking of Raja Rammohun Roy who had told the House of Commons Select Committee of 1831 that "a large sum of money is now annually drawn from India by Europeans retiring from it with the fortunes realized there." He held that if this money had not been going out of India, the country could have been in a better position to develop! It was Naoroji who made it a really forceful theory to lay bare the mechanism of colonial exploitation. He produced his monumental work *Poverty and Un-British Rule in India* (first published in 1901) which embodied a coherent and convincing exposition of the Drain Theory. He "conceived of economic drain as an external-cum-internal drain. It was a kind of built-in mechanism which extorted resources outof a low-level colonial economy; and the surplus thus generated through a complicated process was drained out of the economy through the process of external trade, the dynamics of which was supplied by the unilateral transfer of funds in an equally complicated kind of way."

The drain of wealth from India took place on various counts such as unrequited exports, that is, trade with no equivalent returns, remit-tances to England by European employees as savings and for the support of their families, remittance for the purchase of British goods for their own consumption, expenditure by them in India on the purchase of British goods, the purchases' by the Government not included under "Home Charges" (the expenditure on the maintenance of India Office in England), charges in England, which included interest on public debt held in India, loss in exchange and debt incurred for productive works, the cost of maintenance of the British army in India, and the cost of British expeditions to extend the empire with the help of the Indian army.

All this was possible basically because India was not politically free and the nature of its economy was colonial. Had it been politically independent, the nature of its economy would have been different. Its resources would have been used to generate domestic employment opportunities and incomes which could have been spent on goods produced in the country, promoting India's economic development.

Dadabhai Naoroji pointed out that most of the top posts in the administration, army and public utilities were occupied by Englishmen, for which they received fat salaries and perks. He did not accept the claim that their "services" were an "invisible export" for which legiti-mate payments were received.

He held that these salaries and perks were not in any way commensurate with the services rendered by them. Secondly, since Indians were not associated with any of these services, they could not acquire any experience or training.

Replying to the British propagandists who were making much of the loans incurred by India for the development of railways which would help modernise the economy, he said: 'British India's own wealth is carried out of it, and then that wealth is brought back to it in the shape of loans, and for these loans she must find so much for interest; the whole thing moving in a most vicious and provoking circle. Will nothing but a catastrophe cure this?"[10]

A very distinguished contemporary of Naoroji, Karl Marx, had also reached the same conclusion on the basis of his own calculations. To quote, "India alone has to pay5 million in tribute for'good government', interest and dividends on British capital, etc., not counting the sums sent home annually by officials as savings from their salaries, or by the English merchants as part of their profit to be invested in England."" In a letter to N.F. Danielson in February 1881, Marx had written: "What the English take from them (Indians) annually in the form of rent, dividends for railways...pensions for military and civil-servicemen, for Afghan and other wars, etc., etc. - what they take from them without any equivalent and quite apart from what they appropriate to themselves annually within India- speaking only of the value of the commodities the Indians have gratuitously and annually to send over to England - it amounts to more than the total sum of income of the 60 millions of agricultural and industrial labourers of India."[12]

He campaigned hard to impress upon the right thinking people, be they Indians or the British, the need to stop the wealth of India being drained away from it. On July 1, 1900 he told a gathering in England, attended by a number of the English: "You in England pay something like fifty shillings or more taxes per head per annum. We in India pay only three to four shillings per head per annum. From this you may conclude thatwe mustbe the mostlightly taxedpeople in the world. That is not the case however. Our burden is nearly twice as heavy as yours. The taxes you pay in this country (England) go from the hands of the tax payers into the hands of the government from which they flow back into the country again in various shapes, fertilising trade and returning to the people themselves. There is no diminution of your wealth; your taxes simply change hands. Whatever you give you must get back. Any deficit means so much loss of strength. Suppose you pay a hundred million pounds a year and the government uses that money in such a way that a part only returns to you, the other part going out of the country. In that case you are being bled, part of your life is going away. Suppose out of 100 million pounds only eighty million pounds return to you in the shape of salaries, commerce and manufactures, you will have lost twenty million pounds. Next year you will be so much the weaker and so on each year. This is the difference between taxing the people and bleeding the people.""

Dadabhai rejected the British explanation in terms of Malthusian theory of population that India was poor and was not developing at a faster rate because of high rate of growth of its population. He retorted: "It is not the pitiless operation of Economic laws, but it is the thoughtless and pitiless action of the British policy, it is the pitiless eating of India's substance in India and the further pitiless drain to England -in short it is the pitiless perversion of economic laws by the sad bleeding that is destroying India .... It is absurd to talk of over-population, i.e., the country's incapability, by its food or other produce, to supply the means to support to its people, if the country is unceasingly and forcibly deprived of its capital.""""

According to his analysis, the poverty of India was due to the lack of the expansion of productive activities, especially modem industries, which, in their turn, were absent owing to the lack of capital. Capital formation was hindered by colonial rule and its policies. Thus, Swaraj or political independence emerged as the foremost precondition for the removal of poverty.

India had abundance of natural resources ("natural agents in any quantity") and enough labour. B ut itlacked capital. Withoutcapital,vast areas of cultivable land, "vast mineral and other underdeveloped resources" and ample supply of labour were of no use. If the country had capital which could be carefully and judiciously used, the production would increase, employment opportunities would be generated and poverty would be wiped out.

To solve the problem of capital, it was necessary that the process of economic drain was reversed. For this following steps were needed, namely, India must retain what it produced, the burden of servicing of public debt must be reduced, there must be a ceiling on payments to British officials by way of salaries, perks and pensions, employment of Indians wherever possible and a rational adjustment of Indo-British financial relations must be brought about and so on.

Dadabhai was convinced that without an active intervention of the State, Indian economy could not develop. At the same time, he wanted to allow private enterprise, both Indian and foreign, but within a well-formulated policy discipline. He was of the view that Indian entrepreneurs needed encouragement and guidance. For this two things were needed: first, political independence, and second, proper guidance by the State. To quote, "As long as the people of a country have no share in its administration the powerful stimulus of patriotism and self-interest cannot come into action."" Further, "Indians also would do a great deal if properly guided and encouraged. I am afraid encouraging them to look out does not seem to be much in the line of officials. 1116

He had some inkling that in Independent India, the pattern of economy would be a mixed one. The "association of government and private enterprise in works in which government control is necessary, so that each takes its risks and profits according to its share .... This would be very well adapted to supply the element of self-interest, the want of which has a great deal to do with the evil of waste."[17]

Before we end, let us also note that Dadabhai was not only in favour of State enterprises, but also a protagonist of nationalisation of large foreign-owned enterprises."

Mahadev Govind Ranade was not only a stalwart among the nationalist leaders of his time, but a trained economist also.

He lashed out at the very approach of the British Classical Political Economy to Indian problems and he demolished it logically in one of his lectures. Its assumptions such as the prevalence of individualism, the desire to promote one's self-interest, the free and unlimited competition as the best promoter of efficiency in production, the opposition to State intervention and customary regulation as encroachment on individual freedom, free movement of capital and labour and so on were not applicable to Indian conditions. The economic and social conditions in India were very different and the British policies which were supposed to be based on the approach of British economists did more harm than good to India. [19]

Thus, Ranade pleaded for developing "a Political Economy which took notice of Indian economic conditions instead of the conditions of the West.""

Ranade charged the British with destruction of the Indian economy and reducing it to a miserable situation in a period of just fifty years. "India, fifty years ago, clothed herself with her own Manufactures, and now she is clothed by her distant masters. The same is the case with Wool, Silk and other Textiles, with Oils and Hides .... This is our condition, and when the whole situation is thus taken in at one view, we feel that we are standing on the edge of a precipice, and the slightest push down will drive us into the abyss below of unmixed and absolute helplessness."[21]

The decline of traditional handicrafts increased the dependence of the people on agriculture which was precarious because of its depend-ence on the monsoon. Thus, Ranade pointed out to the phenomenon of de-industrialisation or ruralisation. The increasing pressure of popula-tion on land led to subdivisions of holdings, shrinking of forests and decline in per acre productivity. He also believed that increasing ruralisation had a number of uneconomic and far reaching conse-quences. It meant country's growing "rustication, i.e., a loss of power, and intelligence, and self defence".[22] The economy became colonial in character. It was treated by the British as "a Plantation, growing raw produce to be shipped by British Agents in British Ships, to be worked into Fabrics by British skill and capital, and to be re-exported to the Dependency by British merchants to their corresponding British Firms in India and elsewhere."[2]

Ranade was a great optimist and believed that India would emerge as a great modem nation provided it went in for industrialisation for which the possibilities were immense in the country. He enumerated a number of them. What was lacking was modem technology, methods of organisation of industrial enterprises and capital. He suggested a way out thus: "We have to organise labour and capital by co-operation, and import freely foreign skill and machinery, till we learn our lessons properly and need no help. We have rusticated too long; we have now to turn our apt hands to new work and bend our muscles to sturdier and honester labour. This is the civic virtue we have to learn, and according as we learn it or spurn it, we shall win or lose in the contest We have to work against great odds, which are represented by our old traditions, our poverty of resources, and the hostile competition of advanced races, whose industrial organisation has been completed under more favour-able conditions than our own."[24]

He calculated that between 1830 and 1880 gold and silver worth rupees 450 crore were imported by the Indians. Besides, there was a large-scale hoarding of these precious metals by them. This could be a big source of capital accumulation for productive use. "This hoarding, at least, proves that nearly 8 crores of rupees may be each year turned to capital account if we were only resolved to use it."

He attached great significance to the role of State in India's industrialisation. It was to be"recognised as the national organ fortaking care of national needs in all matters in which individual and cooperative efforts are not likely to be so effective and economical as national effort.' In India, it was not to remain confined only to three functions assigned to the State by Adam Smith, namely, the maintenance of law and order, the defence, and the provision of communal services and infrastructural facilities, but it was to encourage cooperative efforts, provide credit facilities to entrepreneurs, and pioneer new industrial enterprises. The State would buy needed goods from the public enter-prises (Ranade used the term "State factories"). He campaigned for the establishment of an Indian iron industry.

He stood for reforming agrarian relations to increase agricultural production which was crucial for India's economic development and thereupon improvement in the standard of living. He cited the examples of countries like France, Russia and Germany to drive home the point. To him, "The essential condition of rescuing the country from its miserable helplessness was to effect a radical change in the relationship of the soil with the person who cultivated it " He was in favour of the State legislating and working for the protection of workers and peasants from exploitation by capitalists and landlords. He was opposed to the freedom of contract which permitted high rates of interest to be extorted. from "poor, disunited, indebted classes" and was all for debt reconciliation.

Romesh Chandra Dutt was a giant among the intellectuals of his time. A staunch nationalist, who presided over the sessions of the Indian National Congress more than once, had seen the working and motive of British imperialism from very close quarters as a member of the civil service. As a professor and researcher, he had looked into the economic problems of the country very deeply. In his preface to his *magnum opus, Economic History of India,* he stated frankly,

> *Place any other country under the same condition, with crippled industries, with agriculture subject to a heavy and uncertain land tax, and with financial arrangements requiring one-half of the revenues to be annually remitted out of the country, and the most prosperous nation on earth will soon know the horrors of famine. A nation prospers if the sources of its wealth are widened, and if the proceeds of taxation are spent among the people, and for the people. A nation is impoverished if the sources of its wealth are narrowed, and the proceeds of taxation are largely remitted out of the country. These are plain, self-evident economic laws, which operate in India, as in every other country, and the Indian statesman and administrator must feel that the poverty of India cannot be removed until Indian industries are*

revived, until a fixed and intelligible limit is placed on the Indian land tax, and until Indian revenues are more largely spent in India?

He dismissed the argument that increasing population was respon-sible for India's growing poverty as superficial. He also dismissed the charge that Indian peasants were "careless and improvident" and "did not know how to save when there was plenty"? It was colonialism with its ruinous policies that was responsible for growing poverty and misery of the country. It had destroyed India's handicrafts, increased the burden of the peasants and thrown them into the clutches of moneylenders and drained away a large part of country's wealth. In his Presidential Address to the First Industrial Conference held at Benaras on December 30, 1905 he strongly advocated the extension of all modem industries and electrification. He was a votary of S wadeshi whereby "we use our home manufactures, so far as practicable, in preference to foreign manufacturers."

Summing up, the writings of nationalist leaders like Naoroji, Ranade, Dutt and others who studied Indian problems deeply and later came to be the founding fathers of the Indian National Congress reflected not only a grave concern at the deterioration of the economic plight of the common people but provided a comprehensive critique of the British policies and elucidated that without political freedom, socio-economic institutional changes and modernisation, the uplift of the people was impossible. They were aware of the happenings beyond the frontiers of the country, particularly in Europe and America. In view of their investigations and observations, they came to the conclusion that, without industrial revolution, it was not possible to modernise the economy and improve the social life. Without modem industrialisation, it was totally impossible to build an economy which could eliminate India's massive unemployment, low productivity and poverty.

Prof. Bipan Chandra has concluded from an extensive survey of their speeches and writings: "They accepted with near unanimity the complete economic transformation of the country with the help of modem machines as the primary goal of their economic policies and the panacea for all the economic ills of the country." For example, Bholanath Chandra had as early as 1873 called for the boycott of foreign goods and appealed to his countrymen to make industrial enterprise "the ocean to the rivers of all their thoughts". Tilak's *Mahratta* (February 13,1881) wrote: "We must become capital-ists and enterprisers...a nation of traders, machine-makers and shop-keepers". Justice Ranade hoped in 1893 that industrialisation "will soon become the creed of the whole Nation, and ensure the permanent triumph of modem spirit in this Ancient Land."

As Bipan Chandra has found, nationalist leaders held the lack of modem industries as the main cause of the countrywide economic impoverishment, underproduction and underemployment. The scope for further employment opportunities in traditional sectors of the economy was limited, and modem industries alone could lessen the pressure on land and on the fast declining handicrafts. Industrialisation would check excessive dependence on agriculture and drain of wealth from the country and it would be a key element in securing economic independence. Justice Ranade believed, the modern industries would also open vistas for the full and many-sided development of productive powers. Another intellectual of those days opined that industrialisation would take the country to "a superior type and a higher stage of civilisation". He had also held that India's poverty was "essentially an industrial problem."

It was also believed thatindustrialisation would lead to greater unity of the Indian people and help them overcome divisive *pulls. The Bengalee* (January 18, 1902) wrote:

> *The agitation for political rights may bind the various nationali-ties of India together for a time. The community of interests may cease when these rights are achieved. But the commercial union of the various nationalities, once established, will never cease to exist. Commercial and industrial activity is, therefore, a bond of very strong union and a mighty factor in the formation of a great Indian nation.*

As Prof. Bipan Chandra has found, "by the end of the 19th century, the demand for rapid industrialisation of the country along modem lines had assumed national proportions. Not a single important newspaper or public worker of the period...denied or doubted at any time the advan-tages and desirability of introducing and promoting western technique and industry in India."

It does not mean that Indian nationalists were unaware of the evil consequences of the economic system brought in by industrial revolu-tion in the West, such as acquisitiveness, inhuman treatment of workers and growing economic inequalities, but they did not reject it because India had no way out but to fall in line with the historical forces.

A number of nationalist leaders themselves came forward to start industrial and business ventures. In 1855 Dadabhai Naoroji became a partner in the business firm of the Camas, set up in London, and fourteen years later he set up his own firm Dadabhai Naoroji and Company. Justice Ranade played an important role in the establishment of a number of ventures started in Poona, namely, the Cotton and Silk Spinning and Weaving Factory, the Metal Manufacturing Factory, the Poona Mercantile Bank, the Poona Dyeing Company, and the Reay Paper Mill. K.T. Telang and Pherozshah Mehta played an active role in setting up a soap factory in Bombay. Mehta was also connected with textile industry, coming up in Bombay. Tilak was associated, for some time, with a cotton-ginning factory. Dinshaw Eduljee Wacha who presided over the seventeenth session of the Congress, held in 1901, was intimately connected with textile mills. The same was the case with another Congress president, R.N. Mudholkar. Pandit Madan Mohan Malaviya started in 1881 the Deshi Tijarat Company and helped establish the Prayag Sugar Company. Lala Lajpat Rai was similarly connected with a number of ventures. An industrial exhibition came to be organised along with the Congress session forquiteanumberof years.

Indian nationalist leaders were aware of the disastrous conse-quences of the growing penetration of foreign capital into India. Dadabhai Naoroji, R.C. Dutt and G.V. Joshi, and papers like *Bengalee* and *Mahratta* were strongly opposed to the growing hold of foreign capital and warned of its consequences which included increasing dependence. Bipan Chandra Pal warned:

> *The introduction of foreign, and mostly British, capital for working out the natural resources of the country, instead of being a help, is, in fact, the greatest of hindrances to all real improve-ments in the economic condition of the people. This exploitation of the land by foreign capitalists threatens to involve both Government and people in a common ruin .... It is as much a political, as it is an economic danger. And the future offew India absolutely depends upon an early and radical remedy of thistwo-edged evil.*

The leaders firmly believed that reliance had to be placed on Indian enterprise and Indian capital if the country wanted independent eco-nomic development and national prosperity. Foreign capital was inimi-cal to national interests, because, instead of helping and encouraging Indian enterprise, it was suppressing and discouraging it. Foreign capital was imported into India not because the Indians wanted it but as a result of the circumstances created by the alien rule which had destroyed handicrafts and killed all Indian initiatives and efforts to foster the development of indigenous enterprises. Foreign capital was taking away huge resources by way of interest and profit payments, and high salaries and perks to the company officials and technicians.

Prof. Bipan Chandra has rightly observed:

> *Firstly, the Indian national leaders, whether opposing or support-ing the use of foreign capital, had a clear grasp of the economic and political causes and consequences of foreign investments in India. Secondly, the entire national leadership was firmly of the view that real economic strength of the country lay in industrial development based upon Indian effort and Indian capital. Even those Indians who favoured the use of foreign capital did so on the understanding that it was the lesser of the two evils - the other and bigger evil being no industrialisation at all. Most of the Indian leaders would rather consent to a postponement of*

indus-trial development rather than let it be accomplished through the instrumentality of foreign capital. Thus, the point of view of the comprador was more or less entirely absent in the nationalist agitation of the period .... It should also be noted that the nation-alists on the whole supported the growth of industrial capital and not merchant capital. Thirdly, because the early extension of foreign industry, railways, etc., had indirectly encouraged the growth of Indian industry, hostility between the two had not yet become important or decisive and, consequently, it played a relatively minor role in the national economic agitation up to the end of the 19th century .... With the dawn of the twentieth century, however, Indian industrial effort began to outgrow the period of infancy and to come into conflict with the foreign capitalists .... As a result, writers in the nationalist press and orators on the Congress platform began to make, after 1900, frequent and vehement attacks on foreign capital."

Though up to 1930 (before the Karachi session) the Indian National Congress did not have a clear-cut and integrated comprehensive eco-nomic programme, its various economic resolutions did have a unity of purpose, that is, the aim of the Congress was not only to make India politically free but economically independent and free the people from the poverty and misery.

A look at the various resolutions and speeches shows that the Congress consistently stood for the reduction of the burden of land revenue on peasantry and a thoroughgoing restructuring of land rela-tions, introduced by the British. The resolutions, however, were very brief and without any clearly spelt out programme of land reforms. One may have a look at the resolutions of the Congress at Allahabad (1888 and 191 A Bombay (1889), Calcutta (1890,1896,1901 and 1906), Poona (1895), Lahore (1895 and 1909) and Lucknow (1916) to find that the main emphasis was on the fixity and permanence of the land revenue demand. There was no talk of ensuring the clearly-defined rights of the tillers? This was largely the result of the social composition of the Congress leadership which was mostly urban based without much contacts with or the first-hand knowledge of the problems of peasantry. Whatever knowledge the leaders like Naoroji, Ranade, Dutt and others had was derived mainly from government reports and books.

It was in Lucknow, in 1916, that the Congress passed a resolution, urging the government to appoint a committee "to enquire into the causes of agrarian trouble and the strained relations between the Indian *ryot* and European planter" in Champaran (Bihar)[37] which ultimately led to the involvement of Mahatma Gandhi in the first mass peasant movementinthecountry.Itwashereforthe,firsttimethatasemi-literate peasant, Rajkumar Shukla, was allowed to speak from the platform of the Congress in his dialect (Bhojpuri) and move a resolution in Hindi. It is needless to add that the Champaran Satyagraha proved to be a turning point for the Congress. It came face to face with the peasantry of the country. Champaran was followed by Kheda Satyagraha of 1918 and the agitation by the Ahmedabad textile mill-workers. Thus, the Congress had to come out to involve itself with the problems of peasants and workers.

The other issues taken up by the Co;tgress were famines, increasing burden of military expenditure, home charges, the currency and the plight of indigenous industries and industrialisation.

At its Calcutta session (1896), the Indian National Congress held the British rule responsible for the increasing frequency and intensity of famines. To quote:

This Congress deplores the outbreak of famine in more or less acute form throughout India and holds that this and other famines which have occurred in recent years are due to the great poverty of the people, brought on by the drain of the wealth of the country which has been going on for years together, and by the excessive taxation and overassessment, consequent on the policy of ex-travagance, followed by the Government both in the civil and military departments, which has so far impoverished the people that at the first touch of scarcity they are rendered helpless and must perish .... In the opinion of this

Congress the true remedy against the recurrence of famines lies in the adoption of a policy which would enforce economy, husband the resources of the State, foster the development of indigenous and local arts and industries ... andhelpforward the introduction of modern arts and industries. (emphasis added)

It demanded the immediate famine relief work to mitigate the suffering of the people and the formulation of a well-defined famine code. It criticised the government for not restoring the Famine Insurance Fund to the purpose for which it was instituted.

In 1902, the Congress recommended the revival of handicrafts and setting up of modern industries, to lessen the pressure of population on land, establishment of agricultural banks for greater supply and better organisation of rural credit and stop the drain of wealth to reduce the severity of famine.

The Congress consistently asked for the reduction in military expenditure which had nothing to do with the well-being of the people and the defence of the country (Bombay, 1885, Allahabad, 1892 and Madras, 1894) At Nagpur, in 1920, the Congress characterised the military expenditure as "unjustifiable" and responsible for bringing "the national indebtedness to a limit beyond recovery" and the country would not be responsible for the repayment of debts incurred to finance military expenditure, after its Independence.`

One of the most important economic policy issues taken up by the Congress concerned currency and exchange rate. Itopposed the demand for the abandonment of silver standard and its replacement by gold standard and the closure of mints. It asserted that these steps would prove injurious to the interests of the country.[43] Dinshaw Eduljee Wacha told the ninth session of the Congress at Lucknow in 1893 that the currency policy of the British government was responsible for "all the economic evils from which the people at large and the banking and mercantile communities have suffered and are suffering."

The partition of Bengal in 1905 and the movement of Swadeshi which arose in its wake gave a new turn to the economic thinking of the Congress, which was reflected in the

Congress resolution at its Calcutta session of 1906. It accorded "its most cordial support to the Swadeshi movement" and called upon "the people of the country to labour for its success by making earnest and sustained efforts to promote the growth of indigenous industries and to stimulate the production of indigenous articles by giving them preference over imported commodities even at some sacrifice."

This stand was reiterated and elaborated at the Madras session of 1914 and the Bombay session of 1915. At the latter, the Congress called for the expansion of the facilities for industrial and technical education, the grant of fiscal autonomy to the country, the removal of artificial barriers to the development of indigenous industries, erected by the policies of the government and the constitution of industrial advisory committees atprovincial level. It may be noted here thatas early as 1901, the Congress had constituted a committee consisting of Tilak, Madan Mohan Malaviya, Bhupendra Nath Basu, Ranade and others to examine whether "the present state of economic depression of the country is owing to want of knowledge of the methods of production and distribu-tion which prevail in foreign countries" and whether the Indians should "adopt means to bring advanced knowledge and exact information within the reach of the people." The committee was also to look into the problem of scarcity of capital and the ways and means to mobilise it and make it available to both industry and agriculture.'"

At this session itself, the Congress underlined the need to apply scientific know how and better inputs to agriculture. It held that agronomical practices prevalent at that time were out of date and not equal to the task of increasing productivity. It called for the establish-ment of demonstration and experimental farms, and the award of scholarships to those wanting to join institutes of agricultural science.

Gopal Krishna Gokhale, in his presidential address to the Benaras session of the Congress (1905), had defined "the true Swadeshi move-ment" as "both a patriotic and an economic movement." He had called the "idea of Swadeshi or one's own country " as "one of the noblest conceptions that have ever stirred the heart of humanity." As an economic movement it was "to ensure a ready consumption of such articles as are produced in the country and to furnish aperpetual stimulus to production by keeping the demand for indigenous things largely in excess of the supply, the difficulties that surround the question economi-cally are so great that they require the cooperation of every available agency to surmount them."

He went on to add: "The question of production is a question of capital, enterprise, and skill and in all these factors, our deficiency at present is very great. Whoever can help in any one of these fields is, therefore, a worker in the Swadeshi cause and should be welcomed as such."Thus, he made the S wadeshi movement a much wider one rather than keeping it confined to the boycott of foreign goods and the consumption of indigenous goods.

The emergence of Indian enterprises in cotton textiles, the setting up of the Tata Iron and Steel Company and a number of Swadeshi units and the outbreak of the First World War cutting India off from Western Europe brought about a radical change in the situation. The Government appointed the Indian Industrial Commission on which the prominent Congress leader, Pandit Madan Mohan Malaviya, sat as a member and voiced the nationalist opinion.

The Congress at its Delhi session of 1918 adopted a comprehensive resolution on "Industrial Development" which called for an active role to be played by the government *"in promoting the Industrial development ... the object kept in view will be the encouragement of Indian capital and enterprise and exploitation with the sole aim of making India industrially and economically self-contained and self dependent."*[47] (emphasis added). It underlined the need to start industrial banks to meet the demand of industrial development for financial resources.

One may discover the seeds of a future public sector in industry here. The purpose, however, was to facilitate the investment of Indian capital in industrial enterprises. The other things emphasised by the Congress included the reconstitution of industrial advisory boards to give repre-sentation to Indian trade associations and chambers of commerce, setting up of industrial and chemical services to be fully manned by Indians and establishment of commerce colleges.

To sum up the Congress thinking up to the First World War, the Congress and its leaders tried to analyse the nature and causes of India's deteriorating economic conditions and growing poverty and misery of the people and found that colonialism and its policies were the prime cause, and, unless India became politically independent, there was no hope for India arresting the decline in its socio-economic life. Thus, political independence must be the foremost item on its agenda. Political independence was the indispensable precondition for regeneration of the nation and reconstruction of its socio-economic life's

They emphasised the need for socio-economic institutional changes like land reforms, provision of irrigation facilities and latest agronomical knowledge, but they hammered again and again the point that India could not go back to the days of yore. It must look around and outside the frontiers to see how industrial revolution was bringing about a radical change in the socio-economic life of the people. India must reconstruct its economy on the basis of modern industries and latest achievements of science and technology. For this the role of State was indispensable in the existing circumstances. This reconstruction of the economy must be based on Swadeshi with the sole aim of achieving self-reliance.

They were, however, not very clear about the nature of political independence they were striving for. Most of them wanted self-govern-ment within the British empire. In the beginning many of them thought that the positive results of the British rule outweighed the negative consequences, reflected in growing poverty and misery. They hoped, in the course of time, the British would adopt benevolent policies to mitigate the sufferings of the country. But with the passage of time their expectations were belied and their thinking started showing shifts. In the words of Prof. Bipan Chandra, "gratefulness and praise began to give way to constant carping and grieving so far as economic issues were concerned." They realised that the plight of India was not due to any lack of understanding of the Indian situation on the part of the British but because of the very nature and mechanism of their rule. One could find the dilemma of our leaders in the title of Dadabhai Naoroji's book *Poverty and Un-British Rule in India.*

Bipan Chandra has rightly concluded that there was a great deal of divergence between the political and the economic thinking of nation-alist leaders. The latter was much more radical and basically anti-imperialist. Swadeshi, establishment of modem industries, the opposi-tion to the various elements which constituted the Drain and the demand for changes in Indo-British economic relations aimed at undermining the foundations of British imperialism in India, which could not be in harmony with their wish to retain India as a self-governing entity within the British empire. This contradiction could be resolved only during the concluding years of the 1920s.

The nationalist leaders and the Congress could not evolve a comprehensive integrated economic programme in which the place of different sectors and their relative roles were properly defined. May be they did not have sufficient data and theoretical acumen to do so.

It is noteworthy that their approach to the problem of socio-economic transformation of the country was truly national. They did not view the problem from the angle of any particular region, community or group. Since at that time neither the working class nor the peasantry was organised and conscious section of the society, the thinking of the national movement was not in any way influenced by either the working class or the peasantry. However, they did care for the problems of both the sections to some extent.

THE EMERGENCE OF NEHRU

On January 12, 1905 the Grand Old Man of India, Dadabhai Naoroj1, wrote Dinshaw Eduljee Wacha, a very prophetic letter: "The very discontent and impatience it (the Indian National Congress) has evoked against itself as slow and non-progressive among the rising generation are among its best results or fruits. It is its own evolution and progress...." He went on to add: The main task now is "to evolve the required revolution-whether it would be peaceful or violent....'"

The next generation, led by Jawaharlal Nehru, did behave as Naoroji had predicted. It expressed its impatience and discontentat the slow pace of comprehension of the Indian reality by the Congress, the conservative approach to problems and not very radical or traditional solutions. The new generation was more conscious of India's problems largely due to the groundwork done by the older generation. Let us recall what Justice Ranade had told Gokhale in 1891 when the latter was disappointed at a two-line reply to a longish memorial submitted by the Poona Sarvajanik Sabha. Ranade had said: "You don't realise our place in the history of our country. These memorials are nominally addressed to Government, in reality they are addressed to the people, so that they learn how to think in these matters. This work must be done for many years, without expecting any other results because politics of this kind is altogether new in this land."

The new generation continued the work begun by the older one in the context of the qualitatively new situation and conditions. It solved the contradiction faced by the older generation between its economic thinking and analysis on the one hand and the political approach on the other. It knitted together the various elements, thought of by the predecessors, of a comprehensive economic programme, and supplied the missing links. It removed the vagueness and ambiguities. It linked India's fight for its political freedom with the worldwide struggle of the oppressed and enslaved peoples against imperialism. It made the Indian people and national movement aware of the changes taking place in the world at large.

To appreciate the transition to a new stage of economic thinking in the national movement, let us have a look at the objective situation as it emerged after the First World War.

Soon after the end of the First World War, it became clear that there was no possibility of reforming the British rule in India internally so that a modern industrialised economy could be built and institutional reforms carried out to uplift the oppressed people. More and more people became convinced that the main aim of the British was to keep India and its economy subservient to the mother country. In this situation it was impossible for India to make any progress. The famines, plague, influenza and other epidemics were taking a heavy toll of lives, but the government seemed to be unconcerned. Thanks to the efforts of Swami Vivekananda, Tilak, Naoroji and others the people of the country had gradually become more self-respecting and self-confident. The message of Vivekananda: "The only hope of India is from the masses. The upper classes are physically and morally dead", had influenced a large number of the youth. Gradually, it came to be realised that without the involve-ment of the masses, the Congress and the national movement were not going to be effective. With the spread of English education, increasingly people came into contact with the developments in the West and the ideas like democracy, nationalism, independence started attracting and influencing them. A powerful desire to make India a strong, independent and modern industrialised economy took root in them

The rise of a small Asian country like Japan as a modern economy thrilled and inspired the Indians. The defeat of the Italian army by the Ethiopians in 1896 and of the Czarist Russia in 1905 convinced that the British imperialism also was not invincible, that European superiority was just a myth. Tilak's *Kesari* had written on December 6, 1904:

It was up to this time supposed that the Asiatics lacked the sentiment of nationality and were, therefore, unable to hold their own before the European nations in spite of their individual courage and heroism. It was further believed that the continents of Asia, Africa, and America were created by Providence to be dominated by European nations .... The Russo-Japanese War has given a rude shock to these beliefs, and those who hold them are now beginning to see that ... there is nothing inherently improb-abie in the Asiatics forming themselves into independent nations and taking rank with their European rivals.

The *Karachi Chronicle* of June 18, 1905 was more candid in its comments: "What one Asiatic has done others can do.... If Japan can drub Russia, India can drub England with equal ease .... Let us drive the British into the sea and take our place side by side with Japan among the great powers of the world.' The Russian Revolution of 1905 attracted the attention of Indian nationalist leaders. Mahatma Gandhi who was at that time in South Africa made several comments on it. He wrote: "We have no voice in conducting the affairs of the state and have to pay taxes without demur, the same is true of the Russians also. Seeing such oppression, some Russians do come out bravely against it from time to time. Some time ago, there was a rebellion in Russia.' He tried to draw inspiration from it and compared the Viceroy in India with the Czar and declared that "We can also show the same strength that the Russian people has done."

Dadabhai Naoroji in his presidential address to the Calcutta session of the Congress in 1906 took note of the First Russian Revolution as well as of the happenings in China and Japan and asked: "While China in the East and Persia in the West of Asia are awakening and Japan has already awakened and Russia is struggling for emancipation-and all of them despotisms-can the free citizens of the British Indian Empire continue to remain subject to despotism—the people who were among the first civilizers of the world?"

Tilak and his followers had studied keenly the methods of the Russian revolutionaries and tried to explore the possibility whether they could be adopted in India. He was convinced that they needed to be adopted in India even though the conditions in the two countries were not completely identical: "Howsoever poor the soil of India might be, it is, however, certain that the tree of oppression and repression will bear the same fruits in India, as it has borne in Russia."

After the October Revolution, a number of Indian revolutionaries such as Madame Cama, Virendranath Chattopadhyay, Shyamji Krishna Verma, Ranoji Rao, Raja Mahendra Pratap, Baraktullah and others established contacts with Russian revolutionaries and a few of them met Lenin. Lala Lajpat Rai believed that "with a Republican China in the north-west and a Bolshevik Russia in the remote north, it will be extremely foolish to rule India despotically. Not even gods can do it."

It must be noted that the lack of information about the October Revolution and the socialist regime, following it, was responsible for certain misgivings in the minds of a number of nationalist leaders. For example, C.R.Das told the Gaya session (1922) of the Congress:

> *The recent revolution in Russia is very interesting study. The shape which it has now assumed is due to the attempt to force Marxian doctrines and dogmas on the unwilling genius of Russia. Violence will again fail. If I have read the situation accurately, I expect a counter revolution. The soul of Russia must struggle to free herself from the socialism of Karl Marx. It may be an independent movement, or it may be that the present movement contains within itself the power of working out that freedom. In the meantime the fate of Russia is trembling in the balance.*

It is obvious, certain changes took place in the objective conditions which affected the character of the Congress. The emergence of Mahatma Gandhi as its supreme leader transformed it into a mass party and it could no longer remain as an exclusive preserve of the urban nationalist elite. Gandhiji made it a militant organisation for throwing out the colonial domination and bringing about social, cultural and economic regeneration. His stress on constructive programme, espe-cially khadi and village industries, brought about a reorientation of the economic thinking of the Congress. The problems of peasantry started figuring in the Congress thinking more prominently. The Congress leaders at various levels involved themselves in their agitations. Ma-hatma Gandhi himself was involved in peasant movements in Bihar and Gujarat.

The first organised national body of industrial workers came into being on October 31, 1920. Lala Lajpat Rai presided over the inaugural session of the All India Trade Union Congress anditwas attended among others, by Pandit Motilal Nehru, Sardar Patel and Annie Besant. Thus, industrial workers were brought into the national movement and their problems and their thinking found place in the deliberations of the Indian National Congress.

The rejection of Montagu-Chelmsford reforms, the agitation against the Rowlatt Act, the Jallianwalla Bagh massacre and the Khilafat and Non-cooperation movement took the Congress and freedom movement to a great height. The establishment of national schools and national universities like Kashi Vidyapith, Gujarat Vidyapith, Bihar Vidyapith and others where the medium of instruction and examination was an Indian language and the constructive programme of Gandhiji not only took the message of the Congress to the grassroot level but produced a large band of dedicated workers. The Congress and the masses became identified with each other.

During this period a new generation of workers and leaders entered the Congress. Though they accepted Gandhiji as their supreme leader, their immediate leader was Pandit Jawaharlal Nehru who not only helped the Congress broaden its vision, but solved the dilemma arising out of the demand for economic independence while not willing to go out of the British empire and linked the Congress and freedom move-ment as a constituent of the worldwide struggle against imperialism and for economic and political independence of the colonial countries. He brought in the idea of socialism, political democracy and planning and linked them with the Congress demand for Swadeshi and Swaraj. He contributed towards removing the confusion in the thinking of the Congress. The credit goes to him for evolving a comprehensive, integrated economic programme and concretising it. He looked far ahead of many of his contemporaries and into the future.

Nehru's Congress connections began in 1912, the year he arrived in India, after completing his education in England. He attended the Bankipore (Patna) Congress, presided over by Gokhale. Though he was impressed by the sincerity, commitment and seriousness of Gokhale, the Congress gathering could not impress him in any measure because "it was very much an English-knowing upper class affair where morning coats and well-pressed trousers were greatly in evidence. Essentially it was a social gathering with no political excitement or tension."

Nehru, from the very beginning, held the British rule responsible for India's poverty, misery, exploitation and cultural and intellectual decline and had no confidence in the leadership the national movement had. He was extremely dissatisfied with the activities of these Congress leaders. "All these people lived in a world apart, cut off from the masses and even the lower middle class. Politics was confined to this upper strata." Thus, when Gandhiji came on the scene and brought the masses into the Congress politics and national movement as a major determin-ing factor, Nehru was attracted to him even though he differed with him on many an occasion. Even before he came into contact with Gandhiji, he had started taking interest in politics and was searching for his moorings. The Moderates repelled him because of their timidity and cowardice. They represented the upper middle class which was for slow changes.

At that time Nehru was a pure nationalist, though "fresh reading was again stirring the embers of socialistic ideas" in his head, but "They were vague ideas, more humanitarian and utopian than scientific."

He has himself admitted that, in the beginning, "My politics had been those of my class, the bourgeoisie." The industrial workers were not nationally organised and had very little influence over national politics. "The peasantry were a blind, poverty-stricken, suffering mass, resigned to their miserable fate and sat upon and exploited by all who came in contact with them-the Government, landlords, money-lenders, petty officials, police, lawyers, priests."

The newspapers were, by and large, not concerned with the problems of the people. They voiced the interests of capitalists, landlords, native princes and the British. The few who dared to take up the national and popular interests, had always to live in fear and were constantly terrorised.

The situation was depressing, but three things saved Jawaharlal and cheered him up. They were his coming into contact with Gandhiji, his involvement in the Kisan movement in Awadh (central U.P.) and the happenings in the Soviet Union.

With the special session of the Congress in 1920 at Calcutta, began the Gandhi era in Indian politics. "The whole look of the

Congress changed; European clothes vanished and soon only khadi was to be seen; a new class of delegate, chiefly drawn from the lower middle classes became the type of Congressman; the language used became increas-ingly Hindustani, or sometimes the language of the province where the session was held...and a new life and enthusiasm and earnestness became evident in Congress gatherings."

Gandhi instilled courage into India. He brought discipline and endurance and the will to self-sacrifice. He drove away fear from the hearts of the people. "He came to represent India to an amazing degree and to express the very spirit of that ancient and tortured land. Almost he was India, and his very failings were Indian failings."

Gandhi represented the vast masses of the country, especially the peasantry. Nehru was attracted to him because of his courage, frankness and self-sacrifice. He realised that Gandhi understood India best and had .become "the quintessence of the conscious and subconscious will of those millions." He found Gandhi "A man of keenest intellect, of fine feeling and good taste, wide vision; very human..." who "knows his India well and reacts to her lightest tremors, and gauges a situation accurately and almost instinctively, and has a knack of acting at the psychological moment.""

It seemed Gandhi was the leader for whom Nehru had been waiting. He immediately became his follower though not agreeing with all his views. Even disagreements did not diminish his deep regard forand faith in Gandhi. In a letter to Gandhi on January 23, 1928, while voicing his differences with him, Nehru admitted that he was Gandhi's "child in politics, though perhaps a truant and erratic child".

In June 1920, Nehru was drawn into the Kisan movement of Awadh, which brought him face to face with enormous poverty, misery and exploitation of the peasantry, the degrading conditions in villages, the callous attitude of the British government and the intermediary tenure-holders who constituted strong pillars of support for the Raj, but also realised the tremendous power of organised peasantry. This experience moulded his life and outlook radically. He was himself to admit it in the following words: "Looking at them and their misery and overflowing gratitude, I was filled with shame and sorrow, shame at my easygoing and comfortable life and our petty politics of the city which ignored this vast multitude of semi-naked sons and daughters of India, sorrow at the degradation and overwhelming poverty of India. A new picture of India seemed to rise before me, naked, starving, crushed, and utterly miser-able. " Further, "What amazed me still more was our total ignorance in the cities of this great agrarian movement. No newspaper had contained a line about it; they were not interested in rural areas. I realised more than ever how cut off we were from our people and how we lived and worked and agitated in a little world apart from them.

Though his involvement in Kisan movement gave him the feeling that he was "re-Indianizing himself and functioning in a wholly Indian situation", "he had made no study of economic and land problems, and had no economic ideology to offer." It seems, he was not clear how to integrate the peasantry with national movement and make theirdemands a part and parcel of the national charter of demands, though, as already noted, he was aware of their potential and their fighting capacity.

Till this time, he was not clear about the socio-economic dimensions of Swaraj. His study of and acquaintance with scientific socialism was almost non-existent. According to S. Gopal, he even believed that "Life under socialism would be unacceptable to him as it would prove joyless and soulless, regulated by bureaucracy to the minutest detail.

As he has himself admitted, he was more under the influence of anarchism of Bertrand Russell who was his favourite author and the concept of village government, propagated by Gandhiji. He saw the conditions in native states, which were much worse than those in British India. He also saw the divisive forces like communalism at work. He was trying to understand the factors behind them which sustained them. He was worried at the prospect of India's unity and its modernisation, though he was till then not in a position to work out an integrated outlook. The turning point in his quest for such an outlook came when he left for Europe in 1926. He went there after a gap of thirteen years during which the old order which he had known had given way to a completely new world, the correlation of forces had changed, balance of power had altered, British imperialism was in a phase of decline and the forces of anti-imperialism were on the rise. A socialist revolution, the first of its kind in the human history, had taken place in Russia and this had heralded the beginning of the end of imperialism and colonial domination. He attended the Congress of Oppressed Nationalities at Brussels in February 1927 as the official representative of the Indian National Congress. There he came into close contact with socialists and commu-nists of Europe and Indian revolutionaries abroad. The Congress of Oppressed Nationalities decided to form a permanent organisation, the League Against Imperialism, to continue the work and execute the decisions at Brussels. AlbertEinstein, Madame Sun Yat Sen and Romain Rolland were among the patrons of the League.

The Brussels Congress and the subsequent committee meetings of the League had a deep impact on the thinking process of Nehru. They widened his mental horizon and deepened his understanding of the problems of colonial and dependent countries. He could understand better the inner conflicts of the socialist and labour movements in the West when he saw their reflections in the deliberations. His attitude underwent a transformation:

> *As between the Labour worlds of the Second International and the Third International, my sympathies were with the latter. The whole record of the Second International from the War onwards filled me with distaste, and we in India had sufficient personal experience of the methods of one of its strongest supporters-the British Labour Party. So I turned inevitably with goodwill towards Communism, for, whatever its faults, it was at least not hypocritical and not imperialistic. It was not a doctrinal adher-ence, as I did not know much about the fine points of Commu-nism, my acquaintance being limited at the time to its broad features. These attracted me, as also the tremendous changes taking place in Russia.*

At Brussels, he tried to impart a new dimension to Indian nationalism and link it to the question of the freedom of all oppressed and dependent countries. In fact, he tried to internationalise the problem of India's independence and make it a matter of concern for the world at large. In a statement to the press on February 9, 1927 at Brussels, he said: The Indian National Congress is necessarily national and has nationalism as its basis, but as our great leader Gandhi has said, our nationalism is based on the most intense internationalism. The problem of Indian freedom is for us vital and urgently essential, but at the same time it is not merely a national problem. India is a world problem and as in the past so in the future other countries and peoples will be vitally affected by the condition of India.

Today the strongest and the most far-reaching imperialism is that of England and English imperialism and policy always have India as their cornerstone. Both Egypt and other parts of Africa have suffered domination because British imperialism wanted to strengthen its hold on India and to protect its sea routes to that country.

From the Continent, Nehru with his father, wife and younger sister went to Russia in November 1927. He remained in Moscow for four days and studied the changes in socio-economic life of the people brought about by the October Revolution and the Soviet regime. Even though the visit was too short to acquire a detailed knowledge and deep appreciation of the tremendous changes in the Soviet life, Nehru was happy and later recorded in his *Autobiography:*

> *But we were glad we went, for even that glimpse was worthwhile. It did not, and could not, teach us much about Russia, but it did give us a background for ourreading. To my father all such Soviet and collectivist ideas were wholly novel. His whole training had been legal and constitutional, and he could not easily get out of that framework. But he was definitely impressed by what he saw in Moscow*

On his return, he not only wrote a series of articles on his impressions of the Soviet visit, but the ideas and insights which he had acquired began reflecting themselves in his outlook and approach and his political and economic stand inside and outside the Congress.

In his very fast article "The Fascination of Russia" *(The Hindu, April* 3, 1928), he admitted that, since his return, he was frequently asked to speak on the Russian Revolution and the changes it had brought about in the life of the people in the Soviet Union. Such was the curiosity of the people and Nehru "welcomed this spirit of enquiry and this interest in a country which has many points of contact with ours, and which has launched on one of the mightiest experiments in history. All the world is watching her, some with fear and hatred, and others with passionate hope and the longing to follow in her path." This was because:

> *Itisdifficultto feel indifferent towards Russia,anditis still more difficult to judge her achievements and her failures impartially. She is today too much of a livewire to be touched without a violent reaction, and those who write about her can seldom avoid superlatives of praise or denunciation. Much depends on the angle of vision and the philosophy of life of the observer; much also on the prejudices and preconceived notions which he brings to his task. But whichever view may be right no one can deny the fascination of this strange Eurasian country of the hammer and sickle, where workers and peasants sit on the thrones of the mighty and upset the best laid schemes of mice and men.*

Nehru was certain that the Russian experiment would help India find solutions to its own problems because there was a great deal of similarity in the situations of the two countries. The old approach and the old mode of thinking had to be discarded and new lessons had to be learnt and here the experiences of Russia would be of great help. To quote Nehru:

> *For us in India the fascination is even greater, and even our self-interest compels us to understand the vast forces which have upset the old order -of things and brought a new world into existence, where values have changed utterly and old standards have given place to new. We*

are conservative people, not over-fond of change, always trying to forget our present misery and degradation in vague fancies of ourglorious past and an immortal civilisation. But the past is dead and gone and our immortal civilisation does not help us greatly in solving the problems of today. If we desire to find a solution for these problems, we shall have to venture forth along new avenues of thought and search for new methods. The world changes and the truths of yesterday and the day before may be singularly inapplicable today. We have to follow the line of life in its ever-varying curves and attempt to adhere rigidly to an outworn creed may take us off at a tangent from this curve of life and lead us to disaster. Russia thus interests us because it may help us to find some solution for the great problems which face the world today. It interests us specially because conditions there have not been, and are not even now, very dissimilar to conditions in India. Both are vast agricultural countries with only the beginnings of industri-alisation, and both have to face poverty and illiteracy. If Russia finds a satisfactory solution for these, our work in India is made easier.

In November 1927, thus, Nehru's conversion to scientific socialism was complete. He was no longer a believer in a somewhat vague, humanitarian kind of socialism, drawn from the books of Bertrand Russell. The same Jawaharlal who was not capable of working out a revolutionery programme because he had no clear idea, was now more confident and itching to undertake the task. One may recall that on April 25, 1923 he had admitted his inability to produce any kind of blueprint for the national movement. He was full of optimism, and was confident of India winning its freedom and changing the face of the country. He saw some kind of similarities not only between Russia and India but also between Lenin and Gandhi. In his very first letter to his daughter - Indira - with which he began his story of mankind's struggle for advancement, he wrote:

The year you were born in-1917-was one of the memorable years of history when a great leader, with a heart full of love and sympathy for the poor and suffering, made his people write a noble and never-to-be-forgotten chapter of history. In the very month in which you were born, Lenin started the great Revolu-tion which has changed the face of Russia and Siberia. And today in India another great leader, also full of love for all who suffer and passionately eager to help them, has inspired our people to great endeavour and noble sacrifice, so that they may again be free and the starving and the poor and the oppressed may have their burdens removed from them.

About ten weeks later, he told his daughter, while referring to the French and Russian revolutions:

We want independence, of course. But we want something more. We want to clear out all the stagnant pools and let in clean and fresh water everywhere. We must sweep away the dirt and the poverty and misery from our country. We must also clean up, as far as we can, the cobwebs from the minds of so many people which prevent them from thinking and co-operating in the great work before us.

Independence was an indispensable precondition for India's socio-economic transformation, but what kind of independence should it be? He did not accept the view that there was not much difference between Dominion Status and complete independence. Under the former, the British domination on India in every vital field and sphere was to be maintained. The goal of the British was to continue to keep India subservient to them and its economy a dependent one. Under this kind of arrangement, there was no possibility for India to sweep away all the outdated and antiquated institutions and relations which hindered its modernisation because they had proved to be very dependable props of the British rule. The examples of Canada and Australia were not applicable to India because the circumstances were different. The former were peopled largely by the Europeans and their relations with the British had evolved on a different footing. Nehru had detailed the differences in an article in *The Review of Nations,* published from Geneva, as early as January 1927. He had ruled out any worthwhile cooperation between India and Britain within a framework of Dominion Status for India because they could not be equal partners. "Cooperation to be productive of good mustbe the cooperation of equals, not the miscalled cooperation which is based on the master-fulness of the rulers and the servility of the ruled."

In India there was no love lost between the Indians and the British, "the two races are as apart from each other as ever, and today each views the other with resentment and hostility." True, British rule had given India railways, telegraph, telephone and brought in some kind of order and peace, but "there are other things, of the mind and the spirit, not to mention material good, more vital than railways and the like ... other countries even in the East have developed railways and the telegraph and the telephone without England's help, and perhaps India also might have done so if Providence in its inscrutable wisdom had not thrust England on her. And peace is good, but even the terrors and the misery of the battlefield are better than the peace of the graveyard."

He pointed out to the British policies which strangled Indian entrepreneurship and initiative in commerce and industry. The facilities for technical education were scanty and the exchange and financial policy had injured Indian interests.

In December 1927 the 42nd session of the Indian National Congress was to be held at Madras and the British government had decided to send a commission, headed by Sir John Simon, to look into the Indian situation. The proposed commission was not to have even a single Indian as its member. Nehru rushed back to India from Europe and went to Madras.

Nehru was now in a different mood. He felt himself "full of energy and vitality, and the sense of inner conflict and frustration that had oppressed me so often previously was, for the time being, absent." In his own words: "My outlook was wider, and nationalism by itself seemed to me definitely a narrow and insufficient creed. Political freedom, independence, were no doubt essential, but they were steps only in the right direction; without social freedom and a socialistic structure of society and the State, neither the country nor the individual could develop much. "

He rejected the Dominion Status for India and was firmly for complete independence as the political goal. He was of the view that political independence was only a precondition for achieving the social goal which was still vague and at the level of generalities because "The Congress was a purely political and nationalistic body, unused to thinking on other lines. "[31] But this had to be changed. The Congress had to be induced to think more deeply and systematically of the problem of the socio-economic transformation of the country and define its con-tours. The ever-gaining strength by the All India Trade Union Congress, the fast growing Kisan movement which was now brought out of its sectional attitude and was linking a permanent solution to the problems of the peasantry with the struggle for political independence and subsequent socio-economic transformation of the society and the youth movement enthused Nehru to act boldly.

This thinking resulted in his bold initiative at the 42nd session of the Congress at Madras. At the Subjects Committee on December 25, 1927 he moved his famous resolution on political independence which said: "This Congress declares the goal of the Indian people to be independ-ence with full control over the defence forces of the country, the financial and economic policy and the relations with foreign countries. The Congress demands that this right of the people of India should be forthwith recognised and given effect to, in particular by the complete withdrawal of the alien army of occupation."

The resolution was passed by an overwhelming majority and it signified "a new outlook" and a break from the traditional Congress thinking and he wrote to Gandhiji who had criticised it as "hastily conceived and thoughtlessly passed" that it had "come to mean a very great deal for me and I attach more importance to it than to almost anything else."

There was a passionate discussion between Gandhi and Nehru on not only the independence resolution but also the socio-economic vision to be adopted by the Congress. The latter challenged the socio-economic vision of Gandhi with a great deal of frankness and force, but he was respectful all through, recognising the political sagacity and the unique position which Gandhi had come to occupy in the country. He character-ised Gandhi's socio-economic vision as unrealistic and vague. The new level of understanding which Nehru had reached after his visit abroad and talks with socialists and communists in the Continent and the USSR were clearly reflected in his letter to Gandhi:

> *You have stated somewhere that India has nothing to learn from the West and that she has reached a pinnacle of wisdom in the past. I entirely disagree with this viewpoint and I neither think that the so-calledRam* Raj *was very good in the past, nor do I want it back. I think the Western or rather industrial civilisation is bound to conquer India, may be with many changes and adaptations, but none the less in the main based on industrialism. You have criticised strongly the many obvious defects of industrial-ism and hardly paid any attention to its merits. Everybody knows these defects and all the Utopias and social theories are meant to remove them. It is the opinion of most thinkers in the West that these defects are not due to industrialism as such but to the capitalist system which is based on the exploitation of others. I believe you have stated that in your opinion there is no necessary conflict between Capital and Labour. I think that under the capitalist system this conflict is unavoidable.*

While appreciating Gandhiji's constructive programme which laid emphasis on Khadi, village industries and self-help, he criticised his silence on the necessity for institutional reforms like the abolition of zamindari and capitalist exploitation. So this "child of Gandhi in politics" went ahead of him by enlarging the horizon and vision of the national movement.

The socialist orientation of the nationalist vision was indispensable for making the political independence in the future more than a symbolic affair and he was hopeful that even the Indian National Congress which was "conservative in their social outlook" would "look towards the socialist ideal of society". He saw the commonality of interests among "the peoples of Asia and Africa struggling for freedom" and "the worker of the West" and "imperialism was the common enemy to be fought ceaselessly and rooted out before a better order could be established. The problem with which he now started grappling was the nature or kind of socialism to be adopted in India. What would be its contours? How should it relate itself to the Indian situation and reality? Should it be just a carbon copy of socialism being established in the Soviet Union or would it be different in its texture?

On March 18, 1928 he addressed an appeal to the youth who believed in three things, namely, (a) full independence for India, (b) religion to remain a purely personal matter and must not be allowed to interfere with political, economic and social issues, and (c) equal opportunities for all irrespective of caste, class and wealth. While clarifying the import of (c) to the Congressmen in a circular of April 5, 1928, he wrote:

> *It raises the issue of Socialism versus capitalism. Socialism is a vague term which covers many theories but it is needless to enter into them at this stage. It is generally agreed however that it means the nationalisation of the means of production and distribution so that the whole state may benefit by them and individuals may not seek to amass huge fortunes by the exploitation and impoverishment of others. It means the organisation of the State on a vast cooperative basis so that all avoidable waste, which is so much in evidence in the present state of society, may be prevented. It means friendly cooperation with other countries, not with the desire to exploit one for the benefit of another, but to the mutual advantage of all, so that finally wars may be put an end toand agreat world cooperative commonwealth may be built*

Nehru went round the country, telling the people and the Congress-men about the importance of independence resolution and the necessity of relating India's fight for freedom to the establishment of a new international order. He told the All Bengal Students Conference:

National independence and perfect freedom to develop on the lines of our own choosing is the essential requisite of all progress. Without it there can be no political, economic or social freedom. But national independence should not mean for us merely an addition to the warring groups of nations. It should be a step towards the creation of a world commonwealth of nations in which we can assist in the fullest measure to bring about cooperation and world harmony.

But the international order of this kind could not emerge so long as imperialism remained and exploited weaker countries. Political inde-pendence was necessary but it was only one constituent of the ultimate goal, other constituents being social and economic emancipation and development without any discrimination. In India, for centuries a big segment of the population had been deliberately suppressed and denied all opportunities of growth and advancement in the name of religion and ancient practice. Besides, all over the country millions of working people were deprived of the just fruits of their work and were made to lead a life of poverty and misery. The situation would not change unless "a system which produces poverty and misery" was replaced by a socialist system. "If your ideal is to be one of social equality and a world federation, then perforce we must work for a socialist state...." ...socialism is the only hope for a distraught world today.""

In this endeavour, Russia was anatural ally of Indiabeing "an outcast like us from nations and much slandered and often erring. But in spite of her many mistakes she stands today as the greatest opponent of imperialism and her record with the nations of the East has been just and generous." Around the same time he told the Kerala Provincial Conference that Russia under the socialist government could never be a danger to India. In fact, both Russia and India were bound to be allies in the fight against imperialism and for national independence and co-operation among the nations of the world.

All through his campaign for complete political independence and the socio-economic transformation in the country, he lashed out at the attempts to glorify poverty and tell the poor that they should not care for happiness in this world but for the kingdom of heaven. He tried to drive home the point that poverty was not a good thing, but an evil which needed to be uprooted lock, stock and barrel. The poor required neither petty services nor charity but wanted to be rid of their poverty and the system which produced it. This was possible only when a socialist system was established.

Nehru's new thinking was reflected clearly in an article "Swaraj and Socialism" *(The New Leader,* August 11, 1928), in which he posed the question: "What are we aiming at? What manner of country should we like India to be?"

To answer this question, it was necessary that one looked beyond the boundaries of the country and see the changes which were brought about by industrial revolution in Western Europe. It was a matter to be lamented that "Many of us, regardless of what is happening all around us, still live in the ancient past. Some want the Vedic age, others a reproduction of the early days of Islam. We forget that our ancient civilizations were meant for different conditions .... India will only progress ... when she discards the myths and dogmas of yesterday in favour of the reality of today." He quoted the example of Russia which had been marching on the path of its socio-economic transformation without taking recourse to the capitalist system which in the West had led to imperialism. It was imperialism which was responsible for existing colonial exploitation, unequal terms of trade and wars. Thus, India's socio-economic modernisation could not be had by following the path of capitalism which "necessarily leads to exploitation of one man by another, one group by another, and one country by another. If, therefore, we are opposed to this (British) imperialism and exploitation, we must also be opposed. to capitalism. The only alterna-tive that is offered to us is some form of socialism."

Thus, "As a necessary result of this decision, we must fight British dominion in India, not only on nationalistic grounds, but also on social and international grounds."

Nehru's study of Lenin's works and his keen observation had made him aware of the phenomenon that we now call "neo-colonialism". "Britain may well permit us to have a large measure of political liberty, but this will be worth little if she holds economic dominion over us." Political freedom without a self-reliant economy was meaningless and not worth trying. "We may demand freedom for our country on many grounds, but ultimately it is the economic one that matters."

Throughout 1928 and 1929 Nehru toured the country to educate the masses and generate support for his ideas. He faced opposition not only from the outside, from among the liberals but also from within. Besides, there were doubting Thomases. They thought Nehru to be quixotic, devoted to his ideals and their passionate propagation. The bold initiative in organising the boycott of the Simon Commission made him the darling of the nation. He became popular and a much- loved leader of the masses of the country. Gandhiji put his seal of recognition by writing to him: "My love to you. It was all done bravely. You have braver things to do. May God spare you for many a long year to come and make you his chosen instrument for freeing India from yoke."

Towards the end of 1928, the Congress held its 43rd session at Calcutta under the presidentship of Pandit Motilal Nehru. Here a determined attempt was made by a section of the Congress leadership, led by Pandit Motilal Nehru, with the backing of Gandhiji to water down the resolution of complete independence passed at Madras. Gandhiji himself moved a resolution, asking the British to grant India Dominion Status within two years, though complete independence remained the ultimate goal. Pandit Jawaharlal Nehru attacked the resolution in the sharpest possible words by marshalling strong logic and facts. He was of the view that the acceptance of the resolution meant allowing the British to continue their exploitation for two more years. Ultimately, the supporters of the resolution reduced the time limit to one year and reiterated their commitment to complete independence thereafter. Even though this resolution was passed, Jawaharlal absented himself from the final sitting. His sincerity made Gandhiji remark:

> *He thinks this resolution itself falls far short of what he wants but, a high-souled man as he is, he does not want to create unnecessary bitterness ... how can he help*

feeling dissatisfied? He would not be Jawaharlal if he did not strike out for himself an absolutely unique and original line in pursuance of his path. He considers nobody, not even his father, nor wife, nor child. His own country and his duty to his own country he considers and nothing else.

The Congress had made it clear that it would launch non-cooperation movement after the expiry of one year if the British government did not respond positively. Nobody in his dreams even believed that it would take the resolution seriously. Thus, to all intents and purposes the year 1929 was to be a period of preparation for a bigger confrontation with British imperialism. On the other hand, the British government also started preparing for crushing the movement. The Home Secretary's communication to all provincial governments on February 21, 1929 showed the growing importance of Jawaharlal Nehru in the British government's assessment of the latest developments in the Indian situation: "If the experience of the Calcutta Congress is any guide, the decision of future policy appears to be almost entirely with the younger men, notably Pandit Jawaharlal Nehru and Babu Subhas Chandra Bose, and on their intentions and activities future developments may be expected largely to depend." It was also noted that "There is a tendency for the political and the Communist revolutionaries to join hands, and Pandit Jawaharlal Nehru, an extreme nationalist who is at the same time genuinely attracted by some of the Communist doctrines, stands about at the meeting point. "

The British government tried its best to implicate Nehru in some conspiracy case or the other and paint him as an agent of Moscow. His letters to and from Virendranath Chattopadhyaya were intercepted, his correspondence with others abroad was opened and a fake letter from M.N.Roy was also produced, which was to describe him as "liaison agent between Moscow and India". But the government lawyers could not find anything substantial to get him convicted. Even his articles on the Soviet Union, after 1927, could not help because there was nothing to help the prosecution in a court of law.

Nehru helped, maximum possible, the accused in the Meerut Conspiracy Case. He organised the legal assistance while continuing his political education and propaganda work. He told a meeting of the youth in Delhi on February 5, 1929 that the world was moved by ideas and ideas were more powerful than even the most powerful and best organised despotism. Their beginnings might be feeble but in the course of time they were bound to be mighty. "The British Government is afraid of Soviet principles and is trying its best to uproot socialist ideas and not to allow any communist to preach this gospel" He was sure that "In spite of all effort to suppress the ideas of socialism they are making great progress because society is suffering from numerous social and eco-nomic evils which require immediate eradication. Swaraj was only a means to attain the goal of human happiness and human equality through socialism.

Only through socialism, the problem of bread and butter could be solved and the cultural life of the people could be bettered. Political freedom without socialism was of not much use if it did not change the order of society. Only socialism could "raise our people to the same level as the modem nations of the world." Nationalism must be' combined with socialism to make it more powerful and meaningful. "The spirit of nationalism has existed in India for many years, but if nationalism is combined with socialism the day of freedom would be hastened. I know that if we spread socialistic ideas, we are bound to come into conflict with the capitalists.

But this should not deter us from working for the welfare of the peasants and the workers. These are the real sons of the soil and they truly represent the Indian nation. If they are organised, we will have the real sanction of the people behind us. It is clear that the big landlords and talukdars and the Rajas and the Maharajas will not join us and support our cause; but as soon as we are able to organise the workers and create a mass consciousness among the people, these capitalists will themselves come down from their places of privilege and join us. The workers and the peasants are the only people who would stand by us at all times of difficulty."

During 1929 Gandhiji came to U.P. on a tour in connection with the khadi work. Nehru got a number of occasions to discuss with him his socio-economic ideas. While they agreed on many things, their differ-ences on two points were glaring. It was not surprising in view of the development of Nehru's own economic outlook. While Gandhiji talked of DaridranarayanrandIsoughtl funds to help himby expanding khadi and village industries which could provide employment opportunities and a sense of dignity as one could earn one's own living, Nehru thought, Gandhiji was glorifying poverty. According to Nehru, "...poverty seemed to me a hateful thing, to be fought and rooted out and not to be encouraged in any way. This inevitably led to an attack on a system which tolerated and produced poverty, and those who shrank from this had of necessity to justify poverty in some way. They could only think in terms of scarcity and could not picture a world abundantly supplied with the necessaries of life; probably, according to them, the rich and the poor would always be with us."

The second issue on which Nehru differed from Gandhiji was that of trusteeship. Gandhiji wanted the rich to treat their riches as a trust for the people and Nehru thought, it was totally impracticable. How could the rich transcend the system in which they lived and which shaped their attitudes, outlook and the value system? There could be exceptions here and there, but they would be only isolated cases.

These differences found their expression during the 1930s and 1940s and there were very interesting discussions and dialogues between the two leaders, to which we shall have occasions to refer to in later chapters. Perhaps, the differences during the late 1920s were more of tactical nature. Gandhiji wanted to go slow and not to alienate any section of the society, that had joined the grand national united front against British imperialism. The consciousness of the poor and deprived, especially the peasantry, was at a much lower level. Even Nehru knew this when he worked among them that they were concerned mainly with their immediate needs and their mental ken was limited. In a way, Nehru's educational tours tried to help the people-youth, industrial workers and peasants-overcome the limitations of their mental horizon and relate their present conditions to the fact of imperialist exploitation and capitalist system and outdated production relations and value systems.

Thus he tried to prepare them for a bigger battle in future, which was to be fought in both pre-independence and post-independence days. Gandhiji was aware of Nehru's work, but his own work was intended to tackle the situation as it existed within the framework of maintaining the broad national united front and not to allow the British and other vested interests to disrupt it. He also knew of the mental level of the people and understood human psychology as at that moment. His approach was more cautious. Nehru himself admitted later that Gandhi's approach appealed to the people more:

> *It is not surprising that this astonishingly vital man, full of self-confidence and an unusual kind of power, standing for equality and freedom for each individual, but measuring all this in terms of the poorest, fascinated the masses of India and attracted them like a magnet. He seemed to them to link up the past with the future and to make the dismal present appear just as a stepping-stone to the future of life and hope. And not the masses only but intellectuals and others also .... Thus he effected a vast psycho-logical revolution....*

The year 1929 saw the growing national recognition of Nehru's stature and talents. He was elected president of the All India Trade Union Congress which was to meet at Nagpur. He hoped, he would be a bridge between the organised industrial working class and the Indian National Congress, which would result in the latter moving in the direction of becoming more socialistic and more proletarian while the former would join the national struggle for freedom.

He was chosen to preside over the Lahore session of the Indian National Congress. This was done at the instance of Gandhiji, even though he had only three out of eighteen provincial Congress commit-tees (PCC) eager to back him. Ten of them had favoured Gandhiji and five Sardar Patel. Gandhiji's confidence in Nehru was fully reflected in his statement that

Jawaharlal's being in the Congress presidential chair was as good as his being in that position.

The one year period which was given to the British to make up their mind and grant the Dominion Status to India was coming to an end and the Congress was committed to launching the struggle for complete independence for which Nehru had been campaigning and fighting from 1927. In fact, it was acceptance of the failure on the part of those who had been opposing the demand for complete independence. Gandhiji quickly realised the moral victory of Nehru's position and proposed that the reins of the organisation should be handed over to him notwithstand-ing the fact, that only a very small number of PCCs had favoured him. On September 29, 1929 the All India Congress Committee (AICC) elected Nehru topreside over the 44th session of the Congress which was scheduled to be held in December at Lahore.

4

Nehru's Politics from Lahore to Karachi

The election of Jawaharlal Nehru as president of the forth coming session of the Indian National Congress to be held towards the end of 1929 at Lahore was the recognition of his stature and the force of his political and economic views. All attempts by the moderates and liberals to find some sort of basis for agreement with the British had failed. Even the last attempt in the form of the proposals, advanced by the leaders at Delhi just a few weeks prior to the Lahore Congress had come to a nought.

The Delhi proposals had envisaged that all future negotiations between the Congress and the British would be in the framework of Dominion Status for India. The British government was asked to make its decision before the Congress session opened at Lahore. As.expected, the British government rejected the demand for Dominion Status for India. It had thought, the rejection would split the Congress, but this did not happen. The protagonists of the Dominion Status silently accepted their failure and agreed to follow the line advanced by Nehru that there was no alternative to complete independence if the country wanted to build an independent modem economy.

This was reflected in the resolution which was adopted at Lahore with almost unanimity. It called for a sustained struggle by the Indian people to achieve complete independence. It was decided that on January 26, 1930 meetings would be held throughout the country to explain to the people the import of the resolution and ask them to take a pledge to join the struggle for achieving *Purna Swaraj*.

The Independence Day Pledge, drafted and adopted by the Congress, declared it as:

> *The inalienable right of the Indian people ... to have freedom and to enjoy the fruits of their toil and have necessities of life, so that they may have full opportunities of growth. We believe also that if any government deprives apeople of these rights and oppresses them, the people have a further right to alter it or abolish it. The British Government in India has not only deprived the Indian people of their freedom but has based itself on the exploitation of the masses, and has ruined India economically, politically, culturally and spiritually. We believe, therefore, that India must sever the British connection and attain Purna Swaraj or complete independence.*

Out of the eight paragraphs, it devoted three to focus attention on the economic plight of India as a result of the British colonial exploitation.

To quote:

> *India has been ruined economically. The revenue derived from our people is out of all proportion to our income. Our average income is seven pice (less than two pence) per day, and of the heavy taxes we pay, 20 per cent are raised.from the land revenue derived from the peasantry and 3 per cent from the salt tax, which falls most heavily on the poor.*
>
> *Village industries, such as hand-spinning, have been destroyed, leaving the peasantry idle for at least four months in the year, and dulling their intellect for want of handicrafts, and nothing has been substituted, as in other countries, for the crafts thus de-stroyed.*
>
> *Customs and currency have been so manipulated as to heap further burdens on the peasantry. British manufactured goods constitute the bulk of our imports. Customs duties betray clear partiality for British*

manufactures, and revenue from them is used not to lessen the burden on the masses but for sustaining a highly extravagant administration. Still more arbitrary has been the manipulation of the exchange ratio which has resulted in millions being drained away from the country.'

These three paragraphs showed the understanding of the Congress and national movement since their inception. They contained the essence of the Theory of Drain and of deindustrialisation and of the basic characteristics of the colonial economy of India. It was obvious that the Congress under the leadership of Nehru was taking forward the under- standing of its earlier leaders and trying to enrich it. Earlier, Ranade had told Gokhale that their work was not aimed at making the British realise their folly but to help the future generation of leaders in their fight for independence.

Nehru in his forceful presidential address put the problem of India's freedom in the context of the world situation and changing times and circumstances. Capitalism as the world system had entered a phase of decline and it was in the grip of the severest economic crisis which had begun barely two months ago. This crisis was beginning to bring the entire world except the Soviet Union within its ambit. Nehru contended: "We appear to be in a dissolving period of history when the world is in labour and out of her travail will give birth to a new order." No one could say with certainty what was in store for India, but this much could be asserted with some degree of confidence that Asia and even India would play a determining role in the future world policy. While recalling the glorious traditions and achievements of India, he drew attention to a vital failure, that is, the inability to build an equitable society. "No solution was found for the problem of equality. India deliberately ignored this and built up her social structure on inequality and we have the tragic consequences of this policy in the millions of our people who till yesterday were suppressed and had little opportunity for growth."

This failure could be overcome only by working towards the establishment of a socialist society. "I must frankly confess that I am a socialist and a republican and am no believer in kings and princes, or in the order which produces the modern kings of industry, who have greater power over the lives and fortunes of men than even kings of old, and whose methods are as predatory as those of the old feudal aristocracy." Thus, he rejected the capitalism and capitalist path of development for India. Capitalism would only change the appearance of inequality. It would not abolish exploitation and oppression in the society but would perpetuate and aggravate them. The way out was socialism and nothing else. He was convinced of this after his visitto the Soviet Union and other European countries. He was also aware that the Congress in its existing position could not afford to adopt a full socialistic programme, but without the Congress being converted to socialism, there was no other all-India organisation which could lead the country towards this system. The Congress would have to accept a socialistic programme sooner or later because "we must realise that the philosophy of socialism has gradually permeated the entire structure of society the world over and almost the only points in dispute are the pace and methods of advance to its full realisation. India will have to go that way too if she seeks to end her poverty and inequality, though she may evolve her own methods and may adapt the ideal to the genius of her race."

In the India of his dream there was to be no discrimination based on caste, religion, language and sex. The Indian native States were to be integrated with India and these "most curious relics" of the past were to be abolished. The India of his conception meant "the peasantry and labour, and to the extent that we raise them and satisfy their wants, will we succeed in our task. And the measure of the strength of our national movement will be the measure of their adherence to it." The Congress could win them over by espousing their cause which was identical with the cause of the nation. Here there was a very significant statement by Nehru that the Indian nation for him meant the toiling people of the country, not the handful of the feudal elements and exploiters. The Congress till then had only expressed its goodwill to the toiling people but had not gone beyond that. It was utterly and totally wrong to say that "the Congress ... must hold the balance fairly between capital and labour and zamindar and tenant." Till then this attempt to hold the balance had been weighted towards capital and landholders and had amounted to maintaining the *status quo* and "to maintain the *status quo* is to maintain injustice and exploitation. The only way to right it is to do away with the domination of any one class over another."

He was happy to note that a beginning, though a modest one, was made by the Congress a few months ago at Bombay. On May 24-25,1929 the AICC in aresolution at Bombay said: "The great poverty and misery of the Indian people are due, not only to foreign exploitation in India *but also to the economic structure of society, which the alien rulers support so that their exploitation may continue.* In order, therefore, to remove this poverty and misery and to ameliorate the condition of the Indian masses, *it is essential to make revolutionary changes in the present economic and social structure of society and to remove the gross inequalities.*'" (emphasis added).

Nehru had played an important role in the drafting and adoption of this resolution. It had made it clear that, though the overthrow of the alien domination was the most important step towards ameliorating the sufferings and the uplift of the people, it was insufficient. It must be complemented by bringing about a thorough socio-economic restructuring.

He differed with Gandhiji on the question of trusteeship. He told the Indian National Congress atLahore that merely by increasing wages and doling out charity to the toiling people, exploitation and oppression could not be wiped out. "Paternalism in industry or in the land is but a form of charity with all its sting and its utter incapacity to root out the evil. The new theory of trusteeship ... is equally barren. For trusteeship means that the power for good or evil remains with the self-appointed trustee, and he may exercise it as he will. The sole trusteeship that can be fair is the trusteeship of the nation and not of one individual or a group." Many an Englishman thought the English as trustees for India and wanted to run the administration in a manner they thought to be in the best interest of the Indian people.

Nehru raised the question whether the industry, land and other productive forces should be used in the interestof thepeople who worked or for a handful of non-working proprietors. He asked the Congress "to decide for whose benefit industry must be run and the land produce food." The production must be for the benefit of the toiling people, not for supporting the wasteful consumption of feudal elements, capitalists and foreign rulers.

Nehru answered the question in the following words: "Our economic programme must, therefore, be based on a human outlook and must not sacrifice man to money. If an industry cannot be run without starving its workers, then the industry must close down. If the workers on the land have not enough to eat, then the intermediaries who deprive them of their full share must go." He advocated the provision of a minimum wage for industrial worker, which could enable him to live in moderate comfort. He also pleaded for the limitation of working hours, which helped him preserve his strength and spirit. In agriculture, the urgent need was to bring about a change in production relations by altering land laws and wiping out feudalism.

Obviously, while Nehru put forth a few bold ideas and some important elements of the likely socio-economic programme for the country, their linkages were not elucidated. Perhaps, he did not have time to do so. It is clear that he did not want to break with the Congress even though it was not in a position to accept a socialistic programme or declare socialism as its goal. He knew it well that there was no alternative to the Congress and it must be strengthened while trying to persuade it to accept his views and convert it to his ideology. The Congress was the most important unifying anti-imperialist force. Any break or split would help only the perpetuation of colonialism.

Nehru had begun his efforts to work out an integrated economic programme for the Congress even before the Lahore session, though he could complete his work, to some extent, only in 1931 when the Karachi session of the Congress was held. The Independence for India League was organised by him to propagate the ideal of complete independence and work out a programme for India's socio-economic transformation. The

League had its branches in various provinces and worked within the Congress as a lobby or pressure group.

Nehru emphasised from the very beginning that independence was not only the transfer of political power from the British to the Indians, but a precondition for the reconstruction of both the economy and the polity. The future polity would be republican based on socialism.

The U.P. branch of the League, at its meeting at Farrukhabad on March 31 to April 1,1928, adopted a socio-economic programme which said that "the object of the League is to achieve independence for India and to reconstruct Indian society on a basis of social and economic equality. This necessarily implies that the League is out to remove all political, social and economic barriers between various groups or between man and man and man an4 woman. It means that the League aims at the socialistic democratic state in which every person has the fullest opportunities of development and the state control of the means of production and distribution."

The League resolved to change the existing capitalist and feudal basis of the society and to achieve this end it decided to organise the groups and classes which suffered most and were exploited most under the existing order. These groups and classes comprised vast masses of the people. Only a handful of people wanted the continuation of the existing socio-economic order. The League would have nothing to do "with those classes which are by their very nature parasitical on society. There can be no room for these parasites in the future state."

It emphasised the urgent need of drawing peasants and industrial workers into the fold of the League because they formed the bulk of the population and bore the burden of exploitation most.

The programme, adopted by the U.P. branch, was drafted by Nehru and it was comprehensive. It called for "Direct taxation as far as possible on a steeply graduated scale" and the application of "the principles of income tax...to income from land", imposition of inheritance tax or death duty on "steeply graduated" scale, an "excess profit tax" and annulment of agricultural debts. It advocated the creation of a public sector in industry as a result of the extension of "state control of key industries". It stressed the need of land reforms to remove the interme-diaries between the tiller of the soil and the state.

Other items in the programme were: universal, free and compulsory primary education; adult suffrage; minimum living wage for workers of all categories; the right to form trade unions; the participation of workers in the management; eight-hour day and forty-hour week; special protec-tion to women and young workers; the right to strike; unemployment allowance; insurance against sickness and accident; formation of pro-ducers' and consumers' co-operative societies; abolition of all acts of discrimination on the basis of religion, caste and sect; removal of untouchability; and the uplift of women.

The same year on October 27, Nehru presided over the U.P. Provincial Conference at Jhansi where he tried to explain and elaborate certain aspects of this programme. He underlined that there was no solution for the ills of the country except socialism. "Socialism, therefore, must be our aim." While the social programme should aim at removing the disabilities and discriminations from which depressed classes suffered and creating conditions so that all people got full opportunities for growth, the economic programme must bring about "an equitable distribution of wealth" and remove all inequalities. To begin with, the provision of a living wage for the worker and protection from the economic consequences of old age, maternity, accident and sickness, would have to be ensured. Nehru called for radical changes in the socio-economic structure. Landlordism must be done away with. Nehru accepted the need for the payment of compensation to the landlords, but he was against the payment of the full value of the estate as compensation. "The example of other countries shows us that full compensation for land has brought no relief or solution of the problem. In no event therefore can we give full compensation."

To him the aim of the fiscal policy should not only be the gathering of resources but also the removal of disparities in the distribution of incomes and wealth. The incidence of taxation should be increased on the rich and reduced, to the minimum possible, on the poor. The fiscal policy must lead to the transfer of incomes and wealth from the rich to the poor. It must be seen "that the principle of taxation is such as to preventboth great wealth and great poverty". "Taxation shouldbedirect and as far as possible indirect taxation should be abolished. Further, this direct taxation should be steeply graduated so as to fall mainly on the larger incomes."

He strongly pleaded for the imposition of an inheritance tax or death duty. "This is an eminently just and social tax and should be introduced in India and steeply graduated so as to prevent larger inheritance."

The demand for Swaraj must not be limited only to the political aspect but it must include economic and social Swaraj "and for ... this purpose we must lay down a definite economic and social programme. Only thus can you bring your movement for freedom in touch with reality and make it a dynamic and irresistible force.

He campaigned among the people, especially among the youth, for socialism and a new radical socio-economic programme. He told a rally at Delhi on February 5,1929 that socialist ideas were too powerful to be crushed by the British might. But the progressive ideas were more powerful and lasting than the coercive machinery of the state. He also refuted the mischievous propaganda that the ideas of socialism were in conflict with Hinduism or Islam and tried to clear misgivings about the Soviet Union where socialism was being built. He said: "It is my desire that the spirit that was infused in the youth of Europe after the Great War, and especially by the Russian revolution, should be kindled in every Indian youth." The youth must remember that Swaraj was not the ultimate goal of the country, it was only a means to the ultimate goal of human happiness and human equality which could be brought about as a result of building a socialist society.

Nehru emphasised at Lahore on February 8, 1929 that millions of people in the country were underfed and underclothed and they could not be brought to support the freedom movement by the mere talk of political Swaraj.Theconcept of Swaraj had to be broadened by imparting it social and economic content.

That is why, Nehru and the like-minded people wanted "to change the order of society in India and raise our people to the same level as the modern nations of the world, so that our people can live more comfortably and get sufficient food every day." This attempt to impart socio-economic content and dimensions to the concept of Swaraj had alarmed the British government which was seeing "red" in this and thinking that there was some Soviet hand in it Pandit Nehru told the people who had been talking only of nationalism and ignoring the Socio-economic problems that "the spirit of nationalism has existed in India for many years, but if nationalism is combined with socialism the day of freedom would be hastened." But once the talk of socialism was there, there was bound to be opposition from and conflict with capitalists.

This should not, however, deter one from working for socialism. Peasants and workers "are the real sons of the soil and they truly represent the Indian nation. If they are organised, we will have the real sanction of the people behind us. It is clear that the big landlords and talukdars and the Rajas and the Maharajas will not join us and support our cause; but as soon as we are able to organize the workers and create a mass consciousness among the people, these capitalists will themselves comedown from their places of privilege and join us. The workers and the peasants are the only people who would stand by us at all times of difficulty."

Nehru's imprisonment in 1930, in the wake of the Civil Disobedience Movement, gave him ample time to reflect on the various elements which were to constitute a likely economic programme of the Congress and he started working on such a programme.

The notes prepared by him show the direction in which his mind was working. The Congress which was "the great panchayat" (the equivalent of Soviet') of the whole country had accepted his plea for Puma Swaraj and had started fighting for it. The appeal and the influence of the Congress were so powerful that in many parts of the country even zamindars had stopped paying their land revenue to the foreign govern-ment. After the Swaraj, the legislative powers would pass into the hands of the national government and the question to be considered was: how should these powers be used?

Tracing the history of attempts at tackling this question, Nehru lauded the role of the UttarPradesh Congress Committee (UPCC) which had made pioneering work. It was at the instance of the UPCC that the AICC adopted a resolution in mid-1928 (already referred to in this chapter) which called for socio-economic structural changes in the country, after the attainment of Swaraj, to do away with exploitation and oppression of the workers and peasants. All Parties' Report accepted the provision of a living wage for workers and other measures for their protection.

The Jhansi session of the U.P. Provincial Conference made further progress in the formulation of a socio-economic programme. That was in October 1928. The Council of the UPCC in early days of 1930 went a step further and adopted a resolution on the agrarian question and other aspects of the socio-economic programme and forwarded it to the AICC. It called for the abolition of intermediaries between the peasants and the government. It categorically stated that there should be no place for the zamindar letting out his land to others. The resolution could not be considered by the AICC because of the Civil Disobedience Movement. Gandhiji's letter to the Viceroy, though written in the context of the problems of Gujarat peasantry, contained essential parts of an economic programme.

The preparation and adoption of an all-India economic programme was not easy because it was difficult to secure the agreement of all the leading Congressmen for this. He thought that there was no reason why the UPCC should not take the lead, so far as the province was concerned and work out an economic programme for itself. The work was warranted by the developing situation too.

For example, the spread of the no-tax campaign in the province made it imperative that there was an authoritative statement from the Pradesh Congress Committee (PCC) on the agrarian policy envisaged by it. Moreover, it was only fair that zamindars and tenants were informed of the likely gain or loss for them when the Swaraj came. He stressed: "The battle cry of an economic programme is a far more powerful one for the peasant than that of Swaraj alone."

He talked of the fear among certain circles that it was better not to work out a detailed economic programme because it would irritate some groups or the other. This fear was well-founded as it was "impossible to give an abundance of the good things of life to everyone, at this stage of our civilization at any rate." What was feasible was the redistribution of "good things more equitably". Obviously, the richer sections of the society would suffer as a result of such a dispensation. While addressing the leaders who were afraid that this kind of redistribution would precipitate a class conflict, he said, they were "wise in avoiding it, but it must always be remembered that the conflict has been there and is there. It is the inevitable outcome of existing conditions. Therefore it cannot be wholly ignored, and circumstances might at any time force the issue before the Congress for immediate decision. Those who shape Congress policy must be prepared for such a contingency and must be clear about certain matters. They must have the ultimate ideal clear-cut in their minds."

Even at the cost of alienating the big zamindars and taluqdars, the Congress would have to choose the peasants, agricultural labourers and petty zamindars. Any weakening here "would end the solid and the only real support of the masses for the taluqdar's shadow which we can never grasp. This point has to be stressed as most of us are apt to think too much of the big zamindar."

Nehru advocated a land tax above a minimum taxable agricultural income. The rate of land tax should be 25 per cent and there should be an inheritance tax on big zamindaris (i.e., those paying a land tax of Rs.2000 or more). Village panchayats should be given the powers to settle land disputes and cooperatives should be organised in villages. The ultimate ideal should be "large nationalised farms, and peasant proprietors cultivating their own farms but without the right of aliena-tion" to prevent the growth of big landed estates.

The tenants were promised (1) the right to buy outright from the zamindar their land on instalment plan, (2) transferable hereditary right, (3) the right to plant trees, construct works, build houses, (4) common pasture land in the village, (5) reduction in rent at least in proportion to the reduction in revenue, (6) no *nazaranas,* and (7) no *begar*.

On March 24,1931 *The Hindu* carried an important article by Nehru, entitled "The Economic Exploitation of India", in which he expanded the concept of Swadeshi by saying that "Every rupee which an Indian spends must be spent with discrimination and with a definite desire for creating work in India for our own people, so that the savings of our people may remain in the country and may help nascent enterprises." His treatment of the operations of foreign banks showed that he was aware of the phenomenon of finance capital and financial oligarchy, dealt at length by Lenin in his famous *work, Imperialism: the Highest Stage of Capitalism.* He explained how foreign banks helped the export of British capital to India and assisted British monopolists in the exploitation of Indian resources and Indian labour. These banks discriminated against Indian entrepreneurs and saw to it that Indian banking did not develop.

This situation must be changed by carrying on a persistent and determined struggle for political and economic freedom of the country. He hoped: "A time will come ... when a politically free India will control her economic resources and will not permit anyone to exploit them for the benefit of a tew. The key industries ... will be controlled by the state."

He warned the countrymen that if it was impossible to retain India in the fold of the British empire politically, an attempt would be made to retain economic control "under cover of phrases like' equal rights and opportunities'....It would be a poor gain to us, if gain at all, if in our removing the political disabilities of India we confirm her financial and economic disabilities." Obviously, Nehru wanted the country to beware of the phenomenon of neo-colonialism under which there is a marriage between formal political freedom and economic dependence.

Nehru was released from jail in January 1931, his search for a coherent socio-economic programme was resumed. He continued his dialogue with the people, the various elements of the projected socio-economic programme. He had a series of talks with Gandhiji who agreed with Nehru that there was a need for such a programme. Nehru prepared several drafts before both of them could agree on a common draft. It was placed before the Working Committee and the Subjects Committee by Nehru and was cleared. Gandhiji gave his full backing to it and, as expected, it was adopted by the Karachi Congress. It clearly represented a new outlook for the Congress. Nehru himself, later, recorded in his *An Autobiography:*

> *"So far the Congress had thought along purely nation-alist lines, and had avoided facing economic issues, except in so far as it encouraged cottage industries and* swadeshi *generally. In the Karachi resolution (on Fundamental Rights and Economic Policy-author) it took a step, a very short step, in a socialist direction by advocating nationalisation of key industries and services and various other measures to lessen the burden on the poor and increase it on the rich." Even though "this was not socialism at all, and a capitalist state could easily accept almost everything contained in that resolution," there was a furore in the government circles. It was circulated that the resolution which was called "very mild and prosaic" was the indicator of the growing Bolshevik influence over the Congress, especially Nehru's thinking. Rumours were begun to impress upon the gullible that the Bolshevik gold had been flowing into the coffers of the Congress and corrupting its leaders. Nehru himself was very amused when he heard that the resolution was drafted by a communist with international connections and put into Nehru's hands to get it adopted by the Congress."*

The Karachi Congress took place against the background of the Great Depression which was having a disastrous impact on the Indian econ-omy. The rapidly declining agricultural prices had ruined a large mass of peasantry, resulting in the dispossession of numerous peasants for non-payment of rent and debts. Factories had to down their shutters for lack of demand for their goods and a large number of workers were rendered unemployed. The decline in India's export surplus led to a massive outflow of gold from India to meet Home Charges. During the period of the Great Depression the conflict between the Indian interests and those of the British government and foreign capital further sharp-ened. Strong voices were raised for lowering the rupee-pound exchange rate, according protection to textiles, reserving coastal shipping for Indians, reducing the incidence of land revenue and abolishing the salt tax.

Nehru was also impressed by the fact that while the entire capitalist world suffered from the consequences of the Great Depression, the Soviet Union was, to a large extent, immune from them. Its factories and farms prospered and increased the utilisation of productive capacities. This was because the Soviet Union had done away with capitalism and ushered in a socialist system.

The Karachi Congress Resolution on Fundamental Rights and Economic Programme stressed that "in order to end the exploitation of the masses, political freedom must include real economic freedom of starving millions." It called for the protection of industrial labour and a living wage for it, besides the abolition of all extra-economic compul-sions, protection of women workers, prohibition of child labour and the right of labour to form unions to protect its interests and a substantial reduction in agricultural rent to provide relief to peasants.

It wanted a thoroughgoing reform in the fiscal policy to include "imposition of a progressive income tax on agricultural incomes above a fixed minimum" and "a graduated inheritance tax" and the abolition of duty on salt manufactured in the country. It envisaged reduction in the government expenditure and military expenditure by at least 50 per cent; and exchange and currency policy to be geared to help the growth of Indian industries. Similarly, tariff policy was to subserve the interests of Indian industries. The usury to be controlled and fought in all its forms.

The most important item, however, was the idea of having state ownership and control over vital means of production. The Karachi Congress called for"Control by the state of key industries and ownership of mineral resources". The AICC in its Bombay session in the same year expanded this provision to read as follows: "The state shall own or control key industries and services, mineral resources, railways, water-ways, shipping and other means of public transport."

Thus, for the first time, the Congress tried to spell out what it meant by Swaraj of its conception and how it could bring about a change in the conditions of the people at large. It is relevant to note that, notwithstand-ing the fact that the Resolution was drafted and moved by Nehru and it reflected his thinking, the Congress was not prepared at this stage to accept socialism as its goal."

While the emphasis of the Congress became increasingly pro-nounced on social justice and equitable distribution of wealth and incomes, it took every care to avoid any breach in the grand united front which it had forged against colonialism, for instance, the Congress

Working Committee's resolution (January 1, 1932) saying that "it has no design upon any interest legitimately acquired and not in conflictwith the national well-being," and again on June 18,1934 while deprecating "the loose talk about confiscation of private property and necessity of class war", it made it clear that it had to operate within the limits set by the Karachi Congress resolution which "neither contemplated confisca-tion of private property without just cause or compensation, nor advocacy of class war." But it also added: "At the same time the Working Committee is of the opinion that the Congress does contemplate wiser and juster use of private property so as to prevent the exploitation of the landless poor, and also contemplates a healthier relationship between capital and labour."

When Gandhiji went to England in 1931 to take part in the Second Round Table Conference as the representative of the Congress, he was given a note on behalf of the Congress Working Committee, which was drafted by Nehru. It was, in fact, a brief for Gandhiji. The note wanted complete freedom for the country in the economic and financial spheres. There should be autonomy in fiscal affairs and the matters connected with the control of currency. "The real test should be the freedom from the operations of international financeand the Bank of England resulting in the exploitation of the country. We should be at liberty not only to encourage Indian industries and mercantile interests irrespective of its effect on foreign business interests but also we should have the power to follow economic policy for the betterment of the masses different from the one now in vague.'

Not only the key industries and services but also banking must be controlled or owned by the state in India. All dealings pertaining to foreign capital must be through the state. The Congress could not give the guarantee that there would be no distinction between foreign private capital and Indian capital. Obviously, there would be certain preferential treatment for the latter. Nor would any special rights or privileges be granted to British traders. Gandhiji was told to make it "clear that the Swaraj government shall have the right to organise its industries so as to protect and favour its national interests."

On the question of public debt, the Congress was not prepared to give any undertaking that the government of Independent India would take over all the debts incurred by its predecessor. It would scrutinise them and then decide which ones to redeem. It may be noted that a committee of the Congress, headed by D.N. Bahadurji and comprising Prof. K.T. Shah, Bhulabhai Desai and Dr. J.C. Kumarappa, had gone into the financial transactions between Britain and India and found that Britain owed to India more than 546 million pounds sterling and this amount would have to be recovered after Independence.

Looking back we find that Nehru was successful in influencing the thinking and policies of the Congress. At Lahore, he made it declare Puma Swaraj as its goal and there were no 'ifs' and 'buts' in the resolution. The protagonists of Dominion Status silently admitted their defeat and in two years, he persuaded both Gandhiji and the Congress to adopt its first ever economic programme aimed at creating an independent economy for India to make India's Puma Swaraj really complete and meaningful. These were great achievements for Indian nationalism, but Nehru was not fully satisfied because "socialism" was yet to be accepted by the Congress as its goal. He believed in persuasion and arguments. He thought, there was no force other than the Congress powerful enough to take the country towards socialism after liberation from the British yoke. Any split in or break with the Congress was unthinkable because it would prove disastrous for the country and forces of anti-imperialism and anti-colonialism all over the world. It was his belief that by educating the masses, he would be able to build popular pressure on the Congress leadership to accept socialism.

The failure of the Second Round Table Conference and his involve-ment in the agrarian struggle landed him in jail by the end of 1931 and he remained there till August 1933 and for most part of 1934. The period of incarceration prevented him from indulging in active work, but it afforded much-needed solitude for study and reflection which brought clarity and depth in his thinking.

LUCKNOW AND FAIZPORE

Nehru remained behind the bars for most part of 1932, 1933 and the year 1934-35. In between he was released for a few months in 1933-34. Both inside and outside the prison, he continued to study and reflect over the Indian situation and problems against the changing world political and economic scene. He looked into the past and tried to understand and explain how the British captured and ruled India and made it economi-cally subservient to Britain. He went at length to explain how the traditional economy of India was ruined and the peasant came to be exploited "by everyone who came in contact with him".

Nehru ex-plained the causes of deindustrialisation under which the destruction of handicrafts, in the absence of a concomitant growth of modem industries or other avenues of employment, increased the pressure on land. Rack-renting, lack of irrigation facilities and the low productivity led to scarcities and famines in the event of the failure of the monsoon. He remarked with emotion: "Yes, there can be few sights that are sadder than the sunken eyes of our *kisans*, with the haunted, hopeless look in them."' Mahatma Gandhi had aroused new hope and expectation in them. Thanks to him, they were up at the barricades and fighting for the freedom of the country and ending their own exploitation and oppres-sion. Their expectation would have to be fulfilled by changing the existing land relations and providing better opportunities for improving their lot.

Nehru recapitulated the birth of scientific socialism and the contri-butions of Marx and Lenin to the development of scientific socialism. He had a look at the Russia of the Czars and the development of revolutionary movement since the last decade of the 19th century, cul-minating in the October Revolution. He paid glowing tributes to Lenin: "There was no doubt or vagueness in Lenin's mind. His were the penetrating eyes which detected the moods of the masses; the clear head which could apply and adapt well thought out principles to changing situations; the inflexible will which held on to the course he had mapped out, regardless of immediate consequences."

In the course of his study of world history, when he reached the post-First World War period, his outlook on history had undergone a radical change. His views on other subjects had also altered. The war shook everything and everybody."It upset the old order completely .... It shook the whole system of ideas on which we had grown up and made us begin to doubt the very basis of modern society and civilization. We saw the terrible waste of young lives, the lying, violence, brutality, destruction, and wondered if this was the end of civilization. The Soviet rose in Russia-a new thing, a new social order, and a challenge to the old."[3]

He termed "the rise and consolidation of the Soviet Union" as "the most striking" event since the end of the First World War and he watched its progress in the midst of trials and tribulations. He wrote to his daughter about the "wonders" performed by the Soviet Union. The first was the establishment of the Soviet system throughout the territory of the former Czarist empire on the basis of the principle of self-determination.

Talking of the tremendous progress made by the Union of Soviet Socialist Republics (USSR) in the field of socio-economic life of the people, Nehru wrote:

> *The second wonder that the Soviets performed was to transform great parts of this area out of all recognition by prodigious schemes of planning. There is no instance in recorded history of such rapid advance of a people. Even the most backward areas in Central Asiahavegone aheadwith arush which we in Indiamight well envy. The most notable advances have been in education and in industry. By vast Five Year Plans the industrialization of Russia has been pushed on at a feverish pace and enormous factories have been put up."*

He went on to add:

> *The contrast between this progressive, go-ahead Soviet country and western Europe, with its ever-increasing troubles, is very marked .... To compare Soviet Russia with western Europe today is to compare a youth, carrying a heavy burden but full of life and vigour, with an aged person with little hope or energy left, and going forward, not without pride, but inevitably, to the end of his present state."*

Nehru evinced keen interest in the events in Soviet Russia since the October Revolution. He paid glowing tributes to the Soviet people for their successes in preserving the Revolution from the enemies from within and without. He looked at the period from 1917 to 1921 which covered civil war, the foreign invasion and subversive activities by enemies, as the period of "militant communism". "It was a thrilling and dramatic period of war and revolt and civil war and starvation and death, brightened up by the crusading zeal of the masses and the heroism shown in defence of an ideal. The immediate reward was nothing, but great hopes and promises filled the people and made them bear their terrible sufferings and forget even, for a while, their empty stomachs."

He dealt with the period of War Communism (which he called "militant communism") and the phase of New Economic

Policy (NEP) with a great deal of sympathy and understanding. He did not believe that the NEP was a surrender to capitalist elements nor did he think the' Bolshevik leaders had changed their objective. To him the NEP seemed "a step back to rest and recuperate in order to be able to take several steps forward again later."

He found the Soviet Union a great source of encouragement and inspiration to the oppressed and exploited people throughout the world. This was not liked by the colonial powers. They thought "the Soviet Russia represents an idea which strikes at the root of all imperialism." That is why a powerful vilification campaign was started against the USSR. Nehru exposed the duplicity of the imperialist powers on various issues including the repudiation of foreign debts by the Soviet Union. He concluded that it was the imperialist powers who were pursuing a policy of aggression and hostility against the Soviet Union while "Soviet policy with other nations was one of peace at almost any cost, for they wanted time to recuperate, and the great task of building up of a huge country on socialistic lines absorbed their attention." He showed keen interest in how the Bolsheviks solved their problem of nationalities and formed the USSR. He enumerated the various elements that constituted the solution and also the steps taken to remove regional imbalances in socio-economic development.

The way the agrarian question was sought to be solved in the Soviet Union and the socio-economic backwardness was attacked attracted Nehru's attention, and the thing which struck him most was *Piatiletka* orFiveYearPlan. "It was acolossalprogramme, ambitious anddiffcult of achievement even in a generation by a wealthy and advanced country."

He described how the Plan was framed and the various issues and questions that cropped up in the process. The public or state sector was the surest guarantee of the success in drawing up a single coordinated plan for the country as a whole. Thus, he found the dominance of public ownership overmeans and activities of production as the most important precondition for framing and successful completion of a plan of economic development.

The Soviet model of building a modem industrialised economy with self-reliance as one of the important pillars deeply influenced him. He noted: "The object of the Plan was to lay down the solid foundations of industrialism in the Soviet Union. The idea was not to put up some factories to produce the goods which every one needs, such as cloth, etc. This would have been easy enough by getting machinery from abroad, as is done in India, and fixing it up. Such industries, producing consumable goods, are called 'light industries'. These light industries necessarily depend on the 'heavy industries', the iron and steel and machine-making industries, which supply the machinery and equipment for the light industries, as well as engines, etc. The Soviet Government looked far ahead and decided to concentrate on these basic or heavy industries in the Five Year Plan. In this way the foundations of industrialism would be firmly laid, and it would be easy to have the light industries afterwards. The heavy industries would also make Russia less dependent on foreign countries for machinery or war material."

He was aware that the choice of this model for building a strong, industrialised, independent economy would entail great hardships for the people and would demand sacrifices because of the long gestation periods and heavy investments involved in heavy industries. He was full of admiration for the Soviet citizens who "tightened their belt and starved and deprived themselves of even necessary articles" to pay for the imported machinery and equipment. They struggled against back-wardness and remnants of capitalism. "Almost with enthusiasm they put up with further sacrifices and lived a hard, ascetic life; they sacrificed the present for the great future that seemed to beckon to them and of which they were the proud and privileged builders."

What the Soviet Union was doing was a unique thing in human history. Till then nations concentrated all their efforts only when they wanted to win a war. The nations were enthused to sacrifice their all in times of war. "Soviet Russia, for the first time in history, concentrated the whole strength of the nation in a peaceful effort to build, and not to destroy, to raise abackward country industrially and within a framework of socialism." The beginning of developmental work on a gigantic scale absorbed almost all the able-bodied persons and unemployment disappeared. It was the first country in the world where this happened.

The First Plan was completed one year ahead of the schedule. In four years the face of the Soviet Union changed. It was no longer a feudal country. It was marching rapidly on the path of industrialisation. Tremendous progress was registered in every field, be it social services, health, education, culture or accident insurance. And there was a new sense of security among the people. What the working people had failed to achieve in Western countries after more than a century of develop-ment and tremendous increase in production was achieved in the Soviet Union in a few years.

Nehru's admiration expressed itself in the following words: "The argument about the success or otherwise of the Five Year Plan is rather a pointless one. The answer to it is really the present state of the Soviet Union. And a further answer is the fact that this Plan has impressed itself on the imagination of the world. Everybody talks of planning' now, and of Five-Year and Ten-Year Plans. The Soviets have put magic into the word."

These comments of Nehru were in the context of a powerful campaign started in the West that planning was irrational, it could not allocate the available resources to different economic activities so efficiently as market forces could do and it would not be able to provide enough incentive. In the absence of the primacy of market price, it would be impossible to decide as to what, how and for whom to produce. The planners would have to make numerous calculations which were humanly impossible.

The Five Year Plan of the Soviet Union was undoubtedly a colossal undertaking and, in fact, a number of big revolutions tacked together.

> *But the most interesting feature of the Plan was the spirit that lay behind it, for this was a new spirit in politics and industry. This spirit was the spirit of science, an attempt to apply a thought-out scientific method to*

the building up of society. No such thing had been done before in any country, even the most advanced-ones, and it is this application of the methods of science to human and social affairs that is the outstanding feature of Soviet planning. It is because of this that all the world is talking of planning now, but it is difficult to plan effectively when the very basis of the social system, like the capitalistic system, rests on competition and the protection of vested rights in property."

Another thing which tremendously influenced Nehru was the fact that while the whole capitalist world whether developed or underdevel-oped was ravaged by the Great Depression which "held the world by the throat and strangled or slowed up almost all activities", leading to an increase in the number of suicides in many countries as a result of degrading unemployment and destitution, the Soviet Union escaped its direct effects. "There was unemployment there, and work went on harder than ever under the Five Year Plan. It was outside the area controlled by capitalism, and its economy was different [16] It was the public ownership and control of means of production and financial institutions and foreign trade in the Soviet Union that gave no scope for speculation and the institution of stock exchange which could lead to the situation that was witnessed in the United States of America (USA).

During 1933-34 Nehru wrote his famous pamphlet "Whither India?" which reflected his new thinking. It was widely discussed and com-mented upon. This was written soon after his release from jail in August 1933. He enjoyed freedom only for about five months, but even during this period he wrote and spoke ceaselessly about new ideas and his complete and enriched vision. He was convinced that without deciding on the shape of things to come in India after Independence, nationalism, .however passionate it might be, would remain vague and of not much consequence. Independence for what? This was the question which must be pondered over. The question must be tackled realistically on a scientific basis.

India must seek independence only to become an independent economy. There was no use of independence if the economy remained dependent. He refered to Egypt which was politically free but economically dependent. It remained an economic colony of imperialists.

Secondly, he posed the question: For whose freedom was the Congress fighting?

> *There is the feudal India of the princes, the India of the big zamindars, of small zamindars, of the professional classes, of the agriculturists, of the industrialists, of the bankers, of the lower middle class, of the workers. There are the interests of foreign capital and those of home capital, of foreign services and home services. The nationalist answer is to prefer home interests to foreign interests but beyond that it does not go. It tries to avoid disturbing the class divisions or the status* quo. *It imagines that the various interests will somehow be accommodated when the country is free."*

Obviously, the nationalist answer was not only irrational but far from the reality of the situation. The interests of various sections and classes were irreconcilable and there was no use trying to reconcile or harmo-nize them. Nationalism had failed to make the people realise this.

Similarly, one must be clear about the form of government to be adopted after independence. The form of government must act as an appropriate means to the attainment of the ultimate goal. He was happy that the limitations of nationalism were being over-come. "Gradually the nationalist struggle for political freedom is becoming a social struggle also for economic freedom. Independence and the socialist State become the objectives, with varying degrees of stress being laid on the two aspects of the problem.

He rejected capitalism which had given birth to imperialism and was based on exploitation. Socialism was the only course to be followed by. India after independence. India must transcend the narrow confines of nationalism and stand for internationalism and cooperation among nations. Independence of India and other enslaved countries must be followed by fundamental changes in politics, economics and social life.

There were sharp reactions to 'Whither India?' in the Anglo-Indian press. *The* Statesman and *The Pioneer* accused him of being a propagan-dist for Communist ideas and of the Soviet Union. He was sought to be painted as a person preaching for a Communist revolution. But Nehru could not be intimidated. He wrote to *The Pioneer* on November 23, 1933: "I do not admire all that has occurred in the Soviet Union but I do admire their objective and the vital urge that is driving them to it. I think also that in spite of many mistakes and failures the Soviets have an amazing amount of success to their credit."

His thoughts had become clearer. In an article, published in *Daily Herald* of London (October 12, 1933) Nehru stated:

> *Essentially ... our struggle for freedom is a struggle for a radical change of the social structure and the ending of all exploitation of the masses. This can only be done by divesting of the great vested interests in India, and the biggest of these is that of the British Government. A mere process of changing officials, or'In-dianisation', as it is called, of giving a high office to an Indian instead of an Englishman, has no interest whatever for us. It is the system which exploits the masses of India that we object to and which must go before any effective relief comes to the masses.*

So long as there was foreign domination over India, nationalism was bound to be there, but it must be combined with socialism. In other words, independence was needed in order to bring about a socio-economic transformation of the country with the aim of building a socialist society. This transformation was not an easy task so long as the country was saddled with feudal vestiges in every walk of life."

This work could not be accomplished by either shunning the Congress or just indulging in catchy phrases. The Congress had no alternative. It must be persuaded to accept the necessity of working towards socialism. He was convinced that "the natural consequences of our mass struggles" would force the Congress to think in terms of economics and there were signs that it had already started doing so. He wrote to Minoo Masani on December 19:

> *Our direct action struggles were, to begin with, purely political; however, the political aspect became tinged with the economic. The Congress, nationalist as it was, began to talk rather vaguely and idealistically in terms of some social change. That process of change of ideology is proceeding apace and is being hastened by economic conditions as well as the continuation of direct action. The time has come now when we must think more clearly and develop a scientific ideology. This is, so far as I am concerned, one of socialism and I would, therefore, gladly welcome the formation of groups to spread this ideology. But it is not enough to talk merely in terms of an academic ideology especially at a moment when our country is in the midst of a struggle for freedom. This ideology must be tacked on to action and this action, if it is to bear fruit, must be related to the Congress struggle. Otherwise the socialist group will become an ineffec-tive, academic and sterile study centre. Even to spread the ideology the effective method is through action which is co-ordinated to the direct action of the Congress and labour and peasant organisations.*

Nehru's freedom ended on February 12, 1934 when he was re-arrested and put behind bars till September4,1935 when he was released in view of the illness of his wife who was hospitalised in Europe.

This time Nehru went to Europe with more clarity of mind and maturity. He was no longer a vague, humanitarian socialist of the early 1920s, but a firm believer in scientific socialism. Besides a scientific approach to history which was evident in his *Glimpses of World History,* he clearly understood the relations and correlations of various national and international socio-economic factors and forces. Hg noted in his *Autobiography:* "My thoughts travelled ... to other countries, and I watched and studied, as far as I could in gaol, the world situation in the grip of great depression. I read as many books as I could find on the subject, and the more I read the more fascinated I grew. India with her problems and struggles became just a part of this mighty world drama, of the great struggle of political and economic forces that was going on everywhere, nationally and internationally. In that struggle my own sympathies went increasingly towards the communist side."

He frankly admitted that he "had long been drawn to socialism and communism, and Russia had appealed to me. Much in Soviet Russia I dislike-the ruthless suppression of all contrary opinion...." But the record of the capitalist world was much worse. Violence and suppression were the very foundation stones of capitalism which had given birth to imperial-ism and colonialism. Without violence capitalism could not survive for long. So long as the fear of starvation remained, political liberty was of not much consequence. Violence in Russia was temporary and not the basis of the socialist system.

"With all her blunders, Soviet Russia had triumphed over enormous difficulties and taken great strides towards this new order. While the rest of the world was in the grip of the depression and going backward in some ways, in the Soviet country a great new world was being built up before our eyes." He also noted that the successes and failures of Soviet Russia, though very important they were, did not affect the soundness of the theory of socialism. He cautioned the Indians that "it was absurd to copy blindly what had taken place in Russia, for its application depended on the particular conditions prevailing in the country in question and the stage of the historical development." They must look into the Soviet experience to profit by and avoid mistakes.

He was very much convinced that reformism could be of little help in India where the need of the hour was a radical restructuring of the socio-economic system. "In India, only a revolutionary plan could solve the two related questions of the land and industry as well as almost every other major problem before the country."

This time he went to Europe as a great admirer of Marxism which, he recorded, "lighted up many a dark corner of my mind. History came to have a new meaning for me. The Marxist interpretation threw a flood of light on it, and became an unfolding drama with some order and purpose, howsoever unconscious, behind it. In spite of the appalling waste and misery of the past and the present, the future was bright with hope, though many dangers intervened. It was the essential freedom from dogma and the scientific outlook of Marxism that appealed to me.

His attraction towards Marxism increased during the Great Depres-sion because "the great world crisis and slump seemed to justify the Marxist analysis. While all other systems and theories were groping about in the dark, Marxism alone explained it more or less satisfactorily and offered a real solution."

Certain Left circles in India and abroad were of the view that social and economic questions were equally important as the question of national freedom and the issue of socio-economic transformation of the country must not be allowed to come only after independence of the country was achieved. This meant opening two fronts simultaneously, one against the British and, the other against the national and foreign bourgeoisie. This could have split the grand united front forged against British imperialism in which national bourgeoisie was an important partner, and could have led to the break-up of the Congress. This was not acceptable to Pandit Nehru.

To him: "Nationalism still was the dominat-ing thought." And it would remain so till political freedom was achieved. If it was so, there was no alternative to the Congress and, notwithstand-ing all vagueness and ambiguities in its ideology, it had no alternative as the all-India revolutionary force and it must be strengthened and, on no pretext, weakened. Any attempt to weaken the Congress only meant, consciously or unconsciously, helping British imperialism. "To desert the Congress seemed to me thus to cut oneself adrift from the vital urge of the nation, to blunt the most powerful weapon we had, and perhaps to waste energy in ineffective adventurism."

Talking of Gandhiji who was the focus of Leftist criticism, Nehru asserted that, irrespective of his superficial backwardness ideologically "he had been the greatest revolutionary of recent times in India. He was a unique personality, and it was impossible to judge him by the usual standards, or even to apply the ordinary canons of logic to him. But because he was a revolutionary at bottom and was pledged to political independence for India, he was bound to play an uncompromising role till that independence was achieved. And in this very process he would release tremendous mass energies and would himself...advance step by step towards the social goal."

Analyzing the failure of the Leftists to evaluate the role of Gandhiji and that of the Congress and assess the Indian situation correctly, Nehru underlined that it was not due to any fault in the general principles of scientific socialism, but inability to keep in mind that the Indian society was radically different at that time from the Western societies of the nineteenth and early twentieth century. In the latter, industrial working class was a very dominant and important segment. It was a grave error to look at the Indian national movement from European labour standards.

During this sojourn, he broadened his circle of friends with whom he discussed wide ranging issues. He met Andre Mairaux and Gide in Paris and Leonard Woolf and his friends in London. He formed his life-long friendship with V.K.Krishna Menon. At the sanatorium where Kamala Nehru was admitted, he met two intellectual giants of European labour movement. Ben Bradley was a patient there and Rajani Palme Dutt was a frequent visitor. It seems, Bradley and Dutt were influenced by Nehru's views and it was clear when they wrote an article "The Anti-Imperialist People's Front in India" in *Labour Monthly* (March 1936) advocating the need for communists to join hands with the Congress which was the main mass political party in India and was playing an anti-imperialist role.

Nehru was further convinced that the problem of India's independ-ence could not be viewed separately from the struggle of other colonial peoples and oppressed nations for freedom. The same way the question of India's socio-economic transformation could not be discussed or solved in isolation. He was fully convinced that "any real solution of our Indian problems is vitally connected with the world solution of present-day problems. It has become difficult for me to think of India (isolated) from the world."[9]

For the solution of India's problems, the forces of nationalism and those of socio-economic transformation must join hands. While the Congress represented nationalism and political freedom, the Left stood for social freedom. The latter was advised to tread cautiously and carefully so as not to alienate the Congress. He conveyed to the All India Congress Socialist Conference, being held at Meerut, on January 13, 1936:

> *Socialism, it is obvious, includes political freedom, for without that there can be no social and economic freedom. But India being unhappily still politically a subject country, nationalism is the dominant urge of most of her politically minded classes. That is a factor of primary importance and any socialist who ignores it does so at his peril. But no socialist need be reminded that nationalism by itself offers no solution of the vast problems that confront our country and the world; it ignores indeed the world and fails to realize that in doing so is makes an understanding of even the national position impossible. For the Indian problem is but a part of the world problem of imperialism, the two are indissolubly linked together, and that world problem is essen-tially an economic problem, though it has many changing faces. To continue these two outlooks and make them an organic whole is the problem of the Indian socialist. Scientific socialism itself teaches us not to follow slavishly any dogma or any other country's example, which may have resulted from entirely different circumstances. Armed with a philosophy which reveals the inner workings of history and human relations, and with the scientific outlook to guide him, the socialist tries to solve the problems of each country in relation to its varied background and stage of economic development, and also in relation to the world. It is a hard task. But then there is no easy way."*

Nehru was fully convinced that unless capitalism was done away with, profit motive and imperialism could not be got rid of, and a new world order could not be brought about.

Imperialism had given rise to wars and conflicts among nations. The establishment of a socialist system did not mean that there would be no scope for any private initiative. He told Lord Lothian that "It may be that a great deal of private initiative is left ... it must be left. But in all that counts, in a material sense, nationalisation of the instruments of production and distribution seems to be inevitable."" Further, socialists must try to bring about socialism through democratic processes as far as possible. "The rejection of democracy does not or should not come from the socialist side but from the other." It must not be forgotten that one had to secure the goodwill of the vast majority of the people for any socialist transformation. Obviously, it was the duty of the socialists to convert the people to their positions.

Perhaps, to clarify his own views and ideas, he wrote an article in Lausanne on February 21, 1936 which was never published. This article gives a clue to the working of his mind. India had many problems, according to Nehru, but the main problem was political freedom. Behind it were economic problems, namely, the problems of grinding poverty, of immense unemployment of almost all segments of working population. The one and a half century old British rule had destroyed India's rural economy and increased the pressure of population on land. What happened in England during the early phase of Industrial Revolution couldnotberepeated in Indiabecause the latterwas a colony and modem industries could not come up in sufficient number on a large-scale to absorb the people who were displaced from their jobs because of the decline of handicrafts and lessen the pressure of population on land. India was converted into a supplier of raw materials and minerals and a market for British manufactured goods.

The fiscal and tariff policies of the government prevented the emergence of Indian entrepreneurship in many areas of industrial activity. The British interest lay in continuing this situation so that India was kept "as an agricultural background to industrial England." Indians "were told that the true prosperity of India lay in her agriculture and not in modem industry." Thus, an attempt was made by the British to convince the Indians that they could prosper by sticking to the colonial pattern of economic development, as outlined by the British."

Deindustrialisationorruralisation leading to pauperization on amass scale was the root cause of India's poverty. The Great Depression which brought about a sharp fall in prices of agricultural products aggravated the problem of poverty. The existing land system was shaken to its foundations. The closure of industrial units made the workers flee to their villages.

The educated unemployed also increased in number because the industrial development was not fast enough to absorb them and the government services were already very crowded. The unemployed, rural or urban, were looking towards the national movement"in the hope that political freedom would lead to the avenues of escape from the morass of poverty and unemployment. Gradually also the economic issues began to colour the nationalist outlet and a socialist movement sprang up."

Nehru was fully convinced that so long as the whole existing political and economic structure was not changed and the paralysing shadow of imperialism not removed, nothing substantial could happen. A lasting solution of the problem of poverty could not be found within the existing framework. The British government was not willing to think of any institutional or structural changes. Nehru cited the example of the Royal Commission on Agriculture under Lord Linlithgow, which was not allowed to look into the land tenure system and was confined only to superficial things.

Having reached this conclusion, the question arose as to how this transformation, leading to building a socialist socio-economic system, was to be conducted. Profit motive and reliance of the free play of market forces were ruled out as they were not compatible with the goal of socialism. How were the material and human resources of the country to be used? How were the transactions inside and with the outside world to be conducted?

Nehru had pondered over this problem and the logic and the recent experiences of the Soviet Union had convinced him that there was no way out but planning. He had dealt with the problems of planning in a country like India which wanted to go by the consensus and within the framework of a parliamentary democracy in his book *Glimpses of World History* at length.

During his sojourn in Europe, he stated his views on planning more clearly.

> *The development of industry and the land would have to be planned as a whole; it cannot be dealt with in sections. If one tries to tackle one part,one finds something leftover which. one cannot provide for. The whole basis, in my opinion, is not the profit motive, but producing for consumption, because if we produce for profit the result is that we simply glut the market; we cannot sell the goods, because people have no money with which to buy them, and so we get overproduction which at the same time many people have nothing at all. We should organize on the socialist basis and have large-scale agriculture, cooperative or collectiv-ist, big machine industries and cottage industries. The cottage industries must not be such as would be likely to conflict with big industries, because then they would collapse, but-there will be plenty of room for the growth of cottage industries for a long time to come, simultaneously with the growth of big industries. If big industries are not developed on a capitalist basis, they will deal with the essentials which are required and there will be no needless waste of energy. If all these things are taken together, I imagine we might go a little way towards the solution of the various problems that confront us."*

In its endeavour to develop a planned economy, India would have to learn much from the experiences of the Soviet Union and adapt them to Indian conditions after scrutiny. It was difficult to remove the spell of the Soviet Union and one could ignore its experiences only at one's peril. Partly the pull of Soviet Russia"is due to disillusion with the old world and its ways, a desire to escape from a system which has no real hope to offer, even more so we are drawn by the building up before our very eyes of a new civilization, so different from the old, with different values and standards, new motives, hopes and desires.We talk of the Russian experiment, but already it is something much more than that; it has vast achievement to its credit and the history of the world has been changed thereby.

"We stand at the threshold of a new era.... That new era is not a dream of the future; it is the actuality of the present in the USSR with all its defects and mistakes and ruthlessness, it is taking visible, vital shape there, stumbling occasionally but ever marching forward." Even though he wanted large-scale modern industrialisation in India, he was for carving a definite and well defined area for village industries and their coordination with the former.

During his absence from India, Jawaharlal Nehru was elected president of the 49th session of the Indian National Congress to be held at Lucknow in April 1936. His election was, again, at the instance of Gandhiji who described itas "the righ test thing thatcould have happened for the country".

He was conscious that his election did not mean that the Congress was prepared to endorse his social and economic views. It only meant that the Congress had a great measure of trust in him. Nehru believed that the Congressmen were prepared to listen to him and ponder over what he was saying.

He declared from the rostrum of the Lucknow Congress:

I am convinced that the only key to the solution of the world's problems and of India's problems lies in Socialism, and when I use this word I do so not in a vague humanitarian way but in the scientific, economic sense. Socialism is, however, something even more than an economic doctrine; it is a philosophy of life and as such also it appeals to me. I see no way of ending the poverty, the vast unemployment, the degradation, and the subjec-tion of the Indian people except through Socialism. This involves vast and revolutionary changes in our political and social struc-ture, the ending of vested interests in land and industry, as well as the feudal and autocratic Indian States system. That means the ending of private property, except in a restricted sense, and the replacement of the present profit system by a higher ideal of cooperative service. It means ultimately a change in our instincts and habits and desires. In short, it means a new civilization, radically different from the present capitalist order. Some glimpses we can have of this new civilization in the territories of the USSR. Much has happened there which has pained me greatly and with which I disagree, but I look upon that great and fascinating unfolding of a new civilization as the most promising feature of our dismal age. If the future is full of hope it is largely because of Soviet Russia and what it has done, and I am convinced that if some world catastrophe does not intervene, this new civilization will spread to other lands and put an end to the wars and conflicts which capitalism feeds.'"

He was sure that socialism would be established in India but that would be fashioned "after its own way and fit it in with its national genius". There would not be one stereotyped socialism in all countries of the world, though the "essential basis of the order would remain the same everywhere. The spread of socialism to various nooks and corners of the globe would lead to a new world order."

He went on to add:

Socialism is thus for me not merely an economic doctrine which I favour; it is a vital creed which I hold with all my head and heart. I work for Indian independence because the nationalist in me cannot tolerate alien domination; I work for it even more because for me it is the inevitable step to social and economic change. I should like the Congress to become a Socialist organization and to join hands with the other forces in the world who are working for the new civilization.

He frankly admitted his failure to convince the Congress to accept this viewpoint, but he would not give up his efforts. He would not force a split on this issue in the Congress. "The Congress has been in the past a broad front representing various opinions joined together by the common bond. It must continue as such even though the difference of those opinions becomes more marked."

He underscored the inevitability of India's frindship and cooperation with the Soviet Union and othercountries which would opt for socialism, that is new civilization. He had told a press conference at London a few weeks earlier that "Russia is a great friend and not a menace to India." At another point there itself he had underlined that "there is no power in the world today which is more peaceful and less inclined to aggression than Soviet Russia" and "Soviet Russia from an economic point of view does not require India in the least .... Raw materials exist in sufficient quantities in Soviet territories."

He outlined his model of economic development at the Lucknow Congress. It was for rapid industrialization of the country which was indispensable if one wanted to raise the standard of living of the people. It did not mean that there was no place for khadi and village industries in the Indian economy. "They have a social, a political, and an economic value which is difficult to measure but which is apparent..."

Two other economic aspects on which he focussed attention were concerning rural areas. There feudalism was withholding the growth of productive forces and perpetuating an exploitative and oppressive system, and that Indian economy had become a part and parcel of world capitalist system, which was amply demonstrated by the Great Depres-sion affecting even the remote villages of the country.

At Lucknow, the Congress adopted a resolution on the agrarian situation in thecountryandresolved to work outan agrarian programme. It asked the PCCs for detailed information and opinions for working out such a programme until its next session at Faizpore. The Congress also decided to take part in the elections to provincial assemblies under the Government of India Act of 1935. The Election Manifesto, adopted by the All India Congress Committee (AICC) in 1936, reiterated its commitment to the Karachi Resolution and declared its resolve to frame a comprehensive agrarian programme for reforming the system of land tenure and revenue and rent,an equitable adjustment of the burden on agricultural land and solving the problem of rural indebtedness. It promised to industrial workers a decent standard of living, hours and conditions of labour in conformity, as far as the economic conditions in the country permitted, with international standards, suitable machinery for the settlement of disputes between employers and workers, protec-tion against the economic consequences of old age, sickness and unemployment and the right to form unions and to strike for the protection of their interests.

Nehru's whirlwind tour of the country began soon after the Lucknow Congress. He was asked to elaborate his socio-economic views which had aroused the interest of the people and attracted them to him. His popularity soared. Even though he did not command a majority in the Congress Working Committee, there was no one except Gandhiji having a bigger mass base and greater public appeal.

He stated at Bombay that the zamindari and capitalist systems were bound to collapse sooner or later. He did not want that after Independ-ence, Indian capitalists should replace the British capitalists. As in the West, the question was raised that socialism might adversely affect the incentive to work and it might lead to inertia and laziness because there would be assured security for the masses. He emphatically said: "No, I do not agree with this. Look at Soviet Russia. The object of socialism and communism is to bring about a change in human habits, instincts, desires and urges. The whole atmosphere should be changed in that direction."

He lashed out at feudal lords, the princes and the big landlords who "do not fit in with anything modern, whether politically, economically, or culturally. They never think in terms of the masses, but only in terms of their own interests." Big capitalists also, by and large, had kept away from the Congress after Civil Disobedience Movement. A few of them were still in the Congress. The "big bourgeoisie cannot think in terms of the masses and look for support of the British Government."

Wherever he went, he posed the question: why did the country want Swaraj? Was it for perpetuating or eradicating poverty? If the latter was the aim, there was no alternative to socialism. Socialism was emerging as *the* dominant and ascending idea in the world, India could not keep itself aloof from it otherwise it would stagnate. He critised those Left adventurists who wanted to give priority to socialism over Swaraj. Nehru thought that "independence must preclude socialism, because unless we are politically free, we cannot carry out a socialist programme in India. I am perfectly willing to cooperate with any member of any organization that stands for complete independence." The Left adventurists wanted the commitment to socialism as the precondition for cooperation in the fight for freedom. Obviously, their thinking was going to prove divisive.

He had to counteract the vicious propaganda against socialism. Lies were sought to be spread against socialism and the Soviet Union where a system based on socialism was being built. Nehru assured: "In the darkness that prevails around us in the world there is no way except socialism and I can assure you that it will injure nobody but benefit all, except, of course, the vested interests who must now learn to help in a peaceful change."-

Nehru angrily retorted in a press statement on June 5, 1936 that the questions relating to socialism unhappily betray not only ignorance, but passion, which darkens the mind. Socialism is an economic doctrine. It is a way of organizing the production and distribution and other activities of society. It is, according to its votaries, a solution of the ills from which the society suffers today. And yet in considering this economic policy, we are continually having God and religion hurled at us, and Russia, like King Charles's head, is always cropping up. I am perfectly prepared to discuss the Almighty or the strange and mysterious ways in which He is worshipped and I am equally willing to talk of Russia, for Russia is a fascinating country today. Butldoobject tobeing side-tracked from the main issue. That can only be caused by confusion or a deliberate avoidance of the real question.

About religion I am quite convinced that there must be most perfect freedom of faith and observance. People can worship God in any of the thousand ways they like.

> *But I also claim that freedom not to worship God, if I so choose, and also I claim freedom to draw people away from what I consider superstition and unsocial practice. But when religion comes in the garb of vested interest and exploits people, it is not religion and it must be countered.*
>
> *I believe in the basic economic theory which underlies the social structure of Russia. I think also that Russia has made the most remarkable progress, culturally, andeven spiritually, if I may use the word in its real sense.'*

To the people who were counterposing democracy and socialism to each otherand asserting thatthere was nodemocracy in the SovietUnion where socialism was being built, Nehru replied: "I admire the economic transformation of the land there (in the USSR), the development of its social life, its educational and cultural activities. Today the so-called democratic countries in the West are democratic only in apolitical sense. It is not enough to give a vote to a hungry man. That vote can be bought or influenced. In order to have the fullest democracy, you must have an economic democracy." He advised the protagonists of socialism to study the Indian situation in all its aspects and then work out their strategy and tactics. They must speak in the language and manner which would be intelligible to the people at large. Socialism was not the immediate item on the agenda, it had to follow political independence. Socialists must not oppose nationalism but supplement and enrich it in a way to establish an organic link between nationalism and socialism. They must begin a sustained propaganda campaign in a persuasive manner to convince the rank and file of the Congress of the soundness and desirability of socialism.

Only eight months later, Nehru was asked to chair the golden jubilee session of the Indian National Congress at Faizpore. In his presidential address, he again tried to persuade the Congress to accept socialism without which it was difficult to understand and solve India's problems. He was confident that the logic of events would lead the Congress to socialism.

He launched a scathing attack on British economic policies which were antagonistic to the growth of Indian agriculture and industry. He called for a radical reform of the land system without which neither Indian industry could develop nor could the problems of unemployment and poverty be solved.

The Faizpore Congress adopted an agrarian programme which was a step towards an All-India Agrarian Programme framed later. The Congress declared that "the final solution of this (agrarian) problem involves the removal of British imperialistic exploitation and a radical change in the antiquated and repressive land tenure and revenue systems." Even then certain steps could be taken immediately, for instance,the readjustment of rent and revenue to the existing conditions with substantial reductions in both, exemption of uneconomic holdings from land tax, imposition of income tax on a progressive scale on agricultural incomes, subject to a prescribed minimum, substantial reduction in canal and other irrigation rates, abolition of all feudal dues and levies and *begar,* fixity of tenure with heritable rights along with the right to build houses and plant trees, encouragement to cooperative farming, relief from agricultural debts, cancellation of arrears of rents, provision of common pasture lands and the recognition of rural population's rights in tanks, wells, ponds and forests, stop ejection of peasants from their lands for arrears of rents, and statutory provision of a living wage and suitable working conditions for agricultural labourers.

It was, above all, Nehru's ideas and tireless campaigning that attracted people to the Congress and its candidates won the largest number of seats in provincial assemblies. The Congress secured a clear majority in seven out of eleven provinces and emerged as the single largest party in three others. The party formed ministries in seven provinces and a new phase began in the history of the Congress as well as the country.

5

National Planning Committee

In 1937 the Congress formed ministries in seven provinces under the Government of India Act of 1935. The massive vote received by the Party even under arestricted franchise system aroused new expectations and gave it a big moral authority. It created an impression that the day was not far when the country would become independent and the Congress would head the government at the Centre. In 1938 Netaji Subhash Chandra Bose succeeded Nehru as the president of the Indian National Congress and presided over the 51st session at Haripura. In his presidential address, he spoke of the planned economic development of Independent India on socialistic lines. He said:

> *I have no doubt in my mind that our chief national problems relating to the eradication of poverty, illiteracy and disease, and to scientific production and distribution can be effectively tackled only along socialistic lines. The very first thing which our future national government will have to do would be to set up a commission for drawing up a comprehesive plan of reconstruc-tion. This plan will have two parts-an immediate programme and a long period programme. In drawing up the first part, the immediate objectives which will have to be kept in view will be three-fold: firstly, to prepare the country for self-sacrifice; secondly, to unify India; and thirdly, to give scope for local and cultural autonomy.'*

The long-period programme was to tackle the problem of increasing population and concentrate on eradicating poverty which, in turn, would necessitate the reform of land system and abolition of feudalism, liquidation of rural indebtedness, provision of cheaper credit, extension of cooperative movement and modernisation of agriculture. Agricultural improvement alone would not be sufficient to eradicate poverty. "

A comprehensive scheme of industrial development under State owner-shipand State control willbe indispensable. Anew industrial system will have to be built up in place of the old one, which has collapsed as a result of mass production abroad and alien rule at home. The Commission to be set up for planning will have to consider carefully and decide which of the home industries could be revived despite the competition of modem factories, and in which sphere large-scale production should be encouraged. However much we may dislike modern industrialism and condemn the evils which follow, we cannot go back to the pre-industrial era, even if we desire to do so. It is well, therefore, that we should reconcile ourselves to industrialization and devise means to minimise its evils and at the same time explore the possibilities of reviving cottage industries where there is a possibility of their surviving the inevitable competition of factories. In a country like India there will be plenty of room for cottage industries, especially in the case of industries, includ-ing hand-spinning and hand-weaving, allied to agriculture.

"Last but not the least, the State, on the advice of a Planning Commission, will have to adopt a comprehensive scheme for gradually socializing our entire agricultural and industrial system in the spheres of both production and distribution. Extra capital will have to be procured for this, whether through internal or external loans or through inflation.'" The same year the ministers of industries of the Congress-ruled provinces met in Delhi and adopted a resolution which said:

> *This Conference ... is of the opinion tht the problems of poverty and unemployment, of National Defence and of the economic re-generation in general cannot be solved without industrialisation. As a step towards such industrialisation, a comprehensive scheme of national*

planning should be formulated. This scheme should provide for the development of heavy key industries, keeping in view our national requirements, the resources of the country, as also the peculiar circumstances prevailing in the country.

The scheme should provide for the establishment of new indus-tries of all classes and for the development of existing ones'

The Conference also urged that steps should be taken to start basic and heavy industries without delay.

In October 1938 the Congress president Subhash Bose set up the National Planning Committee (NPC) under the chairmanship of Pandit Nehru. Its members included Sri M. Visveswaraya, Sir Purushottam Thakurdas, Prof. Meghnad Saha, Sri A.D. Shroff, Prof. K.T. Shah, Sri Ambalal Sarabhai, Dr. J.C. Kumarappa, Sri N.M. Joshi, Prof. Radha Kamal Mukherjee, Sri Walchand Hirachand, Smt. Vijayalakshmi Pan-dit, Sri G.L. Nanda, Dr. J.C. Ghosh, Sri V.V. Giri and others. At later stages Dr. V.K.R.V. Rao and Dr. Gyanchand were also associated with it.

It is said that Nehru was reluctant to take up the chairmanship of the NPC because his hands were full and he thought he would not be able to do justice to the new assignment. He was busy with sending a medical relief team to China, organising the boycott of the Japanese goods, mobilising support for the Republicans in the Spanish Civil War and looking after the States' People's Conference. He, ultimately, had to yield when Rabindranath Tagore conveyed to him through Anil Kumar Chanda that "there are only two modernists in the High Command-you and Suhhash Babu" and since Subhash Bose had become the Congress president, there was nobody left besides Nehru to head the NPC. Nehru replied to Chanda on December 1, 1938:

I have written to Gurudeva separately. So far as the planning committee is concerned, I shall associate myself with it because I am intensely interested in planning. But all this kind of work requires a certain background, a certain atmosphere and a certain human material. I fear that much of this is lacking here. Still it is a good thing to begin thinking on right lines and make others do so."

Nehru prepared a number of important documents to guide the NPC. He wanted to avoid unnecessary controversies and frictions and chan-nelise the discussions in desirable direction. At the very first meeting of the NPC at Bombay on December 17, 1938 Pandit Nehru cautioned: "I would like to stress the need for the committee to bear in mind that no conflict should arise between village and cottage industries and bigger industries. I would also urge the committee to suggest ways for the coordination of these two kinds of industries. It is also essential that we include a representative of labour in the planning committee.

"I also consider it very necessary that the planning committee keeps in touch with the national movement. The national movement has affected the lives of the people of the country in many respects." If the committee failed to keep in touch with the national movement, he warned, "it would lose itself in the backwaters, and simply discuss individual and isolated bits of industrialisation without the background of nationalism. The problem is indeed a difficult one but it must be faced." Finally, he repeated "the need for the committee to take care that no conflict between cottage industries and large-scale industries takes place."[5]

Obviously, Nehru wanted to avoid any kind of adventurism which might lead to a rupture with the national movement which was a grand alliance of almost all the patriotic Indians against British imperialism, and make the committee irrelevant. Similarly, he did not like the committee to be over enthusiastic about modernising India so rapidly as to do away with cottage industries which not only embodied the artistic legacy of the country but also provided employment opportunities to hundreds of thousands of Indians.

To help the committee avoid any conflict with the national move-ment, Nehru wrote a detailed "Note on Congress Policy" on December 21, 1938. In that he dealt with a number of questions. He referred to the question which was being raised by an important section inside and outside the Congress whether the Party was not opposed to the establish-ment of large-scale modern industries which would be inimical to the interests of cqttage industries and would render a large number of the people unemployed.

> *A question is raised ...as to whether it is open to the Planning Committee ... to consider the establishment or encouragement of large-scale industries, except such as may be considered key industries, in view of the general Congress Policy, in regard to industry. This Congress Policy, as is well-known, shows a strong bias towards the development of cottage industries, specially of hand-spinning and hand-weaving. It follows that the Congress would disapprove of any policy which came in the way of its development of cottage industries. But there appears to be nothing in the Congress resolutions against the starting or encouragement of large-scale industries, provided this does not conflict with the natural development of village industries.*

He reviewed the Congress resolutions from 1920 onwards, showing that the patronage to khadi and village industries did not mean that the Congress was against large-scale modem industries. It only meant that the former were not adequately cared for by either the private capital or the government and the Congress should do as much as possible in its own way to see that they not only survived but prospered. Therefore the Congress Working Committee in a resolution at its meeting at Benaras made it compulsory for the Congressmen to use only hand-spun and hand-woven khadi to the exclusion of any other cloth. It was stated by the Congress Working Committee that "large and organised industries are in no need of the services of Congress organisation or of any Congress effort on their behalf." The same year at the Bombay Congress, the All India Village Industries Association was formed. Nehru con-cluded: "It is clear that the Congress considered it unnecessary to push large-scale industries through its organisation and let this to the State as wellas to their own resources. It did not decide in any wayagainstsuch large-scale industries." After the formation of the Congress Ministries in provinces and the changing situation which indicated that independence of the country could not be delayed any longer, the attitude to large-scale industries would have to be reconsidered. In Nehru's words:

> *Now that the Congress is, to some extent, identifying itself with the State it cannot ignore the question of establishing and encouraging large-scale industries. Every provincial govern-ment has to face this issue and it was because of this that the Working Committee, as early as August 1937, recommended to the Congress Ministries the appointment of Expert Committees for purposes of national reconstruction and social planning. The working Committee evidently had in mind large-scale State planning which included big industry as well as cottage industry. As no action was taken by the Congress Ministries on this resolution for nearly a year, a second resolution was passed by the Working Committee in July 1938, authorising the President to convene a Conference of the Ministers of Industries. It was as the result of this resolution that the Delhi Conference was held, and the resolution under which this Planning Committee is function-ing was passed.*
>
> *It is clear, therefore, that not only is it open to this Committee and the Planning Commission to consider the whole question of large-scale industries in India, in all its aspects but that the Committee will be failing in its duty if it did not do so. There can be no Planning if such Planning does not include big industries. But in making our plans we have to remember the basic Congress policy of encouraging cottage industries.*

It may be mentioned here that India was the only country besides the Soviet Union, which had declared its intention of going in for planned socio-economic transformation. This was the first country under colo-nialism to take to the path of planned economic development after independence. Its conditions were different from those of Russia on the eve of the October Revolution or from those of the Soviet Union in the

1920s. Yet there were certain similarities. All these similarities and differences were briefly indicated by Nehru in his very first article on his visit to the Soviet Union (referred to earlier). Obviously, the contours of planning in India could not be exactly similar to those in the Soviet Union. They had to be drawn according to the genius of India and its historical and prevailing socio-economic conditions. Nehru had under-lined this aspect several times before.

The NPC with Nehru's help defined planning for India in the following words: "Planning under a democratic system may be defined as the technical coordination, by disinterested experts, of consumption, production, investment, trade and income distribution in accordance with social objectives set by bodies representative of the nation. Such planning is not only to be considered from the point of view of economic and the raising of the standard of living, but must include cultural and spiritual values and the human side of life."'

To do a thorough job, the NPC set up a number of subcommittees and associated a number of experts in various fields with them. Detailed questionnaires were framed and circulated to elicit the opinions and views of as many people as possible.

Nehru proved to be a great mobiliser of the public opinion in favour of planning, he cleared many a misconception and countered misleading propaganda. In fact, he emerged as a great educator. He told a gathering of students and teachers of the University of Delhi on February 14 that planning was not merely for industrialising the country, but it concerned almost all aspects of socio-economic life of the people. Even if one began with industrialisation, one would have soon to concern oneself with other areas of life.

Nehru illustrated this thus: "The opening of new factories would not usher in the millennium till the purchasing capacity of the masses, which is very low at the moment, is apparently raised. That brings us face to face with the problems of currency, exchange and prices." Not only this, but one must deal with the vested interests hindering the development of productive forces.'

There were two importantpoints which occurred throughout Nehru's speeches and writings on planning. First, planning would be undertaken only after the country became independent and political power was transferred to the Indians.

> *It is clear that the drawing up of a comprehensive national Plan becomes merely an academic exercise, with no relation to reality, unless the Planning Authority, or those to whom it is responsible, are in a position to give effect to that Plan. If this authority is powerless or is circumscribed and restricted and its activities limited, it cannot plan.*
>
> *It follows, therefore, that the National Authority which plans must also have full power to give effect to its planning. An essential prerequisite for planning is thus complete freedom and independence and the removal of all outside control. This,implies that the country possesses in itself full sovereign authority to take any measures, adopt any policies, and form any relations with other countries as may seem best to its government authority in the interests of the country and its people.'*

Thus, the NPC had to draw up a plan only for a free and independent India. But this did not preclude any reflection on what shape and direction economic planning would take. "Even under existing condi-tions we must make every effort to adoptall measures and policies which develop the resources of the country and raise the standard of our people."

Second, planning in any real sense could be possible only within the framework of socialism. He wrote to Prof. K.T. Shah, the secretary to the NPC:

> *Real planning...is hardly possible under the ordinary capitalist structure of society where so many vested interests intervene. Some measure of planning might be done in a fascist state. But planning, as most of us conceive it, is inevitably connected with a socialist society.*
>
> *Obviously, constituted as we are, and constituted as the planning committee is, we can hardly begin tackling the question on a socialist basis. We have to accept to a*

large extent the present structure, at any rate, as a jumping-off ground. At the same time, we must aim at something different, though that need not be, so far as the committee is concerned, full-bloodied socialism. Even according to the present Congress policy it is our objective to nationalise key industries and key services and banking, etc. That is something definite to go upon .... Further, we should try to aim at, as far as possible, producing for consumption rather than for profit. In any event, the profit motive should be subordinated to the social motive."

Nehru was of the view that, for tactical considerations, too much stress should not be laid on the fact that real planning was possible only under socialism because this would frighten a number of "people and irritate the ignorant". He thought, if consideration was given solely to planning without talking much of socialism, socio-economic develop-mental process might lead to the inevitability of socialism. Develop-ment of productive forces at a faster rate might necessitate the changes in relations of production, more oriented towards socialism. If this happened, it would convert many more to socialism. Even the ignorant who were weary of any talk of socialism might be softened.

He suggested this tactical approach without frontally "challenging the existing structure. At the same time, it should be folly to strengthen the vested interests in the existing structure. We should do nothing to create fresh barriers in the way of the change-over."

He enquired of Prof. Shah whether the Committee should concen-trate only on a few major items of policy, which did not obviously conflict with the basic structure of the day, yet they worked towards considerably changing it.

He was aware of the existing correlation of class forces. The working class was not only numerically small but had not been conscious of its interests and role in socio-economic transformation. The rural proletar-iat was unorganised. Only peasants were organised and knew the importance of doing away with feudal and semi-feudal exploitative relations of production and of the liberation of the country from the foreign yoke because the British were sustaining feudalism in the country. Even they had not been converted to socialism. In these circumstances, Nehru held:

> *I feel that in India today any attempt to push out the middle class is likely to end in failure. The middle class is too strong to be pushed out and there is a tremendous lack of human material in any other class to take its place effectively, or to run a planned society, for even in most countries in Europe where conditions apparently are much more favourable, such an attempt has not succeeded and has given place to reaction. Here, in India, a premature conflict on class lines would lead to a break-up and possibly to prolonged inability to build anything."*

Nehru also visualised that some day in the distant future there might come up a world union of free and equal nations. Then the national sovereign authority might be voluntarily limited to some extent by each constituent unit in the interests of world planning and cooperation.

Though the Congress had not accepted socialism as its goal, it was committed to the ideal of a free and democratic state on the basis of an egalitarian society and an adequate minimum of a civilised standard of life would be assured to everyone so that the attainment of this equal opportunity was made a reality. This accepted ideal should form the background of the proposed Plan.

While due regard for and coordination with cottage industries must be there, stress should be on modern large-scale industries. "A large number of essential industries, which are necessary for the independ-ence and well-being of the country, must inevitably be on a large-scale."

According to Nehru, the task of the NPC was "to expedite this industri-alisation and to indicate how and where key and basic industries are to be started...to demonstrate, in so far as is possible, the domains of large-scale and cottage industries, and where the latter have been especially fathered by the national movement, to give them every protection and encouragement." Nehru visualised a strong and ever-expanding public sector in industries. He referred to the Karachi Congress Resolution which mentioned State ownership of key industries and services, mineral resources, railways, waterways, shipping and other means of public transport. The Resolution could be safely interpreted to encompass "large-scale industries and enterprises which are likely to be monopo-listic in character. A legitimate extension of this principle would be to apply it to all large-scale enterprises. It is clear that our Plan must proceed on this basis and even if the State does not own such enterprises, it must regulate and control them in the public interest."

While he did not favour wholesale nationalisation of industries, he was strongly in favour of extending State control and regulation.'.. wherever even an established industry, under private control, receives aid or protection from the State, or tends to develop into a monopoly, comes into conflict with the general policy of the State in regard to workers or consumers, the State should take necessary steps to assure conformity in all such ventures with its basic policy and with the objectives laid down in the Plan."

In a "Note for the Guidance of Subcommittees of the National Planning Committee", Nehru elaborated some of the points. For ex-ample; he dismissed that there was any basic conflict between cottage industries and modern large-scale industries. The "conflict" was largely due to the difference in the emphasis. Large-scale modern industries were vital for protecting political freedom and proceeding towards achieving economic independence. Without them, even cottage indus-tries could not be made viable and modernised. Nehru wrote:

> *It is clear that in Indiatoday the development of cottage industries on a vast scale is necessary for the well-being of the masses. It is equally clear that the rapid development of large-scale machine industry is an urgent need of the country. Without industrialisa-tion no country can have political or economic freedom, and even cottage industries cannot develop to any large extent if economic freedom is absent. Without industrialisation also the rapid and effective raising of the standard of the people*

is not possible. Key industries, defence industries and public utilities must be devel-oped on a large scale. Even the development of cottage industries is helped greatly by the supply of cheap power and suitable machinery for cottage use which are obtainable from the working of large-scale enterprises. To some extent, handicrafts and large-scale industrial enterprises are complementary to each other. The problem before the country, therefore, is one of coordinated growth in both directions and the avoidance, so far as possible of conflict between cottage industry and large-scale industry."

Nehru said the principal objective of economic planning in India should be to attain national self-sufficiency or self-reliance. This, of course, should be reflected in the balance of external trade and pay-ments. But the main thing was avoiding economic imperialism. The first charge on the country's produce, agricultural and industrial, should be to meet the domestic needs of food supply, raw materials and manufac-tured goods." India must find outlets for its surplus goods to meet its import bills and avoid external indebtedness."

Coming to the details, he wanted a national minimum standard of living to be fixed and assured. In ten years national income and national wealth should go up by two to three times. The State in Independent India must guarantee 2,400 to 2,800 calories to every person daily, 30 yards of cloth every year, and a covered area of 100 square feet for housing. The importance of agriculture must be underlined for achieving food sufficiency, raw material sufficiency, expansion of the rural market and releasing labour for industries.

Planning should aim at liquidating illiteracy, eliminating epidemics, expanding health facilities and raising the average life span. A rational population policy would have to be framed to enable economic growth to improve the standard of living of an average Indian. Labour must be assured better and hygienic conditions of work and protection from sickness and accidents. Unemployment insurance and minimum wages must be provided for statutorily. Regional imbalances must be removed as fast as possible so that the national unity was strengthened and divisive forces and elements kept at bay. Investment policies and the location policies of both the public and private sectors should be formulated by keeping this objective in view.

For raising resources there should be coordinated efforts by the Central and Provincial governments and by banking and insurance companies. Fiscal and tariff policies should also be rationalised and used to mobilise resources. There was an emphasis on promoting scientific and technological research. Institutions were to be established to achieve this end. Latest technologies could be imported on selective basis but only to promote self-reliance in the years to come.

Peasants were to be guaranteed remunerative prices for their prod-ucts and a reasonable relation was to be established between the prices of agricultural products and manufactured goods. Radical land reforms were to be carried out. Minimum wages were to be guaranteed to landless labourers. The Subcommittee on land policy pleaded for cooperative farming so thatresources could be used rationally. Cooperative farming was to be applied first to the culturable wasteland.

Regarding the model of economic growth under planning, Nehru was of the opinion that the Indian model could be formulated in the context of Indian conditions but the Soviet model could be a vital reference point. He wanted that the country would have to give priority to basic and heavy industries, the development of infrastructural facilities, etc. to lay down the foundations for self-reliant economic development of the country. So far as possible, the development should be financed with internal resources.

A stormy meeting of the chairmen and secretaries of the subcommit-tees of the NPC took place under Nehru's chairmanship on February 12, 1940. It was decided by the majority that the key industries should be under the ownership of the State and the private sector industries aided or supported by the State, there should be greater measure of State control than in the case of unaided private industries. "The State may appoint directors or representatives to see that the State Policy in regard to planning is carried out. Such representatives of the State will not be supposed to interfere in the day to day administration of the industry, but, i6will be their function to see that the industry is coordinated with the National Planning Scheme and the general policies of the State are being carried out by the industry."

For two years the NPC went ahead with its task at a remarkable speed. Its twenty-nine subcommittees drew specialists from all over the country. It was in fact a truly national endeavour. Despite the fact that the British government remained indifferent and did not help the NPC in any way and there was lack of data and statistics, it went ahead with its work and did a remarkable theoretical work. But the exercise proved to be of "a highly educative value" for the members of the NPC and "the general public".

Nehru impressed upon the mind of the people the importance of country's industrialisation. He warned: "For a country to try to do away with industrialization would lead to that country falling a prey, economi-cally and otherwise, to other more industrialised countries, which would exploit it."'

In 1940 the work of the NPC had to be suspended because of certain political developments. The Congress Ministries in the Provinces resigned as a result of the differences with the British government on the question of making India a party in the Second World War without taking the Indian people into confidence.

Consequently, the support extended by provincial governments to the NPC ceased. Second, the businessmen who were associated with the NPC engaged themselves in making money by taking advantage of the situation of scarcities. Third, the Congress launched the Individual Satyagraha movement and most of the Congress members of the NPC and its chairman, Nehru, were arrested. The work of theft NPC could be resumed for a while in 1945. The seventh session took place on November 8-10, 1945. This session adopted an important resolution on "Foreign Capital Investment in India", which laid down the policy of the Congress towards foreign capital investment after Independence. The NPC said:

> *It is important that the investment of foreign capital in Indian enterprise should not ordinarily be permitted hereafter in a form which would entitle it to ownership and management in respect of industries of national importance.*
>
> *In particular in the case of key industries, involving the use of secret processes which would not otherwise be available to the country, foreign participation in ownership and management may be permitted. Such participation should be subject to the approval of the State, which will lay down the conditions and limitations to safeguard adequately Indian national interests'*

This statement was perfectly in accordance with the Congress thinking. As early as 1927 the Congress had declared that Indian resources and Indian market were to be used solely for the benefit of the Indians. The Congress and its leaders like Nehru were very clear in their mind that Britain was ruling India on behalf of British financial, mercantile and other vested interests.

By the beginning of 1946, the political situation in the country radically changed and the negotiations among the Congress, the Muslim League and the British government started and after a few months, an interim government came into being. Nehru became the head of the interim cabinet. Independence seemed to be round the confer. The NPC came to an end. The Congress and the country faced the new situation with new challenges.

The activities of the NPC attracted attention not only in India where even the big business came out with a Blueprint of its own for the planned development of the national economy (the Bombay Plan or the Tata-Birla Plan) and a, section of the Left, headed by M.N. Roy published its own People's Plan. But outside too, Nehru was questioned by the British and the American media on planning in independent India. On April 6, 1946 Nehru was interviewed by the British Broadcasting Corporation (BBC) which asked him to elaborate his views on economic plans for India and the attitude towards foreign capital.

Nehru told the BBC that real problems of the country were economic and plans were being formulated to get rid of appalling poverty and to raise the standard of living of the people. The feudalism in agriculture had to be ended and there would be attempts to organise the agricultural economy on the basis of cooperative farms "at the same time leaving peasant proprietorship in large areas. We want the goodwill of the peasantry and their consent."

He said, development of industries would take place in a big way all over the country. There would be a state sector which would encompass, to begin with, mineral resources, communications, waterways, defence and key industries. Small industries, though free, would be subject to State control and coordination. Regarding the role and place of foreign capital in the economy of independent India, Nehru's view was, "For the sake of rapid industrialisation we would welcome foreign capital." But "we would rather do without foreign capital if any foreign control is to be imposed."

A few months earlier, he had stated at a press conference that there was a general agreement in the NPC that "we should keep out foreign economic control and that control and development of Indian industries should be in Indian hands. Foreign capital brings in a certain amount of foreign interference and should be zealously watched. It may be necessary, to develop India rapidly, to have foreign capital. But if thin is to be accepted, it can be accepted only on the express condition of Indian control.

> *I think the percentage of investment or share of control is irrelevant. In every exceptional case, involving secret processes, the country will have to make the choice as to whether it will develop the industry or not, and whether it will use the secret process on these conditions, but generally control by foreign capital should not be allowed. And national government that comes into being should examine these questions and should not allow present agreements, involving foreign participation, to continue. The future Government of India is going to be strong enough to take such a decision?'*

Nehru stressed that, after independence, India would neither exploit other countries and their resources nor would it allow outsiders to exploit India and its resources. He also had certain ideas about a new interna-tional economic order to be brought in to replace the existing one. He wrote in *The New York Times Magazine* (March 13, 1946) that "there should be no monopolies in materials or markets or in the natural resources of the world. These should be shared equitably for the advantage of all. But it must be remembered that the peoples of Asia and Africa have been exploited and deprived of their natural riches and resources for many generations and others have profited enormously by these one sided transactions. It has to be remembered that this had resulted in terrible poverty and backward conditions. The balance has to be righted." He asserted, "It was essential to recognise that the entire world must be based on freedom and cooperation of free peoples in a world order, that the economic order must be changed to prevent exploitation and promote the fullest use of the world's resources for human betterment"

A lively debate ensued between Mahatma Gandhi and Pandit Jawaharlal Nehru regarding the shape of Independent India. It began during 1930s but it assumed a definite focus during the 1940s and ultimately, Nehru succeeded in convincing Mahatma Gandhi. According to available documents, a discussion took place among Gandhiji, Nehru and Dr. V.K.R.V. Rao at Wardha some time in April 1940. Rajkumari Amrit Kaur who was present there recorded the discussion.

Nehru made astrong case for an industrialised economy in Independ-ent India. The objective of planning must be to raise the standard of living of the masses by increasing production and for this, in a country like India, State would have to be powerful and it could not be powerful in the present world unless it was based on a strong industrialised economy. No country in the modern world could retain its independence without being industrially developed. Defence of the country could not be ensured and strengthened. One should not take a static view of the world situation and the developments which were in store for it. New discoveries might knock the bottom out of the cottage industries. Hence the country should have not only the whole line of modern industries but they must be constantly renewed and innovated and their technologies updated. Thus, he told Gandhiji, "I want to push cottage industries to theextent we can. But I cannot conceive India coming into her own without industrialisation. These very industries will help cottage industries." He warned: "You may sit on your large-scale industries, but other countries will sit on you."

He did not see in his scheme of development any scope for violence. There could be economic coercion, but it should not be equated with violence Gandhiji, while maintaining that encouragement should be given to hand-spinning to the exclusion of mill industry, stated that there was not much difference between him and Nehru as regards industrialisation. He had "no quarrel with industrialisation of India or heavy industries. I subscribed to the Karachi Resolution of which I was a part-author."

Prof. Rao supported Nehru by underlining that cottage industries would not increase India's national income at the desired pace. Hence, there was no question of dispensing with modern industries altogether.

Then Nehru explained the necessity of planning for India, if one wanted to avoid wastage of resources and use them rationally. He also allayed Gandhiji's fear about modern industrialisation debasing the traditional values and bringing in violence and greed for wealth and money. He said that Gandhiji's fears arose because he bracketed industrialisation and capitalism together. One must oppose capitalism but not industrialisation. It was capitalism that led to unemployment. If industrialisation took place on the planned lines, there could not be unemployment.

> *The moment you talk of unemployment you talk in terms of capitalism. No man is really unemployed in a socialistic order. Take Russia. Every man is a producer he is part and parcel of the nation's wealth. You must see that in theory a certain economic structure will give you ideal conditions. And we proceed towards it non-*

violently. Bapu's approach as far as conversion is concerned is right. But you can't make a convert to give up his vested interests. I hate the idea of trusteeship on principle.'

In January 1942, at the AICC meeting at Wardha, there were sharp attacks on Nehru by Dr. Rajendra Prasad and others, obliquely accusing him of departing from the ideas of Gandhiji. Nehru vehemently reacted and defended his views. He refuted that socialism meant application of abstract ttleories based on Western experiences to this country disre-garding India's specific traditions and conditions. On non-violence versus violence, he stated:

> *I fail to understand the attitude of those who talk of 'hundred per cent non-violence' but tolerate the present economic and social structure based on violence and injustice and hope to build up a new structure by means of bringing abouta mental change among the capitalist and propertied classes. I disagree with Babu Rajendra Prasad and his friends who said that they did not want that type of freedom which England and America were having. I, for one, will any day accept that type of freedom, imperfect though it is, and would then try to remedy the defects and build up a new structure of society which will be free from periodical wars and the use of violence.*

The final round of debate between Gandhiji and Nehru took place during September-November 1945, that is, soon after the release from jail. Gandhiji's letter to Nehru followed a discussion in the Congress Working Committee in September 1945 on socio-economic objectives of Independent India. Gandhiji felt that there appeared to be some fundamental differences between the views of the two and it was better to make them known to the people.

There was a personal reason also for him to bring out the differences in the open. He had grown old and "I have, therefore, named you as my heir. I must, however, understand my heir and my heir should understand me. Then alone shall I be content." This letter was penned by Gandhiji on October 2,

1945, his seventy-seventh birthday. It appears that he wanted to leave the leadership of the country into such hands which could continue his legacy.

Gandhi ji was apprehensive that Nehru's scheme of socio-economic transformation of Independent India might destroy the simplicity of village life and plant Western ideas and values which would ultimately lead to violence and untruth, negating basic human values.

Nehru replied with full respect for his mentor. He wrote:

> *Briefly put, my view is that the question before us is not one of truth versus untruth or non-violence* versus *violence. One as-sumes as one must that true cooperation and peaceful methods mast be aimed at and a society which encourages these must be our objective. The whole question is how to achieve this society and what its content should be. I do not understand why a village should necessarily embody truth and non-violence. A village, normally speaking, is backward intellectually and culturally and no progress can be made from a backward environment. Narrow-minded people are much more likely to be untruthful and violent. Then again we have to put down certain objectives like a sufficiency of food, clothing, housing, education, sanitation etc., which should be the minimum requirement for the country and for everyone. It is with these objectives in view that we must find out specifically how to attain them speedily. Again it seems to me inevitable that modem means of transport as well as many other modem developments must continue and be developed. There is no way out of it except to have them. If that is so inevitably a measure of heavy industry exists. How far will that fit in with a purely village society? Personally I hope that heavy or light industries should all be decentralised as far as possible and this is feasible now because of the development of electric power. If two types of economy exist in the country either there should be conflict between the two or one will overwhelm the other?*

Further, Nehru raised the question of country's political and eco-nomic independence and its defence. He thought, it was not "possible for India to be really independent unless she is a technically advanced country." He was not thinking only in terms of armies "but rather of scientific growth" which was indispensable for cultural regeneration of the country in the context of the existing world conditions.

The conflicts and wars in the world were not the result of industri-alisation but of "a tremendous acquisitive tendency both in individuals and groups and nations" and the way out was discarding this basis and bringing in its place a new basis of cooperation. "If this admitted and is found feasible, then attempts should be made to realise it not in terms of an economy which is cut off from the rest of the world but rather one which cooperates. From the economic or political point of view an isolated India may well be a kind of vacuum which increases the acquisitive tendencies of others and thus create conflicts. "

Gandhiji was afraid that the objective of industrialisation was urbanisation and building palaces for the people, which wasnot feasible in a country like India where people should better be allowed to remain in villages undisturbed. To this Nehru very persuasively replied: "There is no question of palaces for millions of people. But there seems to be no reasons why millions should not have comfortable up-to-date homes where they can leadacultured existence. Many of the present overgrown cities have developed evils which are deplorable. Probably we have to discourage this overgrowth and at the same time encourage the village to approximate more to the culture of the town."

Referring to Gandhiji's views, expressed in his book *Hind* Swaraj (1908), Nehru wrote:

> *It is.38 years since* Hind *Swaraj was written. The world has completely changed since then, possibly in a wrong direction. In any event any consideration of these questions must keep present facts, forces and the human material we have today in view, otherwise it will be divorced from reality. You are right in saying that the*

world, or a large part of it, appears to be bent on committing suicide. That may be an inevitable development of an evil seed in civilisation that has grown. I think it is so. How to get rid of this evil, and yet how to keep the good in the present as in the past is our problem. Obviously there is good, too, in the present.

After some more discussions in November 1945 Gandhiji wrote to Nehru that there was not much difference between the two and their outlooks were identical though expressed differently since they were agreed upon the goal of bringing about "man's highest intellectual, economic, political and moral development" and "an equal right and opportunity for all."

Hence the later day accusations against Nehru by Charan Singh and certain sections of Sarvodaya workers who claimed to be self-appointed custodians of Gandhi's conscience were totally false. Gandhiji, as was quoted above, claimed joint authorship of Karachi Congress Resolution which had put forth the idea of public sector. He did not denounce industrialisation and application of modem science and technology but yielded to Nehru's persuasive logic to accept them without reservation.

There were two more points which exercised Nehru's mind. First, for any successful and rational plan, its data base must be accurate and reliable. Without adequate, correct and comprehensive statistics, no projections could be made nor was it possible to evaluate the progress of plan implementation. Hence, he stressed the need for having organisations for the collection and processing of data on scientific basis. During the period when the NPC was at work, Prof. P.C. Mahalanobis helped by making whatever data the Indian Statistical Institute had available to the NPC. He also assisted the NPC technically in making projections.

Second, while the Planning Commission which was to be a body of disinterested economists and other experts, working within the frame-work of guidelines and objectives laid down by the political leadership, might frame a good and feasible plan, its success depended on the people entrusted with its implementation. There must be a right sort of people to translate the plan into reality. This aspect must not be neglected at all because "The very best plan, if run by wrong persons, will harm the country." The Congress Working Committee met in 1945 in Calcutta to prepare the Election Manifesto for 1946 elections to Provincial and Central legislative assemblies. The Manifesto accepted a number of ideas of the NPC and its thinking permeated it. It underlined, "The most vital and urgent of India's problems is how to remove the curse of poverty and raise the standard of the masses." To this end, "Industry and agriculture, the social services and public utilities must be encouraged, modernised and rapidly extended in order to add to the wealth of the country and give it the capacity for self-growth without dependence on others." It included planning, and prevention of the concentration of wealth and powers in the hands of individuals and groups and curbing the vested interests. It wanted, "the State must... own or control key and basic industries and services, mineral resources, railways, waterways, shipping and other means of public transport. Currency and exchange, banking and insurance must be regulated in the national interest.

Even though poverty was widespread, it was mainly a rural problem and it could be tackled by launching an all-out attack on its causes. The Manifesto mentioned the dangers of concentrating industries only in a few provinces, leading to regional imbalances. It emphasised proper coordination and balance between industrial and agricultural sectors and the need to promote the development of science and technology.

In the rural sector, the reorganisation of agrarian relations was promised to be done on the basis of co-operation. While individual farming or peasant proprietorship was to continue, it was underlined that progressive agriculture as well as the creation of new social values and incentives require some system of cooperative farming suited to Indian conditions." But, "Any such change can ... be made with the goodwill and agreement of the peasantry concerned." To impress upon the peasantry the benefits from cooperative farming, experimental cooperative farms were to be established.

6

Making of an Independent India

Political independence of the country was accompanied by its partition. There was communal frenzy, leading to enormous loss of lives and property and serious dislocation of the economy, especially the closure of a large number of cotton textile and jute mills for want of raw materials. In the wake of partition came an attack on Kashmir by the Pakistan backed tribals from across the borders.

Notwithstanding these immediate political and economic difficul-ties, the Congress grappled with the problem of creating an independent industrialised economy. Nehru was anxious to channelise the "tremen-dous flood of energy" of the people, released by freedom of the country, "in right and useful directions" for building a new India. There should not be any rest or complacency. "We must not rest on our hard-won laurels, nor let self-complacency grip our ranks. We must not be static, but keep pace with the march of time. We should be up and doing and let our grip on freedom grow firmer." For carrying on the work of building a new India, world peace was an essential condition. The Meerut session of the Congress (November 1946) called for disarmament and world peace. It warned: "Civilization is likely to destroy itself unless it gives up its imperialist and acquisitive tendencies and bases itself on the peaceful cooperation of free nations and on the maintenance of the dignity of man."

In the context of the failure of capitalism, India would have to opt for a new order of society, which would be for peace and freedom and full cooperation of free nations. The Congress stood for the removal of political and economic inequalities between nations and peoples. It ruled out any secondary or inferior position for India in the World. Obviously, it ruled out any neocolonial status for India. The problem, as Nehru told the AICC in January 1947,was "to prepare a concrete picture of what should take" the place of the political and economic system established by the British. He started a nation wide campaign in favour of land reforms, industrialisation, planning and adoption of a model of economic growth which could make India self-reliant.

Countering the mischievous propaganda that planning meant regimentation and the rise of totalitarianism, he declared that planning meant the most rational use of available resources to achieve certain nationally accepted goals which could bring about an improvement in the standards of living of thepeople and strengthen political independ-ence of the country. It did not mean the negation of freedom of the people. He cleared many a confusion about what planning meant. He was appalled at the ignorance of even those who were involved with planning.

> *I would say that most of the people have no conception of what planning means. With all respect to those who use the word planning frequently enough even members of the Planning Department and the like - I would say that most of them have not the remotest conception of what planning means. Each person moving about in a little circle is not planning. Planning is a conception of the whole and developing each aspectof that whole in relation to other parts. You cannot plan separately, you cannot plan departmentally, you cannotplan in any way unless you grasp that planning means an all-round development of national econ-omy and national life. You must bear the whole picture in mind and then you have to consider the basic things first on which the rest of the superstructure may be built. We shout a lot about our industries. In India they started mostly with jute, cotton textiles and the likes. They did some good and a lot of harm. But they are more or less auxiliaries, superficial industries, dependent on other countries for*

machinery, etc. You cannot industrialise a country by these superficial industries.'

The requirement was primacy to basic and heavy industries and infrastructural facilities like power which alone could lay down the foundations of a self-reliant economy. Nehru reiterated: "Let us have as great a measure of self-sufficiency as possible. If we are not self-sufficient, we are dependent on other countries, maybe for food, maybe for other things. If we are dependent we may get into conflicts while we may avoid them if we have a large measure of self-sufficiency .... Self-sufficiency does not mean cutting the international trade which will increase but not in the basic things that we require."

Replying to those who wanted to divert India from the path of economic development to achieve self-reliance because they asserted that India was a country of spiritualism and non-material values and the emphasis on the development of material production would destroy these long-cherished values, Nehru retorted: "For a hungry man or a hungry woman truth has little meaning. He wants food. For a hungry man, God has no meaning. He wants food. And India is a hungry, starving country and to talk of truth and God and even of many of the fine things of life to the millions who are starving is a mockery. We have to find food for them, clothing, housing, education, health and so on - all the absolute necesssaries of life that every man shoud possess. When we have done that we can philosophise and think of God.` In this endeavour to build anew India, the Soviet Union was a natural ally and India could learn much by cooperating with the USSR. Even months before the achievement of political independence formally, Nehru, while addressing the Soviet delegation to the 34th session of the Indian Science Congress, held in January 1947, said:

You are our neighbours and as neighbours we must take interest in each other; we must know each other and develop closer contacts with each other.

But apart from being neighbours, you have been pioneers in many fields and you have transformed the vast tracts of your country before our eyes with a speed that has astonished human-ity. Inevitably, when we want to produce great changes in India, we want to learn from your example. We want to know what you have done and how you have done it. Among the many things that you have done is this tremendous flowering of science in the Soviet Union and the application of that science to the betterment of human beings who live in those vast territories.

It is our purpose also to better the lot of the millions who live in India and we want to utilise science to that end and want to learn from you what you have to teach in that respect.

Internally, Nehru was of the view that there was no hope for the transformation of the Indian economy into a modem one without planning and without active State intervention. The role of the State in the economy was perfectly justified "because, after all, State is the expression of society." Ever since the days of Adam Smith the whole conception of the role of State had undergone a big change. It was no longer confined to protection of the citizens from external dangers and internal turmoil and the provision of certain communal services like roads, health and medical facilities, educational and training institutions.

The extent of State intervention might be a matter of detail and of argument. "But it is obvious that the State will intervene more increas-ingly in the future because life has become complex. You must have planned authority otherwise there will be chaos. Itis quite impossiblefor the State not to interfere in the trade and commerce. It has interfered in the past and it will interfere more and more in the future."

In Indiaplanning and the active intervention by the State in economy were indispensable. The "key industries must inevitably be controlled very closely by the State." "Talking of industry as it is in India today sometimes seems to be a misnomer. Most of our so called industrialists are hardly industrialists. They are in reality financiers; that is not industrialisation. They are buying up industries here and there but there is hardly any industry as such. The prime need in India is industrial power. Without power we can achieve little. It is power that we want and there are big schemes to be operated: unless we have planning, we cannot achieve anything." The increasing skewness in the distribution of incomes and wealth in the country also necessitated the State intervention if the future social turmoils were to be avoided and harmony to be maintained. During the war this skewness had sharply increased and fiscal policies had failed to make any appreciable impact on the situation. Obviously, this happened because a handful of people could amass wealth and incomes by resorting to illegitimate methods and indulging in black marketing.

"There is something wrong in this and the thing must be brought under human nature control. Maybe it is a fault of human nature; century demanded that the be controlled. The spirit of the twentieth profit motive should go and give place to planned distribution. It is not good to have such enormous discrepancies between individuals in India. How it has happened I do not know; I cannot understand it by any mathematical calculation."

Nehru was among the few top leaders of the Congress, who compre-hended the mechanism of colonial exploitation of India and its changing features since the middle of the nineteenth century. He was determined that the economy of Independent India must be out of the colonial shackles. He put his foot down on the question of giving or maintaining any kind of safeguards to British commercial and industrial interests in Independent India. He categorically stated that "no Indian Government can possibly approve of putting up with any form of safeguard or any kind of protection for anybody."

The interests of Indian nationals would be given primacy over those of foreign nationals. The latter would have to operate within the framework of rules and regulations and priorities laid down by the Government of India. The British private enterprise would not enjoy any position of superiority and preference. The aim of Independent India would be "to make India as little dependent on external agencies in the economic sphere as possible and also to make her as self-sufficient as possible.

Independent India of his conception was to follow a different road while developing its economy than that followed hitherto by other countries of the world, except the Soviet Union. "I want India to be an advanced country and develop her trade, not in an aggressive spirit or by creating any vested interests in other countries, but in a cooperative spirit. I dislike imperialism, political or economic. I do not want my own country to indulge in economic aggression because I think that leads to conflicts and war with other countries. In order to avoid such conflicts I want India to develop on more cooperative lines." At the same time, he categorically stated: "I do not want India to be a suppliant country."" In a significant communication to Asaf Afi who was for sometime India's ambassador to the USA, Nehru wrote:

> *The United States are a great power and we want to be friendly with them for many reasons. Nevertheless I should like it to be made clear that we do not propose to be subservient to anybody and we do not welcome any kind of patronage. Our approach, while being exceedingly friendly, may become tough if necessity arises, both in regard to political and economic matters. We hold plenty of good cards in our hands and there is no need whatever for us to appear as suppliants before any country."*
>
> *Till then India did not have any significant official level contacts with the Soviet Union and Nehru wanted that this situation must be remedied. In a message to the people of the Soviet Union on January 12, 1947, he stated: "It is inevitable that free India should develop friendly relations in cultural and other matters with the people of the Soviet Union. If there is no other compulsion, there is the compulsion of geography and our being neighbours. But there are other reasons also, for we have much to learn from them." He felt that both the countries had interest in and responsibility for maintaining world peace. Their mutual friendship would be useful for world peace."*

World peace, however, could not be brought in so long as nations were not free and human beings in large parts of the world were denied security and opportunity in economic matters. Urgent steps must be taken to solve the problems of poverty and backwardness of the people "or else crisis and disaster might overwhelm us. We have, therefore, to think in terms of the common man and fashion our political, social and economic structure so that the burdens that have crushed him may be removed, and he may have full opportunity for growth."

There were misgivings and misconceptions in the minds of Indian big businessmen about the policies of the government of Independent India and most of these arose out of ignorance. It fell on Nehru to enlighten its members and he tried to do it in his inaugural address to the annual session of the Federation of Indian Chambers of Commerce and Industry (FICCI) in March 1947. He explained:

> *Planning means having some conception of the goal we are striving for, of the kind of society we are aiming at, trying to work up towards that end harmoniously and peacefully with as few upsets as possible, laying down targets so that on all sectors we may advance simultaneously. If we advance on one sector and do not advance on others, even that one sector will come to a stop, and we will face bottlenecks and difficulties."*

The policy of the government was oriented towards encouraging industrialisation of the country so that India's manpower was most rationally and fully utilised, no one who wanted and was capable of adding to the national output was denied the opportunity to do so and in this industrialisation there was no essential conflict between the cottage industries and large-scale industries. As the large-scale industries will notbe in aposition toabsorb the vast manpower of India for along period of time, the development of both types of industries could be adjusted which also necessitated planning. Then, there was another consideration for resorting to planning.

> *It should be remembered that economic factors do not recognise the limitations of boundaries. If we have the Damodar valley scheme, it will affect at least two provinces - Bengal and Bihar. It is not a Bengal scheme or a Bihar scheme. If we have a river commission for the Ganga valley, it will affect three provinces.... If we plan for the whole of India, the only right way to plan*

> *is to bring up the industrially backward parts so that there may be a balanced economy in all parts of India, not that a part of India should be industrialised and a part remain agricultural. That will be bad for India from every point of view, not only for the respective parts but for all. It is acknowledged from the defence point of view that industry should be spread out. Of course, nobody is going to force down something against the will of a province; a province will have to agree to and carry out that plan, but if the conception of a plan is to become provincial, it will become ineffective.*

According to him, the main problem of India was to increase its national output, which was increasing at a minimal rate. But, this did not mean that the problem of distribution would be neglected and it was wrong to say that "distribution would look after itself; in future, if there is no proper distribution and no proper social justice, there are going to be conflicts on an enormous scale. Therefore distribution must be taken in hand and considered as a highly important factor. Nevertheless, I do say that the production is the first thing today.""

Nehru had a solid reason for giving primacy to production over distribution and it had much to do with his conception of building a self-reliant economy for India. The resources for such an operation had to be largely raised from internal sources and the task of capital accumulation would become easier if the production increased at a faster rate to yield a higher rate of savings and capital accumulation.

In this context it is difficult to agree with Prof. S. Gopal that "the enthusiasm was now tempered by the responsibilities of office. Radical theories of distribution gave place to an emphasis on production, and he no longer regarded nationalization as a talismatic concept."" In fact, it was sound economics that informed Nehru's stand. Frankly speaking, on the eve of Independence, there were very few industries which could have qualified themselves for nationalization on the basis of a realistic analysis of their situation. The largest industries, namely, cotton textiles, jute and sugar had already entered their phase of sickness. Their nationalization could have complicated the situation rather than helping economic growth. Both cotton textile mills and jute mills were in the grip of an unprecedented crisis for lack of raw materials because most of the areas which has been supplying raw cotton and raw jute had gone to Pakistan.

Prof. Gopal has ignored Nehru's appeal to industrialists, while inaugurating the annual session of All India Manufacturers' Conference on April 14, 1947. He told them that he was in favour of rapid industrialization of the country but this should be oriented towards bettering the standards of living of the people at large and not towards enriching only a handful of industrialists. "Raising the standard of living of the masses must be the first priority in any scheme of industrial advancement and not a subsidiary benefit that may follow from indus-trial reconstruction."

Referring to nationalization, he pointed out that it "should, of course, be discussed in a practical way and not in a theoretical sense .... At the present moment we have to consider what is the best way to get over the present economic difficulty and not indulge in schemes which may obstruct and delay progress during a very vital period of our existence."

Soon after Independence, the AICC met in New Delhi in November 1947 and appointed the Economic Programme Committee, headed by Jawaharlal Nehru. The members of the Committee included Maulana Abul Kalam Azad, Jayaprakash Narayan, N.G. Ranga, Gulzari Lal Nanda, J.C. Kumarappa, AchyutPatwardhan and Shankar Rao Deo. The Committee, in turn, constituted four sub-committees to deal with the problems of agriculture, small-scale and cottage industries, large-scale industries and organization of distribution network.

The committee was asked to draw up the economic programme of the Congress so that the next task after the achievement of political independence, that is, "the establishment of real democracy in the country and a society based on social justice and equality" could be accomplished. The AICC talked of extending democracy from the political to the social and economic spheres. It made the significant statement that "Democracy in the modern age necessitates planned central direction as well as decentralisation of political and economic power, in so far as this is compatible with the safety of the State, with efficient production and the cultural programme of the community as a whole .... In so far as it is possible, national and regional economic self-sufficiency in the essentials of life should be aimed at. In the case of industries, which in their nature must be run on a large-scale and on centralised basis, they should belong to the community, and that they should be so organised that workers become not only co-sharers in the profits but are also increasingly associated with the management and administration of the industry. Land, with its mineral resources, and all other means of production as well as distribution and exchange must belong to and regulated by the community in its own interest."

The Economic Programme Committee defined the aims and objec-tives of the Economic Programme of the Congress which were to include, among others, (a) a quick and progressive rise in the standard of living of the people to achieve a national minimum standard within a reasonable period, (b) full employment, (c) maximum utilisation of material and manpower resources of the country, (d) equitable distribu-tion of the existing income and wealth and prevention of the growth of disparities in the course of industrial development and the fixation of a ceiling of incomes, not exceeding forty times the national minimum and in the course of time the upper limit to be brought down to twenty times the national minimum, and (e) decentralisation so far as it was possible in the context of country's internal and external security, and national and regional self-sufficiency along with a proper balance between rural and urban economy.

It proposed a radical restructuring of agrarian relations and the establishment of direct relations between cultivators and the State. "Land should be held for use and as a source of employment." The Committee wanted the imposition of a ceiling on landholdings, the replacement of the existing land revenue system by progressive taxation of agricultural income and the promotion of cooperatives. It wanted coordinated development of village and cottage industries with large-scale industries, a strong and ever-expanding public sector, acquisition of excessive margins of profits, stable and friendly industrial relations and the abolition of managing agency system.

It recommended the establishment of a permanent Planning Com-mission which should work for a quick and progressive rise in the standard of living, full employment, increase in production through maximum utilisation of resources, the reduction in the distribution of incomes and widest diffusion of opportunities.

In December 1947, the then Congress president, Dr. Rajendra Prasad, appointed an Agrarian Reforms Committee under the chairman-ship of Dr. J.C. Kumarappa. It went into the agrarian situation, prevailing in the country after the abolition of intermediaries like zamindars, jagirdars, and talukdars. It was of the opinion that there could be a lasting improvement in agricultural production and efficiency only after comprehensive reforms in the land system. It was generally against subletting of land and recommended protection of non-owner cultivators. Any cultivator who cultivated a holding for six years continuously must get occupancy rights automatically. The future pattern of the agrarian economy mustrest on four pillars, namely, (a) it should provide an opportunity for the development of the farmer's personality, (b) there should be no scope for the exploitation of one class by another, (c) there should be maximum efficiency, and (d) it should be practicable.

Among other recommendations were assurance of a reasonable income to farmers through stabilisation of prices, crop insurance, appointment of agrarian reforms commissioners, regulated markets, multipurpose cooperative societies, scaling down of rural debts, provi-sion of alternative sources of rural credit and protection of agricultural labourers. A look at these recommendations reveals that they were just the elaborations of the recommendations of the NPC and its subcommittees. They bore the imprint of Nehru's thinking and influence.

Nehru had to wage a strong battle to establish the Planning Commis-sion. In the second half of 1949, Nehru invited Dr. Solomon Trone, an American, who had considerable knowledge of planning in the Soviet Union to have a look at the Indian economy and recommend how its planned development could be organised.

Dr. Trone submitted a detailed report, recommending strongly the immediate establishment of the Planning Commission which should be an autonomous body, entrusted with the task of formulation and execution of a plan. Referring to the Soviet model of economic growth, the emphasis was placed on the establishmentof capital goods industries in the beginning. Steel plants, machine-tool industry, engineering and heavy electrical industry were to be given priority.

Nehru welcomed these recommendations while the top bureaucracy resisted their implementation. The latter was in favour of setting up a Council of Economic Administration, comprising the secretaries of economic ministries of the Government of India with responsibility to coordinate the activities, concerning economic development. A pro-posal to this effect was made by N. Gopalaswamy Ayyangar, a cabinet colleague of Nehru, who did not have any connections with the Congress or the National Movement. As if to placate Nehru and the Congress, a suggestion was appended that only when it was known that the people could have confidence in developmental schemes originating from an outside agency of experts, largely non-official, the government could consider setting up a Planning Commission.

Nehru could not take this lying down. It seemed, he was being outmanouvred by a group of bureaucrats and his struggle for planned development of the country for more than fifteen years was going to be in vain. He asserted that the failure of India on the economic front was not due to any lack of effort but to the lack of appreciation of a particular situation and lack of data to judge it. This problem could not be solved without having an organised effort at planning. He was convinced that there was no lack of resources in the country, the main problem was to mobilise them and channelise them into various developmental activi-ties according to a scale of priorities determined with a view to achieve certain clear-cut objectives. All this meant having a plan and a planning body. He wrote to his cabinet colleague, John Mathai, on September 13, 1949:

the Indian capitalism had "proved totally inadequate to face things as they are today in the country. They have no vision, no grit, no capacity to do anything big. The only alternative is to try to put forward some big thing ourselves and rope in not only these classes but the people as a whole. Otherwise we remain stagnant and at the most ward off catastro-phe."

He underlined the dangers of dealing with the problems separately and in isolation from the main task of the country's overall socio-economic transformation. What was needed was an integrated approach and its formulation by a planning body. It was sad that the provinces of the country were thinking and working out their schemes of development in isolation from one another and this was not a happy situation. An effective planning machinery could have coordinated their activities and directed by keeping in view the national perspective. These concerns found an echo in his letter to John Mathai, one of the staunchest opponents of planning in his cabinet, on September 29, 1949: "We may make mistakes and pay for them, but surely the greatest mistake is not to view the whole scheme of things in its entirety, realistically and objectively, and to decide on clear objectives and plans. If once this is done, the next step of complete coordination follows much more easily and only by coordinated effort can real results be achieved."'

Mathai did not relent in his opposition to Nehru's efforts at setting up a Planning Commission, which, he thought, would reduce the importance of capitalist class and make it subservient to the State. Nehru did aggravate Mathai's fears when he wrote to him on February 16,1950 that a Planning Commission was needed to "balance the various social forces at work in India, and pay more attention to what might be called the vital forces which will ultimately lead to progress." Three months later, Nehru told Mathai that he was responsible to the masses who had trusted him and put him in the position of leadership and had commit-ment to Mahatma Gandhi's teachings. Gandhi had provided him his sheltering care all these years. He was unlike Mathai and others who had always served the government of the day irrespective of its complexion. It was difficult for Nehru to betray the trust of the people.

In the meantime (January 1950) the Congress Working Committee adopted a resolution calling for the establishment of a Planning Com-mission. Nehru told his opponents in the Cabinet that he was bound by the mandate of the Congress Working Committee and they could decide their course of action. This led to the resignation by John Mathai and the Cabinet approved the proposal to establish the Planning Commission with Nehru as its chairman to enable it to get its recommendations cleared by the government without difficulty.

In April 1950 a conference of chief ministers and PCC presidents took place in Delhi "to formulate an economic programme for the country and to devise the best methods to implement the programme."

To achieve a social order in which there would be justice-social, economic and political- 'it is necessary to formulate not only a short- term but also a long-term plan, initially to cover a period of five years? The resolution at the Conference stated:

While the long-term plan will necessarily have to be well integrated and all-inclusive and will require a clear demarcation of the phases through which it should be worked out by the country and the people, for the purpose of the immediate programme, attention will have to be determined to indicate the order in which action for the fulfillment of the programme can most effectively be taken. For the implementation of such a programme, emphasis should be laid on the rousing of mass enthusiasm and consciousness which alone can make it a people's programme. It will also be necessary to create such institutions as cooperatives in agricul-ture and industries and Panchayats, and to arrange for the training of local leadership to man the institutions. In the background of our limited resources, economic planning presupposes a period of austerity on the part of the people. In order to secure voluntary self-denial on a nationwide scale for the purpose of a programme of planned regional development, efforts shoud be made to create a sense of equality of sacrifice among all sections of the community.

It wanted fast recovery of the economy from the damages of the Second World War and the Partition of the country. It called for the creation of conditions for maintaining a stable and fair price level and for launching a more comprehensive planning with a view to "(a) promoting a balanced economy in agriculture, large-scale and basic industries, village industries and social services; (b) rationalizing production in agriculture and industry and taking steps for the establish-ment and administration of a just and decentralised cooperative econ-omy; (c) bringing a definite rise in the standard of living of the people as a result of planned economy which guarantees a fair remuneration to those who participate in the creation of wealth."

It said the rate of capital formation should be raised and local projects should be linked to local investible surplus. Besides there was the need to promote multi-purpose cooperatives throughout the country.

The Delhi Congress of 1951 declared: "The Congress stands for the progressive extension of the public sector" and "The private sector should function in close accord with the public sector in the fulfilment of common national objectives "and also "Labour should be able to participate in the day to day working of industrial undertakings and in the handling of the general problems cf each industry." It recommended the formation of village production councils charged with the responsibility of developing and increasing production and should serve as the link between the people and the agencies of the State. The Congress wanted incentives for organising small uneconomic holdings into cooperative farms. It emphasised the reorganisation of the whole system of production and distribution with the object of achieving the ends of social justice. The existing disparities in standards of living in the rural and urban areas, the backward and advanced regions and between the different economic strata of the population were to be progressively narrowed down, and a ceiling was to be imposed on incomes and taxation and other economic policies were to be reoriented towards this. There was need to meet the requirements of the planned development of the economy on the basis of internal mobilisation of capital.

The First Five Year Plan was formulated by taking into account the ongoing projects for the rehabilitation of the ravaged economy. Though it was in the right direction, it did not lay down a clear-cut ideological framework and model for self-reliant economic growth. However its various constituent elements were embodied in the Plan. For example, Nehru told the Parliament, while speaking on the First Plan, that he had "no doubt at all that without the development of major industry we cannot raise the level of existence in this country. In fact, I go even a step further and say, we cannot remain a free couhtry without heavy industries, for they are essential for our defence."

He stressed the urgency to remove inequalities because they were inimical to the smooth running and success of political democracy, and adult suffrage would become meaningless.

> *He beseeched the Parliament to look at the Plan from a broader angle and not merely with a critical eye. We must remember that it is the first attempt of its kind to bring the whole picture of India -agricultural, industrial, social, and economic-into one frame-work of thinking. That is a very important thing. Even if it is wrong in parts, it is a tremendous achievement. It has made the whole country 'planning conscious'. It has made us realise mentally and emotionally that we are a united nation. We tend to go off at a tangent and think along narrow provincial, communal, religious or caste lines. We have no emotional awareness of the unity of our country. Our Plan has challenged us to think in terms of the good of the nation as a whole apart.from the separate problems which we have to face in respect of our villages, districts or provinces. Therefore, the mere act of framing this plan and of having produced this report is something for which we can congratulate ourselves.*
>
> *We might remember that when we talked about planning two or three years ago, powerful voices were raised against it. It was said that planning should confine itself just to helping industry by tariffs, by subsidies,*

and so on. It should not interfere with the economy in any other way. While the essence of planning is some kind of controlled economy, our present plan only talks about a public and a private sector. Now, the private sector must function within controls in numerous ways. It must be controlled in regard to the dividends and the profits that it makes, but that is not enough. We have to control the strategic points of the economy of the country, for example banking and insurance ... so as to fit them in more and more within the purview and sphere of a controlled economy."

He promised that the Second Plan would be an improvement on the first. It would be more effective and far-reaching. Its model and philosophy would be clearly spelt out.

These views of Nehru were given an important place in the resolution on Five Year Plan, adopted at the Hyderabad Congress in January 1953. It called upon the people to give their cooperation and assistance for the success of the Plan. The same year in July, the AICC at Agra stressed three important points, namely, the speedy completion of land reforms, change in social structure to induce economic progress and the urgency to mobilise as much savings as possible to increase investments.

All through the period of the First Five Year Plan, both Nehru and the Congress talked of a welfare society or social, economic andpolitical justice and the equality of opportunity as the goal of economic develop-ment. They rejected capitalism and called for institutional changes to end the relations of production, which were exploitative. They, how-ever, did not talk of socialism as their goal or objective. Nehru, as usual, campaigned in favour of socialism and wanted the Congress to accept it as the goal, but, till this happened, he had to go by the accepted position of the Congress. Speaking at a meeting of the National Development Council on November 9, 1954 he said:

Take private enterprise. It is undoubtedly useful so far as our country is concerned; we wish to encourage it, but the dominance it exercised throughout the world, during a certain period, is no more. It is out of date in that sense. For a planner, it has no .secondary place. A system which is based purely on the acquisi-tive instinct of society is immoral. That does not mean we are going away with private enterprise. I think there is much scope for it, and we must give it freedom and encouragement to develop. But we have to realise that the days of the acquisitive element in society are passing; other factors are coming in. Even in the highly capitalistic countries the social element is increasing at a tremendous pace. We have also to think on these lines and get out of the static habit of thinking. We have to be clear about the broad picture we are aiming at.

The picture I have in mind is definitely and absolutely a socialistic picture of society. I am not using the word in a dogmatic sense at all. I mean largely that the means ofproduction should be socially owned and controlled for the benefit of society as a whole.

All through his tenure as president of the Indian National Congress during the 1950s, Nehru had one constant refrain in his speeches, that is, self-reliance. "We must seek to build up our strength on ourselves and not by dependence on others. Dependence in one direction leads to dependence in another. Nations, it is said, by themselves are made. By self-reliance, we shall command respect and we shall make our country more and more our own, of each one of us."

For building a self-reliant economy people have to work hard and make great sacrifices. They have to remain ever vigilant to avoid waste and reserve to increase the investible resources. This attitude would give strength to the country. "Our strength will come not from building up arms or entering into a competition in armaments, but from the development of our country and the well-being of our people."

Retrospectively, the first general elections of 1952, held on the basis of universal adult suffrage, proved that Nehru's economic policies were well received by the people. He was greatly enthused. He directed the Planning Commission to go ahead with the task of preparing the Second Five Year Plan.

The Planning Commission invited experts from the Soviet Union and other socialist countries for discussions and interac-tions. Prof. P.C. Mahalanobis was to prepare the basic framework of the Second Plan which was to lay down the foundations of India's independent economy. As Nehru described later there was, at the meetings of the Commission, 'electricity in the air'. Nehru emphasised the need for a bolder approach in the Second Plan preparation.

Nehru also realised that the time had come for declaring socialism as the primary goal of the country because "welfarism", "egalitarian-ism", "socio-economic justice", "equality of opportunism", etc. were too vague to rouse the enthusiasm of the people and they did not convey the message that India was trying to build a socio-structure which would be alternative to capitalism. The mere rejection of capitalism was not enough, the shape of what was going to come in its place was no less important.

Secondly, after the achievement of political freedom, the horizon of India's liberation struggle had to be widened and for this also the adoption of socialism as its goal was important.

In the years following India's Independence, Nehru tried to develop its political and economic relations with other newly liberated countries and socialist nations. Even though Soviet Union was geographically very close to India, there were very few contacts on State level. The British government had tried to keep India isolated from the Soviet Union.

Soon after the formation of the Interim Government, Nehru estab-lished political relationship with the Soviet Union. Ambassadors were exchanged. The Soviet Union's offer of wheat to India in 1951, when there was an acute shortage of foodgrains in the country, was well-received and the sentiments and fraternal feelings were widely appreci-ated. The Soviet Union had offered to send wheat to the tune of five lakh tonnes in its ships which were to carry back raw jute and cotton in exchange. It is a different matter that India accepted only one lakh tonnes of wheat. It may not be forgotten that Nehru was opposed by a number of his colleagues including C. Rajagopalachari on this issue.

The first formal trade agreement was signed between the two countries onDecember 2, 1953 and it was for a modest turn over of rupees 1.3 crore. In India's total trade with the Soviet Union the share of exports was to be only 0.2 per cent and the imports 0.1 per cent.

These two events which seemed to be inconsequential at that time proved to be of great significance for the ever-expanding and deepening relations between the two and had a far-reaching impact on the pace and direction of India's socio-economic development and on international relations in the years to follow.

AVADI AND AFTER

The Avadi Congress of January 1955 was a major landmark in the history of not only the Indian National Congress but also the country. It fulfilled the long cherished desire of Nehru to get the Congress committed to socialism as its goal for which he had been struggling, arguing, educating and campaigning both inside and outside since 1927. While the Congress accepted industrialisation, planning, the establishment and extension of public ownership over key industries and financial institu-tions, the need for institutional changes and the desirability to bring about an egalitarian society, it did not accept socialism during the pre-Independence era. Nehru, being a democrat, believed in persuasion rather than breaking away from the Congress. He knew that any split in the Congress would only help imperialism and delay the achievement of Independence.

In January 1955, he, ultimately, carried the great organisation with him when he moved a resolution on "Socialistic Pattern of Society" and it was adopted. It said:

> *In order to realise the object of the Congress as laid down in Article 1 of the Congress Constitution and to further the objec-tives stated in the Preamble and Directive Principles of State Policy of the Constitution of India, planning should take place with a view to the establishment of a socialistic pattern of society, where the principal means of production are under social own-ership or control, production is progressively*

speeded up and there is equitable distribution of the national wealth.'

A day after the adoption of this resolution, another resolution on "Economic Policy" was adopted. Its purpose was to bring the future development of the Indian economy in line with the goal of a socialistic pattern of society. It noted with satisfaction the improvement in the general economic situation of the country. The First Plan had exceeded a number of targets. The improvement in the food situation and the progress of river valley projects were heartening. There was social awakening throughout the country and the people had become "planning conscious". A durable foundation for all-round advance of the country was laid down. "The time has now come for a substantial advance on the economic and social plane with the definite objective of increasing production greatly, raising standards of living, and having progressively fuller employment so as to lead to full employment within a period of ten years. The national aim is. a welfare state and a socialistic economy. This can only be achieved by a considerable increase in income and much greater volume of goods and services and employment. Economic policy, must, therefore, aim at plenty and at equitable distribution'

The Second Plan was to keep these objectives in view. It was to try to meet the needs of the people mainly on the basis of production within the country. In other words, the country must aim at self-reliance. "This necessitates the building up of heavy industry, including machine-making industry, as well as a wide extension of small-scale and cottage industries. The success of the Plan depends not only upon careful estimates and planning and proper directions being given, but also on the full cooperation of the people. Planning should, therefore, be based on the widest consultation of the people."

The resolution further said: "In view of the declared objective being a socialist pattern of society, the State will necessarily play a vital part in planning and development. In particular it will:

(i) initiate and operate large-scale schemes providing services such as power, transport, etc.;

(ii) have overall control of resources, social purposes and trends, and essential balances in economy;

(iii) check and prevent evils of anarchic industrial development by the maintenance of strategic controls, prevention of private trusts and cartels, maintenance of standards of labour and production;

(iv) plan the economy of the nation in its basic and broad aspects."

It clarified the roles of the public and the private sectors. "The public sector must play a progressively greater part, more particularly, in the establishment of basic industries."[5] The private sector should continue because, presently, it had an important role to play, that is, to add considerably to production and employment. But this sector had to work within the framework of the national Plan and conform to its discipline.

Speaking in support of this resolution, Nehru spoke of the urgency of increasing production of goods and services, but, at the same time, he wanted this tailored to needs of the masses. This, in turn, necessitated sufficient increase in the purchasing power of the people at large. This would mean an increase in the employment opportunities. He also talked of avoiding inflationary pressures and emphasised the need for physical planning along with financial planning. While heavy industries were necessary for economic independence of the country, cottage and village and small-scale industries were essential for creating employ-ment opportunities and increasing the supply of consumer goods quickly.

Nehru explained to Congress members of Parliament that the Avadi resolution on the goal of the Congress did not mean a change in the policies of the Party "because for a long time past, I should say, a quarter of a century, and in a sense ever since Gandhiji came up to the Congress, the outlook of the Congress was, broadly speaking socialistic.

"I use the word `broadly speaking' not in a scientific sense. And Gandhiji, of course, was always the symbol of the most underprivileged and the lowest on the social scale and he also told us to judge every action we did, every law that we passed, from the point of view of how it affected the poorest and the most deprived and most underprivileged people in the country. That was the basic background which may not, of course, be called cent per cent socialistic."

Pandit Nehru described the Avadi Session of the Congress as "a life-giving Session" which made "the Congress a more dynamic body".'

On March 9, 1955 he addressed a letter to presidents of the Pradesh Congress Committees whioh showed how elated he was after the Avadi Session. He wrote:

> *The Avadi Congress was something more than the triumph of some individuals. It was an expression of the nation's will: it exhibited the dynamic character of the Congress which could adapt itself to changing conditions and keep in tune with the people and their urges. A great organisation, full of years and tra-ditions, is apt to become static and to rest on its laurels. There was this dangerous tendency in the Congress and many of us were apt to become complacent. It is not easy for such a vast organisation, rooted in past habits, to make a fresh move. It is still more difficult for an organisation which has attained success to keep alive to change and growth. Oddly enough, nothing is more dangerous, in a way, than to succeed, for this leads one to think that our work is over."*

He reminded them that in 1947, the Congress completed only one stage of its journey. The second stage of the journey, embarkation on the path of social and economic advance, was more difficult. The goal defined at Avadi had to be kept in mind and everything had to be judged by the yardstick as to "how far it takes us in the direction of the pattern of society that we aim at. If vested interests come in the way, they have to be removed."

In May 1955 the AICC directed the congress Government at the Centre to consider the Avadi resolution on economic policy "in concrete terms in order to draw up an adequate, balanced and planned programme of development."

While the government was engaged in drawing up the outlines of the Second Plan, it faced growing hostility from Western counfrries espe-cially the USA. There were solid reasons for this attitude.

After the Second World War, the US ruling circles found themselves in an unenviable position. On the one hand the accumulation of surplus capital continued to increase. On the other hand, the demand for it sharply declined. The revolutionary triumphs of the peoples in Eastern Europe closed a large area to be used as a market for American goods and curtailed the scope for the export of the surplus US capital. The victory of the Chinese revolution and independence of India, which began the collapse of colonialism and kindled a longing for independent economies by reserving their own market and resources for their own use perturbed the US. As one leading American expert, Stephen E. Am-brose, admits:

American foreign policy after 1945 had this as one of its guiding stars, and therefore, the prevention of these evils i or, put positively, the creation of an open door everywhere. To insure these conditions the nation prepared to use her economic might (as in the 1946 British loan and the 1948 Marshal Plan) or her military (as in Greece, Korea, and elsewhere). The leaders believed that free, private enterprise was essential to a free, open, democratic society, and they would save it at home by imposing it abroad. Truman described the program most succinctly in March 1947. 'The whole world should adopt the American system,' he declared, 'The American system can survive in America only if it becomes a world system."

Ambrose goes on to add:

The politicians looked for areas in which American influence could dominate; the businessmen looked for profitable markets and new sources of raw materials; the military looked for overseas bases. All found what they wanted as America after 1945 inaugurated a program of expansion that had no inherent limits.[12]

The American monopoly capital wanted neocolonialism to replace the old fashioned, discredited arrangement of colonialism. It wanted that formal political independence of erstwhile colonies should be combined with dependent economic development so that it could get access to their markets for selling their finished products and to their raw materials, minerals and foodgrains, and their doors should remain wide open for the penetration of multinational companies (MNCs) and foreign capital. Dan Nabudere has remarked:

> *The events of the next war brought to the US the realisation that her expanded production in key sectors required new markets. With the general offensive by the Soviet Union, particularly after the war when Eastern Europe was no longer under the control of imperialism, imperialism was faced with the need to preserve what remained of its power. The new policy was to intensify the idea of the self-determination of all peoples in order to give a progressive stance to imperialism and take away the initiative from the Soviets. The US could lose nothing by pursuing such a policy, which actually strengthened her economy. It is in this sense that the US multilateral strategy which called for the abolition of colonial preference must be seen and it is from these proceedings, which arise out of imperialism, that the whole neocolonial strategy springs."*

There was, thus, strong opposition from Western quarters to any efforts on the part of newly liberated countries like India which wanted to embark on the path of building their independent modern economies. The Clay Committee Report on Foreign Assistance very clearly recom-mended to the US Congress:

> *We believe that US should not aid a foreign government in projects establishing government owned industrial and commer-cial enterprises which compete with existing private endeavours. While we realise that in aiding foreign countries we cannot insist upon the establishment of our economic system, despite its remarkable success and progress, we should not extend aid which is inconsistent with our beliefs, democratic tradition and knowl-edge of economic organisation and consequences."*

The US was averse to giving aid of any kind to those who refused to join military pacts. The passage of the Mutual Security Act of 1954 set the pattern for the US aid. "To enable allied countries to maintain large military establishments without substantial drains on their economies, sizable amounts of economic aid accompanied military assistance. Section 131 (a) of the Act authorized the President to provide countries receiving military assistance from the US in a regional collective defense arrangement, with commodities, services, financial,, and other assistance necessary to sustain an increased military effort."

Thus it was clear that a country like India which did not have sufficient capital and foreign exchange resources to import machinery, spare parts and technical know-how for setting up modern industries after the pattern dictated by its own national interests had no hope. It was thought, the inescapable fate was a neo-colonial pattern of development and joining the military treaties and pacts sponsored by the USA and other imperialist countries. It was at this juncture that relations devel-oped between India and the Soviet Union and encompassed economic arena.

Prof. S. Gopal notes that, by 1954,

> *Nehru had ... no doubt that the United States was following an imperialist policy, not in the normal sense of conquering a weaker country, but in that she was seeking to force the countries of Asia to conform to her own attitudes. In resisting this, India would have not only to reject offers of military aid and denounce its granting to other nations, but also consider the refusal of economic assistance. Without going out of his way to announce that India would not accept such assistance, Nehru ordered budgeting on the basis that it might not be available. The occasion could also be utilized to press forward with developmental pro-grammes and harness the public emotion which had been aroused for constructive work rather than spend in demonstrations of feeling against Pakistan and the United States.*

The Bandung Conference on April 22-23, 1955 gave Nehru the occasion to propound the philosophy of non-alignment, peaceful co-existence and world peace at some length. He asserted that military blocs and military alliances increased the insecurity of the members joining them, while *Panchshila* promoted world peace, lessened tensions and increased friendship and co-operation among nations.

According to Prof. Gopal, Nehru noted on May 6, 1953: "I dislike more and more this business of exchange of persons between America and India. The fewer persons that go from India to America or that come from the United States to India, the better." He conveyed to C.D. Deshmukh on May 7,1953 his feeling that the Americans in India tended to produce an impression of having partly taken charge of many activities which were normally the responsibility of the government. And he told Rajkumari Amrit Kaur on August 30, 1953 that "We have had quite enough of American superiority." Americans were becoming irritants because of the attempt by them to impose their world outlook wherever they were going."

The agreement between India and the Soviet Union to cooperate in building the Bhilai Steel Plant, on February 2, 1955, heralded the era of economic ties with the Soviet Union, which have played a crucial role in making India move towards economic independence. It also began the rupee-payment arrangement which falsified the Western assertion that the stock of foreign exchange resources was a limiting factor in India's industrialisation to build an independent modern economy.

Prof. Gopal has noted that the USA was so angry with Nehru because of his policies that it wanted to destroy his image and freely distributed an article written by a member of the Nehru clan to denigrate his public standing and turn the people against him. The US embassy in New Delhi paid a handsome amount of money to a language daily to get it published in its Urdu translation.

Nehru, however, was not deterred and he refused to bow before the American machinations. He went ahead with his independent foreign policy based oii non-alignment, world peace and peaceful, friendly co-existence. His stand and speeches were appreciated in the Soviet Union. K.P.S. Menon cabled from Moscow on August 31, 1954 that, unlike the Americans, the Soviets wanted Nehru to remain Nehru and 4ot to toe their line of thinking.

Nehru visited Moscow as India's first Prime Minister in June 1955 and received an unprecedented welcome. The entire presidium of the Supreme Soviet was present at the airport to receive him. He was regarded as the symbol of world's hope for peace.

He himself stated that he came to the Soviet Union, after a lapse of twenty eight years, and was eager to find out what had happened there in this period, and wanted to know as to what were the elements which would endure in the new civilization, coming up there. On the conclu-sion of his visit, he told a meeting in Moscow on June 22, 1955 that "I have been deeply impressed by the great achievements of the Soviet Union. I have seen the transformation of this vast land through the industry of its people and the great urge that drives them forward to better their own condition." He wished: "Let our coming together be because we like each other and wish to cooperate, and not because we dislike others and wish to do them injury. '

The same year the Soviet leaders, Khruschev and Bulganin, paid an official visit to India and lent strong support to its stand on Goa, Kashmir and a number of other issues. This visit further deepened the mutual ties.

The economic ties with the Soviet Union, the nationalization of the Imperial Bank and life insurance companies, setting up of a number of national laboratories and land reforms prepared the congenial atmos-phere for launching the Second Plan with the goal to build a socialist pattern of society. The Indian National Congress which held its annual session in February 1956 at Amritsar adopted a resolution on "Economic Policy and Five-year Plan", noted that the decisions of the Avadi Congress were widely welcomed by the people and had enthused them. The First Plan was nearing its end and most of its aims and targets were realised or exceeded. The national income had gone up by 18 per cent as against the original target of 11 per cent. Industrial production had gone up by 50 per cent and agricultural production had increased by 15 per cent and foodgrains production had recorded a 20 per cent rise. Dependence on foreign foodgrains was over and prices were being maintained at a reasonable level. In the rural areas "a new psychology of hope and self-reliance" had arisen. During the First Plan, the basic and heavy sector could not be propelled on the path of development and this shortcoming along with the shortage of trained manpower had to be overcome. It, however, eould not be denied that the First Plan had not only recorded substantial progress in many directions, but had also prepared the ground for a more rapid advance in the future.

> *The Second Plan has now to build on these foundations and to proceed more rapidly towards the solution of the chronic prob-lems of poverty and unemployment and the achievement of a large measure of economic independence.*
>
> *For this purpose, the rapid progress of industrialisation has become imperative and special stress has to be laid on the development of industry of basic importance, such as, steel, the building of heavy machines, coal and heavy chemicals. The mineral wealth of India still remains largely unexplored and unexploited and it is essential to carry out extensive and intensive mineral surveys with a view to exploiting these resources. Planning necessarily depends upon a full knowledge of the available resources. The generation of power and transport facilities have to be coordinated with the developments in other fields.'*

To create employment opportunities and check the inflationary pressures because of heavy investments in industries with long gestation periods, cottage, village and small-scale industries had to be promoted. This required an improvement in their efficiency and rural electrifica-tion.

The Indian National Congress reiterated its position on the roles of the public and private sectors:

> *The public sector has to expand rapidly, but the private sector also has to play an important part within the framework of the Plan. The two sectors must be viewed*

as parts of a single plan, to be worked in coordination with each other, and not as two independ-ent sectors of our economy. Within the scope indicated for the private sector, encouragement should be given to private initia-tive and enterprise. Thus every effort should be made to increase production, keeping always the social objectives in view. The basic test for determining the lines of advance should be social gain and service of the community and not private profit. Where considered necessary and feasible, there can be joint participa-tion between State and private capital. The public sector should expand to the fullest extent of the country's capacity and the State should, more especially, assume larger responsibilities in regard to industries of strategic importance. The possibility of increas-ing State trading, wherever possible, should be considered'

The basis of organisation of activities in industrial, agricultural and commercial sectors was to be cooperation. To remove the disadvantages resulting From extreme subdivisions of landholdings and secure the economies of scale, co-operative farming had to be promoted.

The problems of backward sections of the society and the backward regions of the country needed to be tackled with a sense of urgency. The efforts must be made to homogenise the society and bring about balanced regional economic growth in order to strengthen the unity.

The Congress approved the approach, policy and proposals of the draft outline of the Second Plan, in whose formulation Nehru had guided. It aimed at increasing the national income by 25 per cent and pushing up the production of basic and heavy industries and infrastruc-tural facilities substantially.

In April 1956, Nehru presented an Industrial Policy Resolution to Parliament. It was to replace the Industrial Policy Resolution of 1948. This was necessary in view of the changed objective situation brought about by the adoption of the Constitution which guaranteed certain fundamental rights and enunciated Directive Principles of State Policy, the completion of the First Plan and acceptance of the socialist pattern of society as the objective of social and economic policy. The Second Plan was to be based on a new industrial policy.

The Industrial Policy Resolution of 1956 stated:

> *In order to realise this objective, it is essential to accelerate the rate of economic growth and to speed up industrialisation and in particular, to develop heavy industries and machine making industries, to expand the public sector, and to build up a large and growing co-operative sector. These provide the economic foun-dations for increasing opportunities for gainful employment and improving living standards and working conditions for the mass of the people. Equally, it is urgent to reduce disparities in income and wealth which exist today, to prevent private monopolies and the concentration of economic power in different fields in the hands of small numbers of individuals. Accordingly, the State will progressively assume a predominant and direct responsibil-ity for setting up new industrial undertakings and for developing transport facilities. It will also undertake State trading on an increasing scale. At the same time, as an agency for planned national development, in the context of the country's expanding economy, the private sector will have the opportunity to develop and expand. The principle of co-operation should be applied wherever possible and steadily increasing proportion of the activities of the private sector developed along cooperative lines.*

The Resolution put all industries of basic and strategic importance and public utilities in the public sector. The Public sector was to cover those industries which required huge amounts of investment. Thus the State was to assume direct responsibility for further development of industries over a wide area. Also the State was to regulate the develop-ment of industries in the private sector in view of the limited stock of capital and other resources available to the country, which needed to be rationally allocated and used according to the priorities fixed by the Planning Commission. Nehru presented the Second Plan to the Lok Sabha for its consideration on May 23, 1956 and in the course of his speech, he made certain significant remarks. First, removal of disparities in the distribution of incomes and wealth and regional imbalances in economic development. Second, socialism is not spreading out poverty but is increasing produc-tion and wealth for distribution. Third, unemployment and poverty of the country were due to backwardness in science and technology. By removing this unemployment and poverty could be removed. This understanding of Nehru was contrary to that of many people who wanted India to adopt only capital-light technologies and set up only cottage, village and small-scale industries. Four, planning was indispensable for India's economic development. The attraction towards free enterprise was fast declining all over the world. Last, the country needed latest technologies, machines, equipment and certain kinds of raw materials which had to be imported. To do that, the country needed foreign exchange resources which had to be earned by increasing export earnings. The country had to practice austerity to increase its exports. It could not afford to be dependent on the benevolence of others. "We cannot live in expectation of the bounties of others. If somebody helps us, we welcome this thankfully, but we do not plan merely in the expectation of others being bountiful." Obviously, the country had to learn to be self-reliant.

Nehru also emphasised theneed for a stable agricultural economy for supply of adequate raw materials and foodgrains. Without this there could not be a stable industrial economy. In agricultural sector, produc-tivity had to be raised substantially by applying modem science and technology and increasing inputs.

He also talked of managing the public enterprises efficiently not only to check waste of public money but also to obtain desired results in terms of production and employment opportunities. He was in favour of giving

> *freedom to the man, to the executive, in charge .... Of course, if there is a major loss, if the whole enterprise goes to pieces, the man in charge will suffer no doubt. But the point is, he is given responsibility .... a great Russian leader like Mr. Mikoyan, has told us, do not*

interfere with your enterprises, give them respon-sibility, give your executive responsibility, do not interfere. Mr. Mikoyan came to me - you know the Russians are putting up a steel plant, it is only at the initial stage yet, but in discussing it he said, 'You do not mind my saying this. But if you do not trust your executive, do not give him fuller responsibility, the work will be delayed, and you will suffer.' He said, 'we have come to the conclusion after considerable experience that we must trust our executives and allow them to go ahead'. Of course, there are all kinds of checks, financial and others, but checks come after-wards. But the chief man must be able to do what he wants to do quickly.

If we are to go in for public enterprises in future in a big way, we must realise this fact. We cannot sit down every day and control public enterprises from Parliament. This cannot be done. Some-times it may be useful; you save some money, but you will lose a great deal of money and the enterprise will not prosper and it will become static, a bad thing for a growing industry?

Soon after the Second Plan was launched, it faced difficulties. They came from three directions, namely, Indian agriculture, world market and West Asia. There was a severe drought in Fastern India, leading to a sharp fall in rice output. The prices of imported machines and equipment registered sharp increases, pushing up the import bill. The Anglo-French action against Egypt to prevent the nationalisation of the Suez Canal resulted in the closure of the Canal and this increased the costs of transportation of India's export and import goods, and proved to be a great impediment for India's foreign trade. The last two difficulties brought a severe foreign exchange problem before India

The output of foodgrains declined by 10 per cent in 1957-58 and the prices of foodgrains registered an increase of 50 per cent between October 1955 and August 1957. The import of foodgrains had to be continued in view of this situation.

It was envisaged in the Second Plan that a sum of rupees 200 crore would be drawn from India's sterling balances over the entire Plan period but within the first year itself the drawals amounted to more than this sum. It was estimated that for the rest of the period of the Plan, the country would need at least rupees 700 crore.

The Government sent the then finance minister, T.T. Krishnama-chari, to USA to seek economic aid. The experience of Krishnamachari convinced that India would have to depend on itself if it wanted to have real political and economic freedom. Self-reliance in basic and heavy industries and in foodgrains production had to be attained as early as possible. Agricultural productivity had to be increased and, till then, the country had to go in for compulsory procurement and regulated distri-bution of available foodgrains.Nehru stressed the need to complete the task of land reforms as soon as possible and then to reorganise agriculture on the basis of cooperation. Service co-operatives and cooperative farming must be the basis of reorganisation to secure economies of scale. Small and fragmented holdings were not only uneconomical but also incapable of benefiting from improved agronomical practices. He told a meeting in New Delhi on April 13, 1958 to catch *kismat* by its neck and bring it under one's control and utilise it.

The All India Congress Committee which met in June 1957 endorsed Nehru's ideas and gave his policies its full support. It emphasised the importance of agricultural surpluses for industrial progress and reduce the impact of vagaries of nature on the people. "Both from the point of view of meeting the needs of the people and keeping the prices of foodgrains at a reasonable level, and also for the success of the Second Five Year Plan, it is essential that the Government and the people should direct the energy and intensify their efforts to meet the situation and increase the production and supply of foodgrains. This must be treated as a matter of national importance.

The AICC recommended the speedy completion of land reforms, augmenting irrigation facilities by constructing and maintaining both major and minor irrigation works, bringing cultivable waste lands under cultivation, increasing productivity in agriculture, ensuring guaranteed minimum prices of crops to peasants, building up reserves of foodgrains with the government, bringing about a change in the food habits of the people and curbing the activities of hoarders and black marketeers. In another resolution the AICC endorsed Nehru's decision of not succumbing to the pressure from Western quarters to give up or curtail the size of the Second Plan or change its pattern of investment. It stated: "The principal targets of the Second Plan are the minimum necessary to create a progressive economy in the country and to provide better living conditions for the people. It is essential, therefore, to implement the Plan without toning down these principal targets or lengthening the period of the Plan.'" The AICC resolved that:

(1) The determination to implement the Plan should not be weakened and the Plan must be implemented within the allotted period, so that the commencement of the Third Plan is not delayed.

(2) Any readjustments of the Plan must be made consistent with the aim of the Congress, that is, the achievement of a socialist society and the building up of an economic structure on a progressively egalitarian basis.

(3) The industrial core of the Plan, namely, the production of steel and coal and the development of transport and power, must be implemented.

(4) Greater production in all spheres should be aimed at. Any process of slowing down production is detrimental to the public interest."

In the face of increasing resource constraints and pressures from the western lobbies, the AICC met informally within a few months and reasserted its determination not to allow any change in the strategy of development or curtailment in its size. In a resolution on the economic situation, it said: Consensus of opinion among the members of the AICC in regard to different problems was as under:

1. Although various difficulties which are inherent in a developing economy had to be faced in a realistic manner without any sense of complacency, the basic economy of India is sound and there is no cause for frustration or defeatism.

2. It will not be desirable to elongate the Second Five Year Plan to six or seven years, although there is room for rearranging the priorities and effecting minor adjustments by pruning the Plan.
3. Every attempt should be made to increase the internal re-sources for the Plan, particularly through the promotion of small savings. Strict economy should be enforced in all Government expenditure by cutting down non-developmen-tal and non-productive projects. There is urgent need for simplicity and austerity in every sphere of national activity. An all-out effort should be made to root out corruption wherever it exists.
4. While external aid would always be welcome for implement-ing the targets of the Second Five Year Plan, our main emphasis should be on self-reliance.
5. Serious efforts should be made to improve the foreign ex-change position by cutting down all unessential imports and promoting exports to the maximum. The spirit of *swadeshi* should be revived in the country.

It underlined that it was urgently necessary to regard self-sufficiency in food as an integral part of national self-defence. Experimental cooperative farms should be set up to demonstrate their efficacy to the peasantry in increasing production. Cooperation in agriculture would broaden the general outlook of peasants and would make them less individualistic and more community-minded. It held that "the real salvation of the Indian agriculturist lies in cooperation."

While the Western pressure for deflecting India from the path of building an independent modern economy increased in view of growing food and foreign exchange difficulties, Nehru's determination not to give in also increased. He told the Gauhati session of the Congress that he would never buckle, come what may. There was no need to be panicky by exaggerating the importance of foreign aid. India had not won freedom to remain static economically and, ultimately become a neo-colony.

The Congress in its resolution on "Economic Situation", adopted at Gauhati endorsed Nehru's stand and expressed its full solidarity with him. It laid stress on increasing the mobilisation of internal resources by increasing production and savings.

> *The dominant factor in the economic situation is the internal strength of the country's economy. The building up of internal resources is, therefore, of the highest importance. Increased production is essential and a substantial part of this should be canalised into savings to provide capital for further development. In an undeveloped economy where people have been living for a long time past on the marginal levels of subsistence, any increase in earnings does not automatically make available a surplus for development. A great part of these increased earnings goes into increased consumption which is bound to add to inflationary tendencies. Thus it is important not only to create a surplus, but to divert it towards saving and investment."*

It emphasised the importance of increasing agricultural production by raising productivity through reorganisation and supply of adequate and better inputs.

Nehru wanted the Congressmen to take an active part in fighting hoarding, black marketing and profiteering and mobilising popular support. He wrote to Dr. Sampurnanand:

> *More and more we become supine and expect the gods to help us or some law to come to our rescue. I am sure we could have dealt with the situation better as a rebellious Congress in the old days than we can today with all the machinery of government .... I wish I was a district magistrate or just the president of the Congress committee in a district so that I could function as I think people ought to function. Unfortunately I am prime minister which in such matters is rather a helpless position."*

He hoped that by the end of the Third Plan, India would be able to cross "that dreadful barrier which separates an underdeveloped country from a developing country, developing through its own resources."

He was extremely happy when the public sector steel plants were commissioned. He thought, India's reliance on foreign consultants and technological assistance would be definitely reduced. S. Gopal has observed:

> *It hurt Nehru that even for project reports they had to rely on foreigners, so that experts from the United States could tell him, with a measure of contempt, that it would take India over twenty years to build a big plant and at the moment, for all her industrial advance, she could not even produce a pin. For training Indians, the Soviet Union would be more helpful than the United States, whose private firms would naturally be concerned with their own interests. Hereafter, except for the occasional individual expert, India should develop greater self-reliance in industrial develop-ment. In this respect, the private sector in India could also be encouraged in preference to resort to foreign agencies.*

Nehru had a bitter experience with Western companies and the World Bank in connection with oil exploration in India. When India realised that one of the important factors aggravating its foreign exchange was the huge import bill for oil, which came to around rupees 100 crore in 1958, it wanted to make explorations for oil deposits in the country. It set up the Oil and Natural Gas Commission (ONGC) and sought the help of the Soviet Union which immediately despatched its experts and equipment to India.

This was "strongly attacked from many quarters, including the oil companies, the business world, the oil journals, as well as the World Bank. The main emphasis in all the criticisms has been placed on the costly nature of the undertaking as well as the high degree of risk associated with it.... Even when the search for oil is successful, the critics point out, the costs of development are also very high and would require the company (or country?) concerned to meet deficits for a period of at least five or six years, at a time when either the required amount of foreign exchange is not available, or such an amount might be more fruitfully employed in other undertakings. Since most of the poor countries cannot afford to gamble with their limited resources, the efforts of the Government should be directed towards less risky and less costly ventures, instead of being sunk in oil exploration."

Biplab Dasgupta, after a careful scrutiny of evidence, has noted, "There are grounds for suspicion that the World Bank put its weight ... in favour of the major international oil companies...."

Nehru believed that the Soviet technology in oil exploration was highly developed and he was confident that India would soon achieve a substantial measure of self-sufficiency. He saw to it that oil exploration work did not suffer for want of funds. He completely ignored all attacks on him from Western quarters about his growing dependence on the Soviet Union.

In fact, the thing which worried Nehru was the state of affairs in the agricultural sector. Agricultural production, especially the production of foodgrains, was increasing at a very slow pace and it was still largely influenced by weather gods. Agriculture had to be modernised and freed from its dependence on the monsoon. Achievements of science and technology could not bring adequate benefits to Indian agriculture so long as holdings were small and fragmented. The way out was coopera-tive farming. He was influenced by what had happened in socialist countries.

He encouraged to think deeply about this problem of introducing cooperative farming to which the Congress had made frequent refer-ences in the past.

The Indian National Congress at its Nagpur session in January 1959 adopted a comprehensive resolution on agrarian reorganisation. It wanted the organisation of the village to be based on village panchayats and village cooperatives, which must have a great deal of autonomy in their functioning. There should be a union of a number of village cooperatives. The cooperatives should promote progressive farming methods and improved techniques of cultivation and activities allied to agriculture. It emphasised:

> *The future agrarian pattern should be that of cooperative joint farming, in which the land will be pooled for joint*

cultivation, the farmers continuing to retain their property rights, and getting a share from the net produce in proportion to their land. Further, those who actually work on the land, whether they own the land or not, will get a share in proportion to the work put in by them on the joint farm."

As a first step, service cooperatives should be organised throughout the country within three years and land reforms completed.

The resolution, for the first time, stated the need to ensure a fairretum to the producer and foodgrains availability to consumers at reasonable prices. It called the fixation of a minimum floor price of each major crop in advance of the sowing season and the arrangements to purchase directly, wherever necessary, from the producer. It wanted the introduc-tion of State trading in wholesale trade of foodgrains. This was meant to eliminate the middlemen to bring down the market prices of foodgrains and regulate the supplies in the market.

To introduce cooperative farming, the concentration of holdings had to be broken by imposing a ceiling on agricultural holdings and surplus land had to be taken over and distributed among those who had no land or very small holding of land. It may be pointed out that, at that time, less than 10 per cent of rural households owned more than 50 per cent of land while one-fourth of the households were landless and another 25 percent owned less than one acre. The State governments were asked by the Congress to enact land ceiling legislations by the end of 1959.

Peasants were not to be coerced but persuaded to see reason and voluntarily join cooperative farming. Nehru himself, in the course of his speech at Nagpur, offered to go from peasant to peasant and beg them to agree to cooperative farming. He aimed at changing their outlook and psychology to a large extent.

It is high time to look into the past and the failure of cooperative farming. Had cooperative farming succeeded, there would have been far-reaching changes in rural socio-economic structure and reduction in the growing disparities in the rural society.

In another resolution, the Congress expressed its concern over greater dependence on foreign loans for financing the Plan. It admitted that foreign loans were not unusual in the development of an under-developed country. "But foreign credits must not be tied up with any political or economic conditions which come in the way of the country following its independent policies." Further, "The main burden of carrying out a programme of economic development must fall on the people of the country, and, therefore, it is to the extent that domestic resources are increased that adequate progress can be made."

While it called for efforts to evolve suitable methods and policies to reduce the rate of growth of population, it cautioned against any sense of panic at an increase in the rate of growth of population, which was bound to come because of the reduction in death rate as a result of improved health and medical facilities. "A lasting solution of the problem of population is to be found in raising standards of living, education, particularly of women, and changes in attitudes and outlook."

It enumerated numerous steps such as making public enterprises to yield an increasing surplus, curbing non-essential imports and expan-sion of life insurance business, to generate resources and conserve foreign exchange. It wanted the pattern of production to be oriented towards fulfilling the needs of the people. It was of the view that steps should be taken to utilise the vast manpower, especially in rural areas, for direct capital formation. It was to be employed in village and cottage industries, construction of irrigation channels, tanks and wells, soil conservation and reclamation, and afforestation.

With the intensification of cold war in the world, the pressures on India from Western quarters to change its foreign policy increased. Nehru realised and underlined the importance of planning to achieve self-reliance in economic affairs. What was urgently needed was to build up a self-sustaining and self-generating economy, both in agriculture and industry. The defence of the country and its foreign policy could be sustained only on this basis. This was the thinking of Nehru, which was echoed by the Congress at its Bangalore session in 1960.

The Third Plan was to be launched very soon, because the Second Plan was drawing to a close. Nehru wanted the emphasis on basic and heavy industries to continue in the Third Plan. Their importance in view of the growing dangers to India's security from its northern borders could be well-appreciated. The public sector was to give increasing importance to steel, oil, power, transport, machine-making and chemi-cals. This line of thinking was endorsed by the AICC at Raipur in October 1960 and the Congress at its Bhavnagar session (1961).

Nehru wanted to add one more steel plant during the Third Plan. He was given the impression by the Americans that the US government would be willing to give aid for another steel plant which was to be set up at Bokaro.

But the Americans wanted a heavy price for it. They wanted achange in the priority given to the public sector and acceptance of US nuclear umbrella over India and facilities for Voice of America to broadcast from the Indian soil. Ultimately, they backed out of their commitment to build the Bokaro steel plant in the public sector and the negotiations were called off. India had to turn to the soviet Union for cooperation for setting up the steel plant.'

With the Chinese invasion of India in October 1962, Nehru and the Congress realized that not only the path and strategy of economic development pursued by India were basically correct, but the pace of economic growth had to be accelerated to strengthen the security of the country. This was the only way to avoid going to others for aid and enter into alliance for ensuring the defence of the country.

Before the death of Nehru in May 1964, the Indian National Congress held its session at Bhubaneshwar and adopted a lengthy resolution on "Democracy and Socialism". It reiterated its commitment to democratic socialism which meant a "revolution in the economic and social relationships" to be brought about "through radical changes in the attitudes and outlook of the people as well as the institutions through which they have to function." It called for the elimination of privileges, disparities and exploitation and ensuring human dignity of every citizen and social justice. The incomes and profits in private hands were to be limited. Inherited wealth and urban property were to be taxed heavily to limit them.

The State was called upon to control and direct the flow of credit and investible resources of the country to conform to the priorities fixed by the Plan. The financial institutions were to be rid of malpractices and various kinds of abuses.

While the public sector was to be the dominant and ever-expanding sector in the economy, the private sector was to be regulated to make it subserve the objectives of the Plan.

For the first time the Congress took note of the growth, proliferation of and dangers posed by the phenomenon of unaccounted or black money. It described it as a threat to democracy and socialism and wanted urgent steps to eliminate it. It felt the need to foster ethical and spiritual values along with economic development. Only then the existing acquisitive socio-economic structure could be gradually replaced by a socialist structure.

Nehru suffered a mild stroke at Bhubaneshwar in January 1964 and breathed his last on May 27, 1964. With his passing away, one long chapter in India's fight for political znd economic independence came to an end. Nehru left a valuable legacy to the country in terms of ideas and a grand vision of a modern nation, and firm foundations for an independent modern economy.

7

Political Integration of India

IMMEDIATE SITUATION POST-1947 INDEPENDENCE

At the time of Indian independence, India was divided into two sets of territories, the first being the territories under the control of the British Empire, and the second being the territories over which the Crown had suzerainty, but which were under the control of their hereditary rulers. In addition, there were several colonial enclaves controlled by France and Portugal.

The political integration of these territories into India was a declared objective of the Indian National Congress, which the Government of India pursued over the next decade. Through a combination of factors, Vallabhbhai Patel and V.P. Menon convinced the rulers of the various princely states to accede to India. Having secured their accession, they then proceeded to, in a step-by-step process, secure and extend the central government's authority over these states and transform their administration until, by 1956, there was little difference between the territories that had formerly been part of British India and those that had been part of princely states.

Simultaneously, the Government of India through a combination of diplomatic and military means acquired de facto and de jure control over the remaining colonial enclaves, which too were integrated into India. Although this process successfully integrated the vast majority of princely states into India, it was not as successful in relation to a few states, notably the former princely states of Kashmir, Tripura and Manipur, where active secessionist movements exist.

PRINCELY STATES IN BRITISH INDIA

The early history of British expansion in India was characterised by the co-existence of two approaches towards the existing princely states. The first was a policy of annexation, where the British sought to forcibly absorb the Indian princely states into the provinces which constituted their Empire in India. The second was a policy of indirect rule, where the British assumed suzerainty and paramountcy over princely states, but conceded some degree of sovereignty to them.

During the early part of the nineteenth century, the policy of the British tended towards annexation, but the Indian Rebellion of 1857 forced a change in this approach, by demonstrating both the difficulty of absorbing and subduing annexed states, and the usefulness of princely states as a source of support. In 1858, the policy of annexation was formally renounced, and British relations with the princely states thereafter were based on indirect rule, whereby the British exercised paramountcy over all princely states with the British crown as ultimate suzerain, but at the same time respected and protected them as allies.

The exact relations between the British and each princely state were regulated by individual treaties, and varied widely, with some states having significant autonomy, some being subject to significant control in internal affairs, and some being in effect the owners of a few acres of land with little autonomy.

During the 20th century, the British made several attempts to integrate the princely states more closely with British India, creating the Chamber of Princes in 1921 as a consultative and advisory body, transferring the responsibility for supervision of smaller states from the provinces to the centre in 1936, and creating direct relations between the Government of India and the larger princely states superseding political agents. The most ambitious was a scheme of federation in the Government of India Act, 1935, which envisaged the princely states and British India being united under a federal government.

This scheme came close to success, but was abandoned in 1939 as a result of the outbreak of the Second World War. As a result, in the 1940s, the relationship between the princely states and the crown remained regulated by the principle of paramountcy and the various treaties between the British crown and the states.

Neither paramountcy nor these arrangements could continue after Indian independence. The British took the view that because they had been established directly between the British crown and the princely states, they could not be transferred to independent India. At the same time, they imposed obligations on Britain that it was not prepared to continue to carry out, such as the obligation to maintain troops in India for the defence of the princely states. The British government therefore decided that paramountcy, together with all treaties between them and the princely states, would come to an end upon the transfer of power.

REASONS FOR INTEGRATION

The Saurashtra and Kathiawar regions of Gujarat were home to over two hundred princely states, many with non-contiguous territories, as this map of Baroda shows.

The termination of paramountcy would have in principle have meant that all rights that flowed from the states' relationship with the British crown would return to them, leaving them free to negotiate relationships with the new states of India and Pakistan "on a basis of complete freedom." Early British plans for the transfer of power, such as the offer produced by the Cripps Mission, recognised the possibility that some princely states might choose to stand out of independent India.

This was unacceptable to the Congress, which regarded the independence of princely states as a denial of the course of Indian history, and consequently regarded this scheme as a "Balkanisation" of India. The Congress had traditionally been less active in the princely states because of their limited resources which restricted their ability to organise there and their focus on the goal of independence from the British, and because Congress leaders, in particular Gandhi, were sympathetic to the more progressive princes as examples of the capacity of Indians to rule themselves. This changed in the 1930s as a result of the federation scheme contained in the Government of India Act, 1935 and the rise of socialist Congress leaders such as Jayaprakash Narayan, and the Congress began to actively engage with popular political and labour activity in the princely states. By 1939, the Congress' official stance was that the states must enter independent India, on the same terms and with the same autonomy as the provinces of British India, and with their people granted responsible government. As a result, it insisted on the incorporation of the princely states into India in its negotiations with Mountbatten.

A few British leaders, particularly Lord Mountbatten, the last British viceroy in India, were also uncomfortable with breaking links between independent India and the princely states. The development of trade, commerce and communications during the 19th and 20th centuries had bound the princely states to British India through a complex network of interests. Agreements relating to railways, customs, irrigation, the use of ports, and other similar agreements would disappear, posing a serious threat to the economic life of the subcontinent.

Mountbatten was also persuaded by the argument of Indian leaders such as V.P. Menon that the integration of the princely states into independent India would to some extent assuage the wounds of partition. The result was that Mountbatten personally favoured and worked towards the accession of princely states to India following the transfer of power, as proposed by the Congress.

ACCEPTING INTEGRATION

The Princes' Position

The rulers of the princely states were not uniformly enthusiastic about integrating their domains into independent India. Some, such as the kings of Bikaner and Jawhar, were motivated to join India out of ideological and patriotic considerations, but others insisted that they had the right to join either India or Pakistan, to remain independent, or form a union of their own. Bhopal, Travancore and Hyderabad announced that they did not intend to join either dominion.

Hyderabad went as far as to appoint trade representatives in European countries and commencing negotiations with the Portuguese to lease or buy Goa to give it access to the sea, and Travancore pointed to the strategic importance to western countries of its thorium reserves while asking for recognition. Some states proposed a subcontinent-wide confederation of princely states, as a third entity in addition to India and Pakistan. Bhopal attempted to build an alliance between the princely states and the Muslim League to counter the pressure being put on rulers by the Congress.

A number of factors contributed to the collapse of this initial resistance and to nearly all princely states agreeing to accede to India. An important factor was the lack of unity amongst the princes. The smaller states did not trust the larger states to protect their interests, and many Hindu rulers did not trust Muslim princes, in particular Hamidullah Khan, the Nawab of Bhopal and a leading proponent of independence, who they viewed as an agent for Pakistan.

Others, believing integration inevitable, sought to build bridges with the Congress, hoping thereby to gain a say in shaping the final settlement. The resultant inability to present a united front or agree on a common position significantly reduced their bargaining power in negotiations with the Congress. The decision by the Muslim League to stay out of the Constituent Assembly was also fatal to the princes' plan to build an alliance with it to counter the Congress, and attempts to boycott the Constituent Assembly altogether failed on 28 April 1947, when the states of Baroda, Bikaner, Cochin, Gwalior, Jaipur, Jodhpur, Patiala and Rewa took their seats in the Assembly.

Many princes were also pressured by popular sentiment favouring integration with India, which meant their plans for independence had little support from their subjects. The king of Travancore, for example, definitively abandoned his plans for independence after the attempted assassination of his dewan, Sir C.P. Ramaswamy Aiyar. In a few states, the chief ministers or dewans played a significant role in convincing the princes to accede to India. The key factors that led the states to accept integration into India were, however, the efforts of Lord Mountbatten, the last Viceroy of British India, and Vallabhbhai Patel and V.P. Menon, who were respectively the political and administrative heads of the Indian Government's States Department, which was in charge of relations with the princely states.

MOUNTBATTEN'S ROLE

Lord Louis Mountbatten played an important role in convincing reluctant monarchs to accede to the Indian Union.

Mountbatten believed that securing the states' accession to India was crucial to reaching a negotiated settlement with the Congress for the transfer of power. As a relative of the British Emperor, he was trusted by most of the princes and was a personal friend of many, especially the Nawab of Bhopal, Hamidullah Khan. The princes also believed that he would be in a position to ensure the independent India adhered to any terms that might be agreed upon, because Jawaharlal Nehru and Patel had asked him to become the first Governor General of the Dominion of India.

Mountbatten used his influence with the princes to push them towards accession. He declared that the British Government would not grant dominion status to any of the princely states, nor would it accept them into the British Commonwealth, which meant that the states would sever all connections with the British crown unless they joined either India or Pakistan. He pointed out that the Indian subcontinent was one economic entity, and that the states would suffer most if the link were broken. He also pointed to the difficulties that princes would face maintaining order in the face of threats such as the rise of communal violence and communist movements.

Mountbatten stressed that he would act as the trustee of the princes' commitment, as he would be serving as India's head of state well into 1948. He engaged in a personal dialogue with reluctant princes, such as the Nawab of Bhopal, who he asked through a confidential letter to sign the Instrument of Accession making Bhopal part of India, which Mountbatten would keep locked up in his safe. It would be handed to the

States Department on 15 August only if the Nawab did not change his mind before then, which he was free to do. The Nawab agreed, and did not renege over the deal.

At the time, several princes complained that they were being betrayed by Britain, who they regarded as an ally, and Sir Conrad Corfield resigned his position as head of the Political Department in protest at Mountbatten's policies. Mountbatten's policies were also criticised by the opposition Conservative Party. Winston Churchill compared the language used by the Indian government with that used by Adolf Hitler before the invasion of Austria. Modern historians such as Lumby and Moore, however, take the view that Mountbatten played a crucial role in ensuring that the princely states agreed to accede to India.

PRESSURE AND DIPLOMACY

Vallabhbhai Patel as Minister for Home and States Affairs had the responsibility of welding the British Indian provinces and the princely states into a united India

By far the most significant factor that led to the princes' decision to accede to India was the policy of the Congress and, in particular, of the two key figures in the States Department, Sardar Vallabhbhai Patel and V.P. Menon. The Congress' stated position was that the princely states were not sovereign entities, and as such could not opt to be independent notwithstanding the end of paramountcy. The princely states, it declared, must therefore accede to either India or Pakistan.

In July 1946, Nehru pointedly observed that no princely state could prevail militarily against the army of independent India. In January 1947, he said that independent India would not accept the Divine Right of Kings, and in May 1947, he declared that any princely state which refused to join the Constituent Assembly would be treated as an enemy state.

Other Congress leaders, such as C. Rajagopalachari, argued that as paramountcy "came into being as a fact and not by agreement", it would necessarily pass to the government of independent India, as the successors of the British.

Patel and Menon, who were charged with the actual job of negotiating with the princes, took a more conciliatory approach than Nehru. The official policy statement of the Government of India made by Patel on 5 July 1947 made no threats. Instead, it emphasised the unity of India and the common interests of the princes and independent India, reassured them about the Congress' intentions, and invited them to join independent India "to make laws sitting together as friends than to make treaties as aliens." He reiterated that the States Department would not attempt to establish a relationship of domination over the princely states. Unlike the Political Department of the British Government, it would not be an instrument of paramountcy, but a medium whereby business could be conducted between the states and India as equals.

INSTRUMENTS OF ACCESSION

Patel and Menon backed up their diplomatic efforts by producing treaties that were designed to be attractive to rulers of princely states. Two key documents were produced. The first was the Standstill Agreement, which confirmed that the agreements and administrative practices that existed as between the princely state in question and the British would be continued by India. The second was the Instrument of Accession, by which the ruler of the princely state in question agreed to the accession of his kingdom to independent India, and to granting India control over specified subject matters. The nature of the subject matters varied depending on the acceding state.

The states which had internal autonomy under the British signed an Instrument of Accession which only ceded three subjects to the government of India—defence, external affairs, and communications, each defined in accordance with List 1 to Schedule VII of the Government of India Act, 1935. Rulers of states which were in effect estates or talukas, where substantial administrative powers were exercised by the Crown, signed a different Instrument of Accession, which vested all residuary powers and jurisdiction in the government of India. Rulers of states which had an intermediate status signed a third type of Instrument, which preserved the degree of power they had under the British.

The Instruments of Accession implemented a number of other safeguards. Clause 7 provided that the princes would not be bound to the Indian constitution as and when it was drafted. Clause 8 guaranteed their autonomy in all areas in which authority was not expressly ceded to the Government of India. This was supplemented by a number of promises. Rulers who agreed to accede would receive guarantees that their extra-territorial rights, such as immunity from prosecution in Indian courts and exemption from customs duty, would be protected, that they would be allowed to democratise slowly, that none of the eighteen major states would be forced to merge, and that they would remain eligible for British honours and decorations. In discussions, Lord Mountbatten reinforced the statements of Patel and Menon by emphasising that the documents gave the princes all the "practical independence" they needed. Mountbatten, Patel and Menon also sought to give princes the impression that if they did not accept the terms put to them then, they would subsequently have to accede on substantially less favourable terms. The Standstill Agreement was also used as a negotiating tool, as the States Department categorically ruled out signing a Standstill Agreement with princely states that did not sign an Instrument of Accession.

THE ACCESSION PROCESS

The limited scope of the Instruments of Accession and the promise of a wide-ranging autonomy and the other guarantees they offered, gave sufficient comfort to many rulers, who saw this as the best deal they could strike given the lack of support from the British, and popular internal pressures. Between May 1947 and the transfer of power on 15 August 1947, the vast majority of states signed Instruments of Accession. A few, however, held out. Some simply delayed signing the Instrument of Accession. Piploda, a small state in central India, did not accede until March 1948. The biggest problems, however, arose with a few border states, such as Jodhpur, which tried to negotiate better deals with Pakistan, with Junagadh, which actually did accede to Pakistan, and with Hyderabad and Kashmir, which declared that they intended to remain independent.

Border States

The ruler of Jodhpur, Hanwant Singh, was antipathetic to the Congress, and did not see much future in India for him or the lifestyle he wished to lead, and entered into negotiations with Jinnah, who was the designated head of state for Pakistan, along with the ruler of Jaisalmer. Jinnah was keen to attract some of the larger border states, hoping thereby to attract other Rajput states to Pakistan and compensate for the loss of half of Bengal and Punjab. He offered to permit Jodhpur and Jaisalmer to accede to Pakistan on any terms they chose, giving their rulers blank sheets of paper and asking them to write down their terms, which he would sign.

Jaisalmer refused, arguing that it would be difficult for him to side with Muslims against Hindus in the event of communal problems. Hanwant Singh came close to signing. However, the atmosphere in Jodhpur was in general hostile to accession to Pakistan. Mountbatten also pointed out that the accession of a predominantly Hindu state to Pakistan would violate the principle of the two-nation theory on which Partition was based, and was likely to cause communal violence in the State. Hanwant Singh was persuaded by these arguments, and somewhat reluctantly agreed to accede to India.

Junagadh

Although the states were in theory free to choose whether they wished to accede to India or Pakistan, Mountbatten had pointed out that "geographic compulsions" meant that most of them must choose India. In effect, he took the position that only the states that shared a border with Pakistan could choose to accede to it.

The nawab of Junagadh, a princely state located on the south-western end of Gujarat and having no common border with Pakistan, chose to accede to Pakistan ignoring Mountbatten's views, arguing that it could be reached from Pakistan by sea. The rulers of two states that were subject to the suzerainty of Junagadh — Mangrol and Babariawad — reacted to this by declaring their independence from Junagadh and acceding to India. In response, the nawab of Junagadh militarily occupied the states. The rulers of neighbouring states reacted angrily, sending their troops to the Junagadh frontier and appealed to the Government of India for assistance. A group of Junagadhi people, led by Samaldas Gandhi, formed a government-in-exile, the *Aarzi Hukumat* ("temporary government").

India believed that if Junagadh was permitted to go to Pakistan, the communal tension already simmering in Gujarat would worsen, and refused to accept the accession. The government pointed out that the state was 80% Hindu, and called for a plebiscite to decide the question of accession. Simultaneously, they cut off supplies of fuel and coal to Junagadh, severed air and postal links, sent troops to the frontier, and reoccupied the principalities of Mangrol and Babariawad that had acceded to India. Pakistan agreed to discuss a plebiscite, subject to the withdrawal of Indian troops, a condition India rejected. On 26 October, the Nawab and his family fled to Pakistan following clashes with Indian troops. On 7 November, Junagadh's court, facing collapse, invited the Government of India to take over the State's administration. The Government of India agreed. A plebiscite was conducted in February 1948, which went almost unanimously in favour of accession to India.

Kashmir

Shown in green is the Kashmiri region under Pakistani control. The dark-brown region represents Indian-administration Jammu and Kashmir while the Aksai Chin is under Chinese administration

At the time of the transfer of power, Kashmir was ruled by Maharaja Hari Singh, a Hindu, although the state itself had a Muslim majority. Hari Singh was equally hesitant about acceding to either India or Pakistan, as either would have provoked adverse reactions in parts of his kingdom. He signed a Standstill Agreement with Pakistan and proposed one with India as well, but announced that Kashmir intended to remain independent. However, his rule was opposed by Sheikh Abdullah, the popular leader of Kashmir's largest political party, the National Conference, who demanded his abdication. Pakistan, attempting to force the issue of Kashmir's accession, cut off supplies and transport links. The chaos in Punjab resulting from Partition had also severed transport links with India, meaning that Kashmir's only links with the two dominions was by air. Rumours about atrocities against the Muslim population of Poonch by the Maharajah's forces caused the outbreak of civil unrest. Shortly thereafter, Pathan tribesmen from the North-West Frontier Province of Pakistan crossed the border and entered Kashmir.

The invaders made rapid progress towards Srinagar. The Maharaja of Kashmir wrote to India, asking for military assistance, offering an Instrument of Accession, and setting up an interim government headed by Sheikh Abdullah. The accession was accepted, but Nehru declared that it would have to be confirmed by a plebiscite although there was no legal requirement to seek such confirmation. Indian troops secured Jammu, Srinagar and the valley itself during the First Kashmir War, but the intense fighting flagged with the onset of winter, which made much of the state impassable. Prime Minister Nehru, recognising the degree of international attention brought to bear on the dispute, declared a ceasefire and sought U.N. arbitration, arguing that India would otherwise have to invade Pakistan itself, in view of its failure to stop the tribal incursions.

The plebiscite was never held, and on 26 January 1957, the Constitution of India came into force in Kashmir, but with special provisions made for it in the Constitution's Article 370. India did not, however, secure administrative control over all of Kashmir. The northern and western portions of Kashmir came under Pakistan's control in 1947, and are today Pakistan-administered Kashmir. In 1962, China occupied Aksai Chin, the north-eastern region bordering Ladakh, which it continues to control and administer.

Hyderabad

Hyderabad state in 1909. Its former territories are today incorporated in the Indian states of Andhra Pradesh, Karnataka and Maharashtra.

Hyderabad was a landlocked state that stretched over 82,000 square miles (over 212,000 square kilometres) in south-eastern India. Whilst 87% of its 17 million people were Hindus, its ruler Nizam Osman Ali Khan was a Muslim, and its politics were dominated by a Muslim elite. The Muslim nobility and the Ittehad-ul-Muslimeen, a powerful pro-Nizam Muslim party, insisted that Hyderabad must remain an independent state and stand on an equal footing to India and Pakistan. Accordingly, the Nizam in June 1947 issued a *firman* announcing that on the transfer of power, his state would be resuming independence. The Government of India rejected the firman, terming it a "legalistic claim of doubtful validity." It argued that the strategic location of Hyderabad, which lay astride the main lines of communication between northern and southern India, meant it could easily be used by "foreign interests" to threaten India, and that in consequence, the issue involved India's peace and security. It also pointed out that the state's people, history and location made it unquestionably Indian, and that its own "common interests" therefore mandated its integration into India.

The Nizam was prepared to enter into a limited treaty with India, which gave Hyderabad safeguards not provided for in the standard Instrument of Accession, such as a provision guaranteeing Hyderabad's neutrality in the event of a conflict between India and Pakistan. India rejected this proposal, arguing that other states would demand similar concessions. A temporary Standstill Agreement was signed as a stopgap measure, even though Hyderabad had not yet agreed to accede to India. By December 1947, however, India was accusing Hyderabad of repeatedly violating the Agreement, while the Nizam alleged that India was blockading his state, a charge India denied.

The situation deteriorated further in 1948. The Razakars ("volunteers"), a militia affiliated to the Ittehad-ul-Muslimeen and set up under the influence of Muslim radical Qasim Razvi, assumed the role of supporting the Muslim ruling class against upsurges by the Hindu populace, and began intensifying its activities and was accused of attempting to intimidate villages.

The Hyderabad State Congress Party, affiliated to the Indian National Congress, launched a political agitation. Matters were made worse by Communist groups, which had originally supported the Congress but now switched sides and began attacking Congress groups.

Attempts by Mountbatten to find a negotiated solution failed and, in August, the Nizam, claiming that he feared an imminent invasion, attempted to approach the UN Security Council and the International Court of Justice. Patel now insisted that if Hyderabad was allowed to continue its independence, the prestige of the Government would be tarnished and then neither Hindus nor Muslims would feel secure in its realm. On 13 September, the Indian Army was sent into Hyderabad in Operation Polo on the ground that the law and order situation there threatened the peace of South India.

The troops met little resistance and between 13 and 18 September took complete control of the state. The Nizam was retained as the head of state in the same manner as the other princes who acceded to India. He thereupon disavowed the complaints that had been made to the UN and, despite vehement protests from Pakistan and strong criticism from other countries, the Security Council did not deal further with the question, and Hyderabad was absorbed into India.

Completing Integration

Central Provinces and Berar, which form part of modern Madhya Pradesh and Maharashtra.

The Madras Presidency was divided and merged with neighbouring princely states to produce Kerala, Tamil Nadu, Karnataka and Andhra Pradesh.

The Instruments of Accession were limited, transferring control of only three matters to India, and would by themselves have produced a rather loose federation, with significant differences in administration and governance across the various states. Full political integration, in contrast, would require a process whereby the political actors in the various states were "persuaded to shift their loyalties, expectations, and political activities towards a new center," namely, the Republic of India. This was not an easy task.

Whilst some princely states such as Mysore had legislative systems of governance that were based on a broad franchise and not significantly different from those of British India, in others, political decision-making took place in small, limited aristocratic circles and governance was, as a result, at best paternalistic and at worst the result of courtly intrigue. Having secured the accession of the princely states, the Government of India between 1948 and 1950 turned to the task of welding the states and the former British provinces into one polity under a single republican constitution.

Fast-track Integration

The first step in this process, carried out between 1947 and 1949, was to merge the smaller states that were not seen by the Government of India to be viable administrative units either into neighbouring provinces, or with other princely states to create a "princely union." This policy was contentious, since it involved the dissolution of the very states whose existence India had only recently guaranteed in the Instruments of Accession.

Patel and Menon emphasised that without integration, the economies of states would collapse, and anarchy would arise if the princes were unable to provide democracy and govern properly. They pointed out that many of the smaller states were very small and lacked resources to sustain their economies and support their growing populations. Many also imposed tax rules and other restrictions that impeded free trade, and which had to be dismantled in a united India. Given that merger involved the breach of guarantees personally given by Mountbatten, Patel and Nehru initially intended to wait until after his term as Governor-General. An adivasi uprising in Orissa in late 1947, however, forced their hand.

In December 1947, princes from the Eastern and Chhatisgarh Agencies were summoned to an all-night meeting with Menon, in the course of which they were persuaded to sign Merger Agreements integrating their states into Orissa, the

Central Provinces and Bihar with effect from 1 January 1948. Later that year, sixty-six states in Gujarat and the Deccan were merged into Bombay, including the large states of Kolhapur and Baroda. Other small states were merged into Madras, East Punjab. West Bengal, the United Provinces and Assam. Not all states that signed Merger Agreements were integrated into provinces, however. Thirty states of the former Punjab Hill States Agency which lay near the international border and had signed Merger Agreements were integrated into Himachal Pradesh, a distinct entity which was administered directly by the centre as a Chief Commissioner's Province, for reasons of security.

The Merger Agreements required rulers to cede "full and exclusive jurisdiction and powers for and in relation to governance" of their state to the Dominion of India. In return for their agreement to entirely cede their states, it gave princes a large number of guarantees.

Princes would receive an annual payment from the Indian government in the form of a privy purse as compensation for the surrender of their powers and the dissolution of their states. Whilst state property would be taken over, their private property would be protected, as would all personal privileges, dignities and titles. Succession was also guaranteed according to custom. In addition, the provincial administration was obliged to take on the staff of the princely states with guarantees of equal pay and treatment.

Although the Merger Agreements were principally intended for smaller, non-viable states, they were also applied to a few larger states. Kutch in western India, and Tripura and Manipur in North-East India, all of which lay along international borders, were also asked to sign Merger Agreements, despite being larger states, following which they became Chief Commissioners' Provinces. Bhopal, whose ruler was proud of the efficiency of his administration and feared that it would lose its identity if merged with the Maratha states that were its neighbours, also became a directly-administered Chief Commissioner's Province, as did Bilaspur, much of which was likely to be flooded on completion of the Bhakra dam.

Four-step Integration

Merger

The bulk of the larger states, and some groups of small states, were integrated through a different, four-step, process. The first step in this process was to convince groups of large states to combine to form a "princely union" through the execution by their rulers of Covenants of Merger.

Under the Covenants of Merger, all rulers lost their ruling powers, save one who became the Rajpramukh of the new union. The other rulers were associated with two bodies, the council of rulers whose members were the rulers of salute states, and a presidium, one or more of whose members were elected by the rulers of non-salute states, with the rest elected by the council.

The Rajpramukh and a deputy Rajpramukh, or *Uprajpramukh*, were chosen by the council from amongst the members of the presidium. The Covenants made provision for the creation of a constituent assembly for the new union which would be charged with framing its constitution. In return for agreeing to the extinction of their states as discrete entities, the rulers were given a privy purse and guarantees similar to those provided under the Merger Agreements.

Through this process, Patel obtained the unification of 222 states in the Kathiawar peninsula of his native Gujarat into the princely union of Saurashtra in January 1948, with six more states joining the union the following year. Madhya Bharat emerged on 28 May 1948 from a union of Gwalior, Indore and eighteen smaller states.

In Punjab, the Patiala and East Punjab States Union was formed on 15 July 1948 from Patiala, Kapurthala, Jind, Nabha, Faridkot, Malerkotla, Nalargarh, and Kalsia. The United State of Rajasthan was formed as the result of a series of mergers, the last of which was completed on 15 May 1949. Travancore and Cochin were merged in the middle of 1949 to form the princely union of Travancore-Cochin. The only princely states which signed neither Covenants of Merger nor Merger Agreements were Kashmir, Mysore and Hyderabad.

Democratisation

Merging the administrative machineries of each state and integrating them into one political and administrative entity was not easy, particularly as many of the merged states had a history of rivalry. In the former Central India Agency, whose princely states had initially been merged into a princely union called Vindhya Pradesh, the rivalry between two groups of states became so bad that the Government of India persuaded the rulers to sign a Merger Agreement abrogating the old Covenants of Merger, and took direct control of the state as a Chief Commissioner's State. As such, the mergers did not meet the expectations of the Government of India or the States Department.

In December 1947, Menon suggested requiring the rulers of states to take "practical steps towards the establishment of popular government." The States Department accepted his suggestion, and implemented it through a special covenant signed by the rajpramukhs of the merged princely unions, binding them to act as constitutional monarchs. This meant that their powers were de facto no different from those of the Governors of the former British provinces, thus giving the people of their territories the same measure of responsible government as the people of the rest of India.

The result of this process has been described as being, in effect, an assertion of paramountcy by the Government of India over the states in a more pervasive form. Whilst this contradicted the British statement that paramountcy would lapse on the transfer of power, the Congress position had always been that independent India would inherit the position of being the paramount power.

CENTRALISATION AND CONSTITUTIONALISATION

Democratisation still left open one important distinction between the former princely states and the former British provinces, namely, that since the princely states had signed limited Instruments of Accession covering only three subjects, they were insulated from government policies in other areas. The Congress viewed this as hampering its ability to frame policies that brought about social justice and national development.

Consequently, they sought to secure to the central government the same degree of powers over the former princely states as it had over the former British provinces. In May 1948, at the initiative of V.P. Menon, a meeting was held in Delhi between the Rajpramukhs of the princely unions and the States Department, at the end of which the Rajpramukhs signed new Instruments of Accession which gave the Government of India the power to pass laws in respect of all matters that fell within the seventh schedule of the Government of India Act, 1935. Subsequently, each of the princely unions, as well as Mysore and Hyderabad, agreed to adopt the Constitution of India drafted by the constituent assembly as the constitution of that state, thus ensuring that they were placed in exactly the same legal position vis-à-vis the central government as the former British provinces. The only exception was Kashmir, whose relationship with India continued to be governed by the original Instrument of Accession, and the constitution produced by the state's Constituent Assembly.

The Constitution of India classified the constituent units of India into three classes, which it termed Part A, B, and C states. The former British provinces, together with the princely states that had been merged into them, were the Part A states. The princely unions, plus Mysore and Hyderabad, were the Part B states. The former Chief Commissioners' Provinces and other centrally administered areas, except the Andaman and Nicobar Islands, were the Part C states.

The only practical difference between the Part A states and the Part B states was that the constitutional heads of the Part B states were the Rajpramukhs appointed under the terms of the Covenants of Merger, rather than Governors appointed by the central government.

In addition, Constitution gave the central government a significant range of powers over the former princely states, providing amongst other things that their governance shall be under the general control of, and comply with such particular directions, if any, as may from time to time be given by, the

President." Apart from that, the form of government in both was identical.

Reorganisation

The distinction between Part A and Part B states was only intended to last for a brief, transitional period. In 1956, the States Reorganization Act reorganised the former British provinces and princely states on the basis of language. Simultaneously, the Seventh Amendment to the Constitution removed the distinction between Part A and Part B states, both of which were now treated only as "states", with Part C states being renamed "union territories." The Rajpramukhs lost their authority, and were replaced as the constitutional heads of state by Governors, who were appointed by the central government. These changes finally ended the princely order to an end. In both legal and practical terms, the territories that formerly were part of the princely states were now fully integrated into India and did not differ in any way from those that were formerly part of British India. The personal privileges of the princes-the privy purse, the exemption from customs duty, and customary dignities-survived slightly longer, but were abolished in 1971.

Post-integration Issues

The Princes

Whilst the progressive integration of the princely states into India was largely peaceful, not all princes were happy with the outcome. Many had expected the Instruments of Accession to be permanent, and were unhappy about losing the autonomy and the guaranteed continued existence of their states they had expected to gain. Some felt uneasy about the disappearance of states that generations of their family had controlled, whilst others were unhappy about the disappearance of administrative structures they had worked hard to build up and which they believed to be efficient.

The majority, however, despite the "strain and tension" of adapting to life as private citizens, content to retire on the generous pension provided by the privy purse. Several took advantage of their eligibility to hold public offices under the central government. The Maharaja of Bhavnagar, for example, became the Governor of Madras State, while several others were appointed to diplomatic posts overseas.

Colonial Enclaves

The integration of the princely states raised the question of the future of the remaining colonial enclaves in India. At independence, the regions of Pondicherry, Karikal, Yanaon, Mahe and Chandernagore were still colonies of France, and Daman and Diu, Dadra and Nagar Haveli and Goa remained colonies of Portugal. An agreement between France and India in 1948 provided for an election in France's remaining Indian possessions to choose their political future. A plebiscite held in Chandernagore on 19 June 1949 resulted in a vote of 7,463 to 114 in favour of being integrated with India. It was ceded to India on a de facto basis on 14 August 1949 and de jure on 2 May 1950.

In the other enclaves, however, the pro-French camp, led by Edouard Goubert, used the administrative machinery to suppress the pro-merger groups. Popular discontent rose, and in 1954 demonstrations in Yanam and Mahe resulted in pro-merger groups assuming power. A referendum in Pondicherry and Karaikal in October 1954 resulted in a vote in favour of merger, and on 1 November 1954, de facto control over all four enclaves was transferred to the Republic of India. A treaty of cession was signed in May 1956, and following ratification by the French National Assembly in May 1962, de jure control of the enclaves was also transferred.

Portugal, in contrast, resisted diplomatic solutions. It viewed its continued possession of its Indian enclaves as a matter of national pride and, in 1951, it amended its constitution to convert its possessions in India into Portuguese provinces. In July 1954, an uprising in Dadra and Nagar Haveli threw off Portuguese rule. The Portuguese attempted to send forces from Daman to reoccupy the enclaves, but were prevented from doing so by Indian troops. Portugal initiated proceedings before the International Court of Justice to compel India to allow its troops access to the enclave, but the Court rejected its complaint in 1960, holding that India was within its rights in denying Portugal military access.

In 1961, the Constitution of India was amended to incorporate Dadra and Nagar Haveli into India as a Union Territory.

Goa, Daman and Diu remained an outstanding issue. On 15 August 1955, five thousand non-violent demonstrators marched against the Portuguese at the border, and were met with gunfire, killing 22. In December 1960, the United Nations General Assembly rejected Portugal's contention that its overseas possessions were provinces, and formally listed them as "non-self-governing territories." Although Nehru continued to favour a negotiated solution, the Portuguese suppression of a revolt in Angola in 1961 radicalised Indian public opinion, and increased the pressure on the Government of India to take military action. African leaders, too, put pressure on Nehru to take action in Goa, which they argued would save Africa from further horrors.

On 18 December 1961, following the collapse of an American attempt to find a negotiated solution, the Indian Army entered Goa, Daman and Diu. The Portuguese took the matter to the Security Council but a resolution calling on India to withdraw its troops immediately was defeated by the USSR's veto. Portugal surrendered on 19 December. This take-over ended the last of the European colonies in India. Goa was incorporated into India as a centrally-administered union territory and, in 1987, became a state.

Secessionism and Sub-nationalism

Whilst the majority of princely states absorbed into India have been fully integrated, a few outstanding issues remain. The most prominent of these is in relation to Kashmir, where a violent secessionist insurgency has been raging since the late 1980s.

Some academics suggest that the insurgency in Kashmir is at least partly a result of the manner in which it was integrated into India. Kashmir, uniquely amongst princely states, was not required to sign either a Merger Agreement or a revised Instrument of Accession giving India control over a larger number of issues than the three originally provided for.

Instead, the power to make laws relating to Kashmir was granted to the Government of India by Article 5 of the Constitution of Jammu and Kashmir and was, under Article 370 of the Constitution of India, somewhat more restricted than in relation to other states. Widmalm argues that during the 1980s, a number of Kashmiri youth began to feel that the Indian government was increasingly interfering in the politics of Jammu and Kashmir.

The elections of 1987 caused them to lose faith in the political process and begin the violent insurgency which is still ongoing. Similarly, Ganguly suggests that the policies of the Indian government towards Kashmir meant that the state, unlike other parts of India, never developed the solid political institutions associated with a modern multi-ethnic democracy. As a result, the growing dissatisfaction with the status quo felt by an increasingly politically aware youth was expressed through non-political channels which Pakistan, seeking to weaken India's hold over Kashmir, transformed into an active insurgency.

Separatist movements also exist in two other former princely states located in North-East India, Tripura and Manipur. These separatist movements are generally treated by scholars as being part of the broader problem of insurgencies in North-east India, rather being a result of specific problems in integrating the princely states into India, as the Kashmir problem is and, in particular, to reflect the failure of the Government of India to adequately address the aspirations of tribal groups in the Northeast, or to tackle the tensions arising from the immigration of people from other parts of India to the north-eastern areas.

The integration of former princely states with other provinces to form new states has also given rise to some issues. The Telengana region, comprising the Telugu-speaking districts of the former Hyderabad State, were in many ways different from the Telugu-speaking areas of British India with which they were merged. In recognition of these differences, the States

Reorganisation Commission originally recommended that Telengana be created as a separate state, rather than as part of a broader Telugu-speaking entity.

This recommendation was rejected by the Government of India, and Telengana was merged into Andhra Pradesh. The result was the emergence in the 1960s of a movement demanding a separate Telengana state, which continues to be strong in the region. A similar movement, although less strong, exists in the Vidarbha region of Maharashtra, which consists of the former Nagpur state and the Berar region of the former Hyderabad state.

Critical Perspectives on the Process of Integration

Jinnah supported the right of princely states to remain independent, a position rejected by Nehru and the Congress.

As this article has discussed, the integration process repeatedly brought Indian and Pakistani leaders into conflict. During negotiations, Jinnah, representing the Muslim League, strongly supported the right of the princely states to remain independent, joining neither India nor Pakistan, an attitude which was diametrically opposed to the stance taken by Nehru and the Congress and which was reflected in Pakistan's support of Hyderabad's bit to stay independent.

Post-partition, the Government of Pakistan accused India of hypocrisy on the ground that there was little difference between the accession of the ruler of Junagadh to Pakistan — which India refused to recognise — and the accession of the Maharajah of Kashmir to India, and for several years refused to recognise the legality of India's incorporation of Junagadh, treating it as de jure Pakistani territory.

Different theories have been proposed to explain the designs of Indian and Pakistani leaders in this period. Rajmohan Gandhi postulates that an ideal deal working in the mind of Patel was that if Muhammad Ali Jinnah let India have Junagadh and Hyderabad, Patel would not object to Kashmir acceding to Pakistan. In his book *Patel: A Life*, Gandhi asserts that Jinnah sought to engage the questions of Junagadh and Hyderabad in the same battle.

It is suggested that he wanted India to ask for a plebiscite in Junagadh and Hyderabad, knowing thus that the principle then would have to be applied to Kashmir, where the Muslim-majority would, he believed, vote for Pakistan. A speech by Patel at the Bahauddin College in Junagadh following the latter's take-over, where he said that "we would agree to Kashmir if they agreed to Hyderabad" suggests that he may have been amenable to this idea. Whilst Patel's opinions were not India's policy, nor were they shared by Nehru, both leaders were angered at Jinnah's courting the princes of Jodhpur, Bhopal and Indore, leading them to take a harder stance on a possible deal with Pakistan.

Modern historians have also re-examined the role of the States Department and Lord Mountbatten during the accession process. Ian Copland argues that the Congress leaders did not intend the settlement contained in the Instruments of Accession to be permanent even when they were signed, and at all times privately contemplated a complete integration of the sort that ensued between 1948 and 1950.

He points out that the mergers and cession of powers to the Government of India between 1948 and 1950 contravened the terms of the instruments of accession, and were incompatible with the express assurances of internal autonomy and preservation of the princely states which Mountbatten had given the princes. Menon in his memoirs stated that the changes to the initial terms of accession were in every instance freely consented to by the princes with no element of coercion. Copland disagrees, on the basis that foreign diplomats at the time believed that the princes had been given no choice but to sign, and that a few princes expressed their unhappiness with the arrangements.

He also criticises Mountbatten's role, saying that whilst he stayed within the letter of the law, he was at least under a moral obligation to do something for the princes when it became apparent that the Government of India was going to alter the terms on which accession took place, and that he should never have lent his support to the bargain given that it could not be guaranteed after independence.

Both Copland and Ramusack argue that, in the ultimate analysis, one of the reasons why the princes consented to the demise of their states was that they felt abandoned by the British, and saw themselves as having little other option. Older historians such as Lumby, in contrast, take the view that the princely states could not have survived as independent entities after the transfer of power, and that their demise was inevitable. They therefore view successful integration of all princely states into India was a triumph for the Government of India and Lord Mountbatten, and as a tribute to the sagacity of the majority of princes, who jointly achieved in a few months what the Empire had attempted, unsuccessfully, to do for over a century—unite all of India under one rule.

FREEDOM AT MIDNIGHT

Freedom at Midnight by Larry Collins and Dominique Lapierre was recommended to me by zackq and KO (who has his own thoughts here). It is a highly readable book with a great writing style. The major fault of the book lies with the authors' reliance on Mountbatten. One of their major sources is a personal interview with Mountbatten. In addition, they got some of Mountbattens personal papers about the events of his viceroyalty in India. In my opinion, the authors seem to be smitten with Mountbatten. Every mention of him has something really nice to say. His charm, persuasiveness, greatness, administrative and military genius are praised over and over again. No skepticism is applied to Mountbatten's account. Since I am not a Mountbatten fan, this turned me off quite a bit.

Freedom at Midnight starts when Mountbatten was appointed Viceroy of India in March 1947 and ends with Gandhi's assassination in January 1948. Thus it is an account of the last year of British India. If you don't know anything about the Indian independence movement, you might be better off reading a more comprehensive account. There is, however, a lot that happened in 1947 and "Freedom at Midnight" covers it in good detail, taking almost 500 pages to do so.

One of the side-effects of the authors' Mountbatten-worship is that most of the major figures, like Gandhı, Nehru, and

Jinnah, are seen mostly through Mountbatten's eyes. One result of this is the extremely negative portrayal of Jinnah. I don't usually have much of a problem with his negative portrayal since that is quite common in history books not written by Pakistanis. But "Freedom at Midnight" tries a negative adjective for Jinnah every time he's mentioned. I know Jinnah was a determined fellow who was arrogant and vain as well, but still the authors lost me there. I do agree with this statement though:

> *Jinnah himself celebrated the day [of independence] by assuming full powers for his supposedly ceremonial office. In the year of life remaining to him, the London-trained lawyer who for years had not ceased to proclaim his faith in the constitutional process would govern his new nation as a dictator.*

This, in my view, was one of the problems with Pakistani democracy since its founding. Contrast Jinnah's behavior with Nehru. Nehru became Prime Minister of India and set up a parliamentary government. In the end, Nehru probably had as much dictatorial power as Jinnah but the foundation of parliamentary democracy had been set up in India while Pakistan became a land of dictators.

The authors also do not seem well-versed in Indian history before the British. For example, they mention that Islam came to India "after the cohorts of Genghis Khan and Tamerlane had battered their way down the Khyber Pass to weaken the Hindus' hold on the Gangetic plain." I guess they are confusing Muslims and Mughals. It was during the slave dynasty and then the Khaljis that the battles with the Mongols took place. Oh and Tamerlane himself was Muslim (not that it matters) and defeated Mahmud Tughluq in 1398. The imperialist attitude of the British is captured well by the authors.

Their rule was paternalistic, that of the old public-school master disciplining an unruly band of boys, forcing on them the education that he was sure was good for them. With an occasional exception they were able and incorruptible, determined to administer India in its own best interests — but it was always they who decided what those interests were.

This description of the Viceroy's travel reminded me of Pakistan's President-General.

Whenever the viceroy's white-and-gold train moved across the vast spaces of India, guards were posted every one hundred yards along its route twenty-four hours in advance of its arrival.

Mountbatten impulsively decided the date of partition (Aug 15, 1947) at a press conference. No prior thought or discussions on this. And this is a guy who, according to the authors, had provided the Congress and Muslim League leaders with a 34-page document titled "The Administrative Consequences of Partition when partition had been agreed on because

He [Mountbatten] had forced these seven men to come to grips with a problem so imposing that it would leave them neither the time nor the energy for recrimination in the few weeks of coexistence left to them.

He had chosen the date because it was the anniversary of Japanese surrender. To top that impulsive decision, he decided not to reveal the Boundary Commission awards until a couple of days after independence. This created a lot of confusion in the provinces of Punjab and Bengal which were being partitioned.

I talked about dual loyalties in a previous post. Two instances in this book provide some food for thought.

- When the tribal irregular forces from Pakistan invaded the state of Kashmir (which was sort of independent at the time) on Ocober 24, 1947, this news was relayed to the British commander-in-chief of the Indian army, Lt. Gen. Sir Rob Lockhart, by the British general commanding the Pakistani army, Maj. Gen. Douglas Gracey. Do you think Gracey was being disloyal to the country he served, Pakistan? Why? Or why not?
- Saḥibzada Yaqub Khan, then a major in the army (later foreign minister of Pakistan), opted to leave for Pakistan from his home in Rampur. He led a battalion of the Pakistani army in the war in Kashmir in 1947-8. His younger brother, Younis Khan, had decided to remain in his ancestral Rampur. He too was an army officer.

> And he too fought in Kashmir. But on the Indian side. What did these two guys think of loyalty? What do you think?

Why did Nehru find difficulty in fitting Jinnah and the idea of Pakistan into his own conception of a 'Modern India'?

The former British colony, India, became independent in August 1947. Indeed two new states emerged from it-India and Pakistan. Jawaharlal Nehru was the first prime minister of India, while Muhammad Ali Jinnah held office as Pakistan's first governor general. Nehru had, as one of the most important leaders, fought many years for India's independence. During this fight, he developed his own views about what modernity meant to him and how a future free Indian modernity would look like. In his opinion, it would be connected with democratic, secular, and socialistic principles, and also with equal rights for every Indian independent of his or her religion, language, caste, sex and so on.

This essay is concerned with Nehru's perceptions about modernity, its features and the role religion should play in it and in politics. The question, which shall be answered, is why did Nehru find difficulty in fitting Jinnah and the idea of Pakistan into his own conception of a modern India. The first of the two main arguments to be discussed is that, in his opinion, all Indians belonged to one nation. The second argument, which Nehru discussed in his writings, is that for him a modern India should be a secular state. In this state, politics and economics should not be mixed with religious matters, and political parties and organisations not be formed along religious lines. Before the author goes into detail with these arguments, it has to be pointed out what modernity meant to Nehru.

Democracy was one basic principle, which Nehru favoured in connection with modernity and with a modern India. As early as the first half of the 1920s, he interpreted *Swaraj*, the objective of the Non-Cooperation-Movement, as "political independence,..., and a democratic form of government". Later in his *Discovery of India*, he stated again that the establishment of a democratic state was one of the important demands made in India.A second basic principle of modernity was, in Nehru's opinion, socialism. During the 1930s, his interest in socialist and communist ideas started. The social issue could, for him, no longer be separated from political freedom and in 1938 he stated:

I am convinced that the only key to the solution ... of India's problems lies in socialism .... I see no way of ending poverty, the vast unemployment, the degradation and the subjection of the Indian people except through socialism. That involves vast and revolutionary changes in our political and social structure, ... Socialism is thus for me not merely an economic doctrine which I favour, it is a vital creed which I hold with all my head and heart.

Socialism was thus, in Nehru's opinion, one of the forces which could lead to a better life for all Indians. It presented for him the only opportunity to bring modernity to India in a fair way. The opposite world order, the capitalist system, he disliked. One last aspect should be shortly mentioned in connection with the question what modernity and, especially Indian modernity, meant to Nehru. This aspect is secularism. The author will go into further detail with it in the following paragraphs when the two formulated arguments will be discussed.

With its manifold cultures, traditions, histories and peoples, India was not easy to grasp for Nehru, but in the course of time he developed his own ideas and concepts about these topics. In his *Discovery of India*, he tried to show that there is continuity in his homeland; that India remains India. He stated that, of course there are distinctive features amongst the Indian people, but he was also convinced that they had a common ground due to the same virtues, national heritage and moral as well as mental qualities. Starting from this point of view, Nehru disagreed with Jinnah's theory that India consisted of two nations.

Jinnah, who led a political party, the Muslim League, argued that a Hindu and a Muslim nation existed in India. As a consequence, he adopted the already existing conception of Pakistan for political claims and as the political objective of the Muslim League respectively. The idea of Pakistan contained the perception that Muslims as a nation should have their own homeland and state where they could live regarding spiritual, cultural, economic, social, and political aspects in accordance with their ideals.

Nehru rejected both ideas, the theory of two nations within India and the concept of Pakistan. In his opinion, the Indian people belonged to one nation, independently of their religion. He argued that if nationality would be based on religion, there would be more nations within the Indian territory than only the Hindu one and the Muslim one. The distinctive feature that separated one nation from another was, in this view, not religion, but rather "a sense of belonging together and of together facing the rest of mankind". He declared that there was no other difference between a Hindu and a Muslim who, for example, both lived as peasants in the same village than a religious one. Their language, customs and traditions were, in his views, the same.

Because of this perception, Nehru believed that a Muslim nation therefore: means that there is no nation at all but a religious bond; it means that no nation in the modern sense must be allowed to grow; it means that modern civilisation should be discarded and we should go back to the medieval ways; it means either autocratic government or a foreign government; it means, finally, just nothing at all except an emotional state of mind and a conscious or unconscious desire not to face realities, especially economic realities.

This statement is, in the author's opinion, a clear piece of evidence for Nehru's view that such a religious based nation would not be a part of the modern world.

In addition, this quotation shows one other facet which is important in order to answer the posed question. In regard to economic realities, Nehru argued that the Indian people have the same concerns and problems independent of their religion. He asked: "In what way are the interests of the Muslim peasant different from those of the Hindu peasant? Or those of a Muslim labourer or artisan or merchant or landlord or manufacturer different from those of his Hindu protype?" He added that the "ties that bind people are common interest, and, in the case of a subject country especially, a common national interest." Nehru believed that in a modern state political participation and claims would develop because of common economic interests and problems, not because of belonging to the same religious group.

In connection with the economic and also with the social issue, one more facet should be mentioned. In Nehru's perception, both could only be solved with the help of socialist methods and the participation of the masses. He believed that the formation of a modern Indian state would only be possible when the masses were involved in the freedom struggle, and in the politics of a future free India. Nehru stressed therefore that "the Congress had further developed agrarian, economic, and social programmes. Neither the Muslim League nor the Hindu Mahasabha had ever considered any such question or attempted to frame a programme." In addition, he added that the Congress, the party which led the Indian struggle for independence from the British colonial masters, "represented not only the nationalist urge of India ..., but also, to a large extent, proletarian urges for social changes." In connection with the Muslim League and Jinnah, he believed that "the communal organizations, ..., were closely associated with feudal and conservative elements and were opposed to any revolutionary social change."

This opinion of his-that the Muslim League was, as a result of their conservative and feudal elements, not connected with the masses and their claims-clearly shows his difficulties in fitting Jinnah and the idea of Pakistan in his own views of modernity. Thoughts about economic and social changes, which would be, in Nehru's perception, inevitable for the constitution of a modern society, were not shared by Jinnah and the Muslim League. Nehru gave, regarding this aspect, the following judgement about Jinnah: "He belonged to an older generation which was hardly aware of modern political thought or development. Of economics, ..., he appeared to be entirely ignorant." This perceived absence of modern ideas in regard to economic and social issues was problematic for Nehru and his views of modernity.

Besides these difficulties, there were also some concerning politics and secularism. Nehru did not believe in the mixture of religion and politics. He rejected communalism, which normally can be described as the policy of a group, or community that is formed along religious lines. Communalism meant, for him, "a narrow group mentality basing itself on a religious community but in reality concerned with political power and patronage for the interested group." This quotation again makes clear that, in his opinion, the religious appeal to win political power for a certain group was an example for a policy which was out of fashion.

It also shows that he had the opinion that a communal party like the Muslim League could not appeal to the masses; neither to all Indians nor only to all Muslims. In this context, Nehru defined the Muslim League as follows: "It represents a group of Muslims, not doubt highly estimable persons, but functioning in the higher regions of the upper class and having no contact with the Muslim masses and few even with the Muslim lower middle classes." The confinement to the interests of special, mostly backward looking groups within the religious community prevented, in Nehru's view, the existence of modern ideas.

Communalism was outdated for him in this aspect. He stated, "... to think in terms of communal groups functioning politically is to think in terms of medievalism." As a result of this opinion, he had difficulties with Jinnah's views and the concepts of the Muslim League. He acknowledged that in fact, the Muslim League was a political organisation, but at the same time he held the view that, because of its confinement to a religious group, it was primarily a religious or communal organisation. Nehru rejected the idea that the religion of a person should also define his/her political view and his/her automatically belonging to a certain party, as obsolete. He believed that among Muslims, Hindus, Sikhs, Christians, Parsees, etc., "one may find Congressmen, socialists, anti-socialists, communists, liberals, direct-actionists, revolutionaries, moderates, extremists, believers in different kinds of economy theory ... ". He stated in this connection that "to appeal to Mussalmans or Hindus as religious groups on politcal matters is obviously the wrong thing. It is the medieval attitude, when politics and economics were in the background, and it cannot possibly fit in with the modern world. It is because of this that I say I find it difficult to think on communal lines."

In conclusion, it can be declared that Nehru had difficulties in fitting Jinnah and the idea of Pakistan into his own conception of a modern India because of his belief that modernity should contain inter alia a secular and socialist order. Jinnah had, in Nehru's perception, a wrong, backward looking political view. Nehru rejected the idea that there were two different nations in India because of religious differences and that the adoptive Muslim nation would need its own homeland, its own state, as being medieval. He had the modern opinion that all Indians belong to one nation. Only with the help of this unified nation could India be liberated and a free state in which every person would have the same rights.

But not only in regard to this aspect did Nehru disagree with Jinnah's ideas. A modern India should be, in his perception, a secular state in which politics and economy should not be mixed with religious matters. Nehru believed that in a really modern society parties and organisations should be formed on the basis of the same economic and political interests, not on the basis of the same religion.

Retrospective it must be stated in connection with the impact of Nehru's views on the further development of the Indian independence struggle that recent historians admire his ideas, but at the same time show that his ideas were not fit to solve all problems and did not respect some of the political, social and religious conditions. B. Zachariah states in this context that Nehru, who was unconcerned with caste, religion and religious nationalism, did not take the communal problem seriously enough, it was a minor problem for him. Michael Mann points out that Nehru, because of his unaccomodating attitude, is blamed to have hindered the unity of India. In conclusion, it can be stated that Nehru's views about a 'modern India' and his denial of concepts like religious nationalism had a strong influence on the events which led to the partition and on the development of an democratic Indian state after 1947 in which emerged a typical Indian type of secularism

IDOLS OF DIVISION

BJP and Congress recently had a war of words about Jinnah and Nehru. The war was about who did it? That is, who was responsible for the partition of India, Jinnah or Nehru? Gandhi although not a principle character in this debate remains firmly placed on the pedestal. It was a historical drama. The time setting was the British Raj.

All three of them were role models of the time. They came from well-to-do families of varying degrees. Jawarharlal's father Motilal Nehru was the wealthiest and the most illustrious. While all three of them went to become barristers, their fathers came from different professions.

Mohandas Gandhi's father was prime minister to the tiny western state of Porbandar in Gujrat. Although, grocers by caste the Gandhis rose by dint of merit and service. Jinnah's father Jinnah Poonja, originally from Kathiawar, Gujrat, was a prosperous merchant of Karachi. They belonged to the Khoja community and the Ismaili sect of Islam. Jawarharlal's father Motilal was a highly placed barrister of Allahabad High Court. He came from a cultured and enlightened family background.

Gandhi's family was the most devout in their faith. He was to become far more religious and developed into Mahatma. Cleanliness of soul and penitence was his way of attaining godliness. Gandhi applied himself to the fullest to attain the attributes of the Hindu god Rama. The path he travelled was 'Satyagrah' or firmness in truth. There was a spiritual content in his struggle. Ahimsa or non-violence, precisely passive resistance or what American writer David Thoreau calls Civil Disobedience was a method of protest, that earned lasting recognition.

Jinnah was a strictly private person modelled on the British. Not much is known about his religious beliefs and practices. For that matter the Ismailias are known to be more businessmen than Muslims. While Jinnah was not a businessman, he preferred doing things the way business is done. Like, 'tell me your business, do your business, and let me do my business'. The Jinnah who fought for Pakistan was for everybody to see, but Jinnah the person was off-limits. The Muslims of British India was his political agenda but he did not fight to establish Islam. Pakistan was to be a country for the Muslims but never did he speak of a land of Islam. He was not irreligious neither was he pious. Jinnah looked on the Islamic identity as a way of empowering the backward Muslims of India. He was much too a 'pucca sahib' to indulge in the obscurantism of religious bigotry and communalism. The most revealing of his statement on the issue was when he spoke in his inaugural address as the governor general of Pakistan. He said, 'You will find that in the course of time, Hindus would cease to be Hindus and Muslims would cease to be Muslims, not in the religious sense because that is the personal faith of each individual but in the political sense as the citizens of the state'.

Nehru on the other hand came from a Hindu Brahmin family. But he was a professed agnostic. Both Nehru and Jinnah shared western thought. He however imbibed himself with Hindu cultural heritage. Both Nehru and Jinnah responded almost in similar fashion regarding the marriage of their daughters Indira and Dina. Gandhi had to lend his family name to Feroz, a Parsi, while Jinnah was even harsh in never accepting Dina's marriage to a Parsi. Indira's marriage ended in separation and Dina as reported was not allowed by Jinnah to see him on his deathbed.

Among the three, Nehru was the politician. He had the gifts for it and was influenced by Hindu tradition of politics. Besides, he was the brightest of intellectuals. His was the sharpest mind of the time. A Fabian (named after Fabian Maximus Verrcusos) Socialist one who believed in gradualist approach, Nehru applied cautious and dilatory tactics and proceeded by meandering ways. He believed in his destiny and worked accordingly. That he was destined to be the Prime Minister of India. If it meant adopting the populist approach, so be it, he gave up western Attire for Khadi. India got two national icons in loincloth-clad sanyasi Gandhi and the impeccably dressed Nehru in Gandhi cap.

The stand of the three against the British Raj was also different. The background and the social context of their participation in India's independence movement varied too. Gandhi was the populist of the three. His contact with the general people was more direct and personal. In fact, the years he spent in South Africa baptized him. Apartheid was not the best of social circumstances. The discrimination in it treated self-respect brutally. Gandhi was appalled by the denial of civil liberties. His soul was not however encumbered by the frailty of his physique. It ruled his spirit. His form of protest did not have a rebel in it but disgraced the wrongdoer by the loftiness of his spirit and the orderly method of his resistance. The world found an apostle of dignity in protest and the mighty were in distress in containing this peaceable form of passive resistance. Even the racist government of South Africa acceded to his demand for the recognition of Indian marriages and the abolition of poll tax imposed on them.

Gandhi then returned to India. Among the three, he was the first to engage the British directly and he kept on doing so to the end of British Raj. His first encounter with the Raj was when the British Parliament passed the Rowlatt Acts in 1919 giving Indian colonial authorities the emergency powers to deal with the so-called Revolutionaries. Gandhi launched a non-cooperation movement, in his words Satyagraha and it spread through out India. Thousands were arrested and Gandhi was jailed. Swaraj (self-rule) or Swadeshi movement further emboldened Indian Freedom movement by spreading the call of boycotting imported goods and thef using homespun fabrics. He kept the freedom movement steaming with his populist form of passive protest.

For the British he was not the ideal man to confer with. Gandhi's undying zeal and lofty spirit in spreading the gospel of self-rule made the British concede with every move. They however looked to it that they retreat with grace. For that, they had Pandit Nehru and Mr. Jinnah to talk to.

Jinnah was more a barrister than a politician. On return from England, he started legal practice at the Bombay High Court and befriended the Parsi community. He made his formal political appearance by acting as the private secretary to the then Congress President Dababhoy Naurozi at the Calcutta session of All India Congress held in 1906. There was very little Indian or for that matter Muslim in him. Leaving aside his origin, he developed his mind and lifestyle in the mould of an Englishman. Physically he was lean and upright with sharp features. Like his features, he was upright, precise, unbending, determined, quick and sharp. His wit and intelligence endowed him with the skill and showmanship of a swordsman. When he believed, he believed with all his faith and determination, leaving no room for doubt, indecision or delay. Those who came across him or had to engage him, it was a matter of black and white. Either to love or to leave him, or even to hate him. To Mountbatten he was a villain and a hero to those who wanted Pakistan.

At the beginning, he worked for Hindu-Muslim unity and is credited for the success of Lucknow Pact in 1916 accepting the principle of separate electorate for the Muslims. He was a strict disciplinarian and rejected brinkmanship. All through he differed with agitation and expressed disapproval of precipitous methods that are destined to fail. By that account, he was never a populist and would not allow his followers to wake him up from sleep at the railway station to accept their adulation. When he came back from retirement in England in 1935, the Muslim League was in dire straits. He galvanized the Muslims of India uniting them in the faith of their separateness as a nation. It is the unbending nature of his resolve and straightforwardness of his method that established the separateness of the Muslims as a nation. The concept of Pakistan, which was in limbo, even few years before madeir into the agenda of Freedom for British India. It prospered with the niggardliness and hesitant approach of Congress. And there was Pakistan, even though moth-eaten as Jinnah called.

Nehru came from the best of circumstances and from a politician's family. Born into an illustrious and wealthy family, he had a privileged upbringing. He received his schooling from Harrow and obtained his law degree from Trinity College Cambridge. Afterward he spent seven years in England to widen his horizons of knowledge. As told earlier, Nehru was influenced by the sceptical and rationalist outlook of Fabian Socialism and drew his patriotic inspiration from Irish Nationalism. His western upbringing was complete. On returning from England, he got into politics as Gandhi's disciple and took part in the Non-cooperation Movement. He also held public office as the President of Allahabad Municipal Corporation and served for two years. Pandit Nehru was outstanding as a politician and remained so. His next move was everybody's guess. The vehicle that carried him forward was Gandhi's sequential engagement with the British. The voice that talked to the British was Nehru who possessed a charming personality. He had the advantage of remarkable enlightenment and a natural rapport with the British, particularly with Lord Mountbatten.

The Congress had everything to gain through Nehru. He added all round balance to Gandhi's populist effervescence and spiritual naiveté. As a devoted disciple of 'Bapuji' Nehru protected Gandhi from the perils and pains of an errant protégé. He was a perfect foil for Jinnah's quick thrust, sharp, and unencumbered judgement. His privileged background and western education enabled him to walk the corridors of power with great ease and grace. He had all the elements in his favour, enlightenment, dignity, poise, confidence and a natural knack for office. He walked the corridors of power as if he had been there for a long time. And then eased into the office of the Prime Minister of India.

There is little doubt that these are the three most interesting personalities of British India-Gandhi, Jinnah and Nehru. These three outstanding leaders dominated a greater and in fact the most important part of the proceedings of the British India with their beliefs, thoughts, actions and utterances. The freedom movement of India was as diverse and complex in its ways as the land itself and the leaders who led it. It is natural that the three men cannot be to everybody's liking. They were patriotic men who judged and acted in accordance with what they believed to be right for the people they led. Those of us who live in a different time cannot, by our judgements of varying nature, take away from them what history has given them. All three of them became what history wanted them to be. A Mahatma, a founder of a new nation and the builder of the largest democracy of the world. They belong to the rank of all time great leaders of Asia along with Mao Ze Dong and Ho Chi Minh.

8

Jawahar Lal Nehru and Jinnah

People who had devoted major part of their adult lives in prison felt themselves getting closer to power and the prospects of an independent India seemed much brighter than ever before and they did not want to postpone what they have been seeking for years. Looking back to 1942, when the Congress rejected the "Cripps Plan", Rajaji came up with his "CR-Plan". He advised the Congress to accept the formation of Pakistan but was violently opposed by the party. Some historians think that if only the Congress had only accepted the CR-Plan, the trauma of Partition in 1947 could well have been avoided. Do you agree?

The CR-Plan anticipated in acute detail what actually happened later in 1947. In a way he paved the way for talks if not a solution. Rajagopalachari largely engineered the Gandhi-Jinnah Talks of 1944. It gave Jinnah much publicity, much propaganda of his cause, much force and increased the chances of formation of Pakistan.

CR was the most brilliant, serious, rational and clever-thinking man India ever produced. Here was a man who could see far ahead but he could not grasp the human frailties in the situation. We now know that Cripps did not have the support of the Home Government in London! Winston Churchill was not for any proposals. And he did not want the Cripps Plan to work. FDR was pressing Churchill that he should do something for India and her demand for freedom. So Churchill knew he had to make some of gesture to the Americans to get them off his back.

So he was trying to please Roosevelt more than anything else! I think that, as far as Churchill was concerned, it was his perceptual objective that there should be no offer to India for freedom especially in the war situation. Cripps was entirely in a false position. He thought it would work. He did not know that Amery (the Secretary of Sate for India) was hand in glove with Churchill!

There is an interesting incident not known to many. Sir C. P. Ramaswamy Aiyer, then the Dewan of Travancore State, met Sardar Patel in Bombay. Both were on their way to meet Sir Stafford Cripps. Patel told Sir C. P. that nothing would come out of the Cripps Plan. The whole thing was a front engineered by Nehru to become the Prime Minister of India and it would not happen for he (Patel) was putting it down and going to kill it! He had already told Gandhi and he had agreed that it should be done! Sir C. P. was taken aback at this revelation. So he wrote a secret communication to Lord Linlithgow who was equally surprised! He narrated it all in a secret letter to Amery in London, which I read in the " Transfer of Power" Documents.

In 1942 Nehru was genuinely anxious that the Cripps proposals should work, though on Congress terms. He was a genuine democrat — anti-fascist. He was anxious to get the Congress to agree to some arrangement with the Raj, He felt that it would help to avert in the future the partition of India.

Talking of Jinnah, do you think that his role on Indian politics was much bigger than Gandhi's?

In terms of their moral presence Gandhi was by far a greater man. Jinnah had two moments of dominance in the Indian story. One was during the First World War (1914-1918), which the Congress just frittered away.

Here was a man who could be a very powerful and useful ally but they alienated him and allowed him to drift into negative relationship with the Congress. And he comes back in 1935 with a new proposition, he has to work extremely hard to build up his position as the all India Muslim leader, and by 1945 he is a key player. But Jinnah was an impossible man to negotiate with. Was it part of his psyche or a mere put-on? He was naturally reserved, he had so many human setbacks, his marriage, the importance that Gandhi got from the "Khilafat Movement", he never really recovered from the serious hurt of the series of injuries he had in life. He was a very secretive man, kept his ideas well in control, a loner. I recognise him as master tactician of real politique. You may not like him but you have to recognise his political talents and manoeuvring skills. In the beginning he didn't want Pakistan but some all-India settlement for Muslims. He allowed the Pakistan Movement to become the vehicle to manoeuvre the politics of the Indian sub-continent.

It was a case of the means becoming the end. Perhaps the means was Pakistan and the end was the Prime Ministership of India. He very much hoped in 1946 and was shattered when Lord Wavell (then Viceroy of India) didn't allow him and Nehru became the Prime Minister of the Interim Government. Gandhi did invite him to take over but it did not happen. We do not know when the tuberculosis he suffered from became rampant—he kept it a closely guarded secret but he knew he had not long to live. That's why he chose to become the President of Pakistan, and not Prime Minister.

I Seek the reader's indulgence for inviting attention to my letter 'Jinnah before and after' (Dawn, June 29). The letter had challenged Mr M. J. Akbar's contention in his article "Jinnah before and after the 1920 Congress session" (Dawn, June 14) that the Cabinet Mission plan of 1946, that would have kept India united and which had been accepted by both the Congress and the Muslim League 'collapsed inexplicably'.

In my letter I argued that the Congress had accepted the plan with disabling reservations and by putting a disingenuous interpretation of its own, in line with Mr Gandhi's thinking. So, it was Gandhi and the Congress leadership who were squarely responsible for the collapse of the plan and that there could not be any two opinions on the subject.

My argument was based on documentary evidence produced by eminent Bombay jurist A. G.Noorani in one of his articles from which I quoted fairly extensively. I was hoping that Mr

M. J. Akbar or some other Indian from amongst Dawn's vast Internet readership would respond to what I had stated. But there has been no response at all. As I had referred to in my letter, Nehru told the Cabinet Mission categorically, on June 10, 1946 that the "Congress was going to work for a strong centre and break the grouping system and that they did not think Mr Jinnah had any real place in the country".

In this context, even more revealing information about Nehru's attitude to Jinnah has come to my notice recently. Mr A. G. Noorani, in his article, 'Punjab and Pakistan', in Frontline of March 12-25, 2005 has quoted what Nehru wrote in his prison Diary on Dec 28, 1943: "Instinctively I think it is better to have Pakistan or almost anything if only to keep Jinnah far away". On this, Noorani has commented: "His aversion to Jinnah was as visceral as was the Congress's to power-sharing. When it wrecked the Cabinet Mission scheme finally in December 1946 (after the London conference convened by the British government), Jinnah had no option but to acquire a 'truncated' Pakistan established in rancour. No alternative was in sight nor was one even offered."

The Third Side of the Partition Coin

There's a third side to the coin that the Partition debate seems to ignore: the British.

The British did 'divide-and rule', and did it quite successfully for two centuries over the Indo-Pak subcontinent. And, we not only had the kind of homegrown 'diversity' such a policy needs but also provided it generously.

The seeds of communalism were already in the fertile Indian soil, long before partition. The British couldn't have ignored them. Besides, you don't build an empire, a far- flung one at that covering nearly a quarter of the world's population and area, without a well-trained eye for such pathology and an ability to exploit it.

We already had slogans: "Quit India" (Congress, 1942) and "Divide and Quit" (Muslim League, 1943), both of which caused, directly or indirectly, sectarian violence and bloodshed. Both sides had extremists. We had satyagrahas and "Direct Action" riots. We had a vocal minority that felt increasingly alienated, and found the majority's promises unacceptable. No matter who initiated or precipitated it or how, such complex situations often have shared responsibility. To consider them otherwise is just politically naïve. We can keep pointing fingers at each other, calling names, throwing around poorly-understood, inflammatory labels, and we seem to have an inexhaustible reservoir of all this, even after some 58 years. We can continue to wallow in the same, or bury the hatchet, learn from our mistakes and start a bold new page as neighbors with a shared heritage.

When Clement Attlee (Labor) was elected Prime Minister of Britain in 1945 (soon after the WWII), he decided that India was strategically indefensible, and Britain could no longer afford to govern it. He also did not believe that Britain had the right to govern it. He sent a Cabinet Mission to India to work out a plan for a Hindu-Muslim working together in undivided India. All parties accepted it initially because the plan provided for protection of Muslim minority rights, but after the elections for the new Assembly, Nehru decided not to have anything to do with the new government. Jinnah also refused and called for Direct Action on August 16, 1946 (a year to the day before Partition).

Amid all this, Attlee appointed Louis Mountbatten as Viceroy to India in March 1947 (just five months before the Partition). He had instructions to keep India united if at all possible. Attlee had even set a deadline for the freedom of India: "No later than June 1948." Mountbatten did one-up, and suggested an earlier date and swifter transfer of power. He also thought the confederal proposals were essentially unworkable and acceded in principle the partition of the subcontinent. He presented a Partition plan to all parties on June 3, 1947, which they accepted. To Mountbatten's annoyance, it seems Jinnah told him (according to Alan Campbell-Johnson, viceroy's press secretary), "I do not agree, but I accept." Basically, no one liked Partition. It wasn't just one of the most desirable options, it was "the only solution," as Campbell-Johnson puts it, and thus they "accepted what they got."

Then, to devise a partition plan, Attlee appointed a distinguished barrister, Cyril Radcliffe, who had never been to the subcontinent, and had no first hand knowledge of the situation, the problems or the people. He was chosen because he was 'unbiased', and was expected to remain so. He was provided with the services of four judges, two Hindu, two Muslim, who almost constantly fought along the partisan lines and weren't much help to him at all. Radcliffe had the 1943 census (the figures were probably old, and never confirmed) and the maps of the region (perhaps out-dated). Radcliffe's former press secretary, Christopher Beaumont, thinks Radcliffe had an "impossible assignment." When Radcliffe met Mountbatten for the first time, he learned that he actually had 36 days. Still, Radcliffe managed to complete the task on 13 August, 1947, two days ahead of schedule.

Karl Meyer, a veteran journalist, scholar and a long-time editorial board member of the New York Times, is quite critical of the British in his book "The Dust of Empires: The Race for Mastery in the Asian Heartland" (May 2003). He concludes that the 'shabby' and 'hasty' departure of the British, together with Mountbatten-Nehru friendship (particularly between Mountbatten's wife, Edwina and Nehru), turned a bad outcome into worse. Meyer rejects the view (promoted by the movie Gandhi) that Jinnah and the Muslim League were "the only culprits." In Meyer's view the "real villain" was Mountbatten, "in collusion" with Nehru, and Jinnah was "nearly blameless by comparison." He thinks Mountbatten's method of drawing borders between these countries was "at best arbitrary, at worst reckless. His timetable for partition left the Indian army on the sideline when communal slaughter began.

Some people in Britain were very critical of Mountbatten, right from the beginning, suggesting that his friendship with Nehru interfered with fairness. Mountbatten supporters obviously disagree. There is no way that the issue can now be independently reviewed, because Radcliffe destroyed all the records when he completed the assignment, refused any discussion of his Commission's work, and never went back to the subcontinent again. His aide, Christopher Beaumont, did however make some things clear in 1992. He gave the British conservative newspaper, The Daily Telegraph, a copy of the memo he had prepared on the deliberations of the Radcliffe Commission, which he had already donated to All Souls College at Oxford. Beaumont confirms that borders were secretly redrawn, to Pakistan's disadvantage, particularly in case of Ferozepore, a 400 sq. mile area, where the canal head-water controlled irrigation in Bikaner. Nehru somehow got the wind of the still-confidential work, and he and Maharajah of Bikaner appealed to the Viceroy. The Viceroy then asked Radcliffe for a private lunch (his second and last meeting with him), and after that, Radcliffe promptly altered the border he had originally drawn. According to this Beaumont memo, "This episode reflects great discredit on Mountbatten and Nehru."

Two other major cases in which Mountbatten intervened were: Chittagong Hill Tracts (CHT) and Gurdaspur District. Despite a higher non-Muslim population, Radcliffe had CHT going to Pakistan and Gurdaspur (with a Muslim majority) to India. In Radcliffe's initial proposal, Gurdaspur District was in Pakistan, but it was changed later because of Mountbatten's intevention.

It's not that the British are suddenly forthcoming with their criticism now. One of the Indian supporters of the British also had some tough words. In the second volume of his autobiography "Thy Hand, Great Anarch !" Nirad Chaudhuri says: (i) " ... then an apologia emerged ex post facto which is the most shameless sophistry I have read anywhere. It was argued, and is still being argued, that if the British had not left – the manner of their leaving being conveniently glossed over – there would have been uprisings and therefore loss of life far exceeding what was seen. Now, the conjuring of the hypothetical bogeys which no one can prove or deny is the best defense of every coward who yields at the first sign of trouble." (ii) [and this is on Jinnah], "I must set down at this point that Jinnah is the only man who came out with success and honor from the ignoble end of the British Empire in India. He never made a secret of what he wanted, never prevaricated, never compromised, and yet succeeded in inflicting unmitigated defeat on the British Government and the Indian National Congress. He achieved something which not even he could have believed to be within reach in 1946."

India received most of the 562 scattered princely states, among other things. Karl Meyer is quite astute when he says there's some "provincial unfinished quality" about Pakistan: 7 different Constitutions, not a single Chief of the State completing his/her term, or managing to have a peaceful transfer of power. Meyer thinks Pakistan got the "loser's share of the Raj spoils." India did receive most of everything (even most of 562 princely states).

Out of the thousands of Indian Civil servants and other elite, Meyers notes Pakistan got just a tiny fraction: about 100 Civil Service and national police, supported by 50 British civil servants, 11 Indian army officers that "overnight had to create Pakistan's administration, judicial and diplomatic realms.

Jinnah was a complex character, much different from Nehru and Gandhi. He was autocratic, aloof, much anglicized and distrustful of the British attitude toward Muslims. His relationship with Mountbatten was stiff, frosty, and decidedly unfriendly (Mountbatten had some choice words, including "awfully cold," to describe an arrogant Jinnah). It's hard to say whether this worked against his cause, but it didn't quite earn him the brownie-points that Nehru seems to have gotten plenty of. He, according to some, was Pakistan's Charles de Gaulle: haughty, impervious, nationalistic and the country, personified.

The question, again, is not whether the British withdrawal was hasty: In the eyes of the Indian group, it was long overdue. As to the British, they saw the light and had their own deadline, announced well in advance. The important questions are: (i) Whether, in haste to withdraw, did the British thoroughly explore ALL options ? (ii) Were adequate security precautions taken to protect the public at large from the inevitable violence and massacre? The answer to both questions is probably NO! Among facile rationalizations offered are: Since independence was announced before Partition, it was up to the new governments of India and Pakistan to keep public order; no large population movements were suspected; the plan did call for the protection of minorities in both countries, but both of them failed; and some Mountbatten supporters hypothesize that by rushing, Mountbatten actually saved more lives than those who died on the eve of Partition, and had he delayed the partion/independence any longer, there would have been a huge civil war, with much greater loss of life. As a rationale, this is unbecoming and bizarre.

For another, non-political perspective from one of my favorite British poets, W. H. Auden ('Partition', May 1966):

> *Unbiased at least he* was when he arrived on his mission, Having never set eyes on this land he was to partition Between two peoples fanatically at odds, With their different diets and incompatible gods. "Time," they had briefed him in London, "is short***. It's too late for mutual reconciliation or rational debate: the only solution now lies in separation. The Viceroy** thinks, as you will see from his letter, That the less you are seen in his company the better, So we've arranged to provide you other accommodations. We can give you four judges, two Muslim, two Hindu, To consult with, but the final solution must rest with you." Shut up in a lovely mansion, with police night and day Patrolling the gardens to keep assassins away, He got down to work, to the task of settling the fate Of millions. The maps at his disposal were out of date And the Census# returns almost certainly incorrect, But there was no time to inspect Contested areas. The weather was frightfully hot And a bout of dysentery kept him constantly on the trot, But in seven weeks it was done, the frontiers decided, A continent for better or worse divided. The next day he sailed for England where he quickly forgot The case as a good lawyer must. Return he would not Afraid, as he told his Club, that he might get shot."*

Flashback to Indian Partition

Astrologers could not decide on an auspicious day for the independence of India so it fell at midnight between 14 and 15 August 1947.

The British colony was divided along religious lines and two nations were born-the secular but Hindu-dominated India and the Islamic Republic of Pakistan. But even as the celebrations were getting under way it was questioned whether partition could lead to peace among the subcontinent's different groups.

Some observers say it has fuelled regional animosities and argue that it established a sinister precedent. Since partition, India and Pakistan have waged three wars against each other-two of them over the unresolved issue of Kashmir.

Peace Declaration

The first ceremonies to symbolise the transfer of power from Britain to one of the new dominions took place in Karachi on the morning of 14 of August. "*At the stroke of midnight hour, when the world sleeps, India will wake up to life and freedom*"

Free India

After the ceremony in Pakistan, Lord and Lady Mountbatten flew to Delhi, where special events to mark the transfer of power took place. He was to stay on as Governor General of India, while Pandit Jawaharlal Nehru became the country's first prime minister. "*That night people were very expectant, very hopeful of things to come*"

Saeed Suhrawardy

The special ceremony began at 11pm in the State Council building.

"At the stroke of midnight hour, when the world sleeps, India will wake up to life and freedom," Nehru said.

As the last chimes of midnight died, an assembly member blew a conch shell and a great cheer rose in the hall.

Tens of thousands of people celebrated outside the building-many more did so in cities around India.

Mahatma Gandhi, regarded as the father of Indian independence, did not attend the celebrations. Instead, Gandhi-who strived for a united India-spent the day with Indian Muslims in Calcutta.

Exodus

Journalist Saeed Suhrawardy, an Indian Muslim from the town of Mirzapur, was 17 at the time and remembers the night clearly.

"I think the whole town was awake," he said. "There was no television at that time and few radios. So radio shops were very crowded with people waiting for the speech of Pandit Jawaharlal Nehru. It was like a festival, at least in my place there was no tension.

"That night people were very expectant, very hopeful of things to come."

But Saeed Suhrawardy recalls that there were also fears that night.

"Reports coming from other places made the minorities fearful for events to come.

"In our town we did not have any record of communal violence. But there were stories of violence, riots, attacks on trains and bloodstained trains arriving with dead bodies."

Saeed Suhrawardy did not think of migrating after partition. Many others did.

As soon as the new borders were known some 10 million Hindus, Muslims and Sikhs fled from their homes on one side of the newly demarcated borders to the other side.

About one million people were killed during the exodus, and to this day many families are separated by the border.

Religious Rivalry

The origin of partition is still a matter of debate.

The name Pakistan-or "Land of the Pure"-did not come into existence until 1933, when it was coined by Rahmatullah Chowdhry, a Cambridge student.

Partition Timeline

- 1930: Alama Iqbal advocates the two-nation theory
- 1933: The name Pakistan is coined
- 1940: Jinnah calls for a separate Muslim state

- May/June 1946: Both parties accept Cabinet Mission Plan
- July: Plan collapses
- Aug: Hindu-Muslim violence kills thousands
- June 1947: Mountbatten plan for partition approved
- July: India Independence Act passed in Britain
- Aug: Separate states of Pakistan and India are born

Three years earlier, the poet Alama Iqbal had advocated the establishment of a separate Muslim state at a Muslim League conference. But it was not until 1940 that his two-nation theory was adopted by the League.

The 1930s saw a growing mistrust between the Muslim League and the All India Congress.

The League's leader, Mohammed Ali Jinnah-until 1940 reluctant to advocate the creation of two nations-is said to have feared that the country's Muslim minority would be subjugated by the Hindu majority.

Deadline

During World War II Britain's mobilisation of the Indian economy and military forces was opposed by Congress.

Fearing the movement's ability to sabotage the war effort, Britain is said to have exploited the Hindu-Muslim rivalry in an effort to curtail the Congress.

After the war, Labour Prime Minister Clement Attlee came to power in Britain.

In 1946, he sent a Cabinet Mission to India that put forward a plan for Hindus and Muslims to work together.

This was initially accepted by both sides, but within week the plan had collapsed. Some say it was Nehru who changed his mind, others say it was Jinnah.

Jinnah called for Direct Action on 16 August 1946 to protest against Congress and the British.

In Calcutta this led to three days of Hindu-Muslim violence-the bloodiest in nearly a century-and thousands of deaths.

A year later, Lord Mountbatten was sent to India to replace Lord Wavell as viceroy, with plans to transfer power no later than June 1948.

Demarcation

The new viceroy is said to have found the situation too dangerous to wait even that brief period, and to have become convinced that partition was unavoidable.

On 3 June 1947, he presented his plan to Nehru and Jinnah. They both accepted it. A month later, the British Parliament passed the Indian Independence Act, ordering the demarcation of the dominions of India and Pakistan by midnight 14-15 August.

Two boundary commissions worked against the clock to partition the states of Bengal and Punjab in such a way as to leave a majority of Muslims to the west of the new Punjab border (what is currently Pakistan) and to the east of the new Bengal border (East Pakistan, which in 1971 would become Bangladesh). Under the partition plan, Kashmir was free to accede to India or Pakistan.

Sharp Reminder

Three days before partition, the Hindu ruler of Muslim-majority Kashmir, Maharajah Hari Singh, said that he wanted to remain independent. However, in a series of events which are still the subject of controversy to this day, a Pathan tribal force entered Kashmir with Pakistani backing. The Maharajah decided to accede to India, allowing Indian troops to be airlifted to the state. Pakistani and Indian forces ended up at the point now known as the Line of Control, splitting the territory unevenly. Nearly 55 years and two wars later, the status of Kashmir remains unresolved-one of the many reminders of a partition that has left thousands of families separated by the line which divides India and Pakistan.

When Edwina met Nehru

The first is a brisk account of Britain's involvement with India and of the backgrounds of those people who were principally responsible for unscrambling that relationship.

It contains most of the facts that matter, if rather too much social trivia that does not, and is generally fair. Where it is unfair is in its dismissal of Mountbatten as a trivial playboy. It is permissible to make fun of some of the wilder schemes which he championed during his time at Combined Operations—notably the iceberg-aircraft carrier Habbakuk—but unreasonable to dismiss the ingenuity, energy and formidable organising powers which created the machine that made possible the invasion of Europe in 1944.

Mountbatten was, indeed, often preoccupied with trifles, or with his status as a member of the royal family, but to claim that he 'engaged himself almost full time' in arranging the marriage between his nephew Philip and the future Queen is absurdly to underestimate the range of his activities and to exaggerate his role as matchmaker.

By the time that the second part of this book begins—dealing with the coming of independence and the partition of India—the reader (or, at any rate this reader) is therefore expecting a hatchet job on the last Viceroy, a reprise of the gospel according to Saint Andrew Roberts.

The contrary proves to be true. Harold Nicolson in his diary remarked how curious it was that 'we should regard as a hero the man who liquidates the empire which other heroes such as Clive, Warren Hastings and Napier won for us'.

But, von Tunzelmann goes on:

Mountbatten was serving his country with as much loyalty, courage and determination as had those other heroes. Mountbatten turned a stagnating mess into perhaps the most successful retreat from empire in history—from the point of view of the imperialist nation, at least.

She examines the three main charges against him—that he mishandled the problem of the Sikhs, failed to make proper use of the British army, and transferred power with disastrously reckless speed—and acquits him on all of them. Certainly she criticises certain aspects of his operations but she is equally ready to show that all the main protagonists—Gandhi, Nehru and Jinnah in particular—were at times guilty of obstinacy, pride, ill-temper and rank bad judgment.

She conveys vividly the terrifying pressures under which they were all working: the massacres that besmirched partition were bad enough, but von Tunzelmann leaves one in no doubt as to how much worse they might have been.

The heroes are all shown to have had their frailties; the heroine, Edwina Mountbatten, is alone almost immaculate. Her achievements were, indeed, prodigious, but the author exaggerates her importance—sometimes it seems as if Mountbatten would have been incapable of performing his task without her constant guidance, if not control.

The remarkable relationship between Nehru and the two Mountbattens is described with sympathetic understanding.

Von Tunzelmann suggests that the 'affair' between Nehru and Edwina began far earlier than May 1948—'the line later perfected by official biographers'. It depends what you mean by 'affair'. No one doubts that a close friendship existed while Mountbatten was still Viceroy but Nehru himself dates to a weekend in Simla in midMay the discovery that 'there was a deeper attachment between us, that some uncontrollable force, of which I was only dimly aware, drew us to one another'.The point is of importance, since Pakistani historians in particular insist that Mountbatten as Viceroy was prejudiced in favour of the Indians because of Nehru's baleful influence, exercised through the Viceroy's wife.

The subtitle of this book, 'The Secret History.. .' suggests that the author has had access to hitherto unknown sources and is offering the reader sensational revelations. If such sources exist they are singularly well concealed.

Von Tunzelmann has, however, worked conscientiously through a mass of published and unpublished material.

From it she has created a compelling narrative, sometimes controversial, occasionally perverse, never boring or unintelligent. It will be interesting to see what she tackles next; there is every reason to hope that it will be well worth reading.

Mountbatten Redrafted Plan for Nehru: Viceroy's Daughter

New Delhi, Jul 19 (PTI) India's last Viceroy Lord Mountbatten had to redraft the plan to give dominion status to both India and Pakistan after Jawaharlal Nehru, who shared a "special relationship" with the Viceroy's wife, Edwina, rejected many points of the plan saying it was tantamount to the "Balkanisation" of the country.

Nehru, who was prone to mood swings, was invited by Lord Mountbatten to Simla to get a feedback on the plan. But Nehru turned down the plan and wrote a "bombshell" letter to the Viceroy, writes Pamela Mountbatten, the Viceroy's younger daughter in her book "India Remembered: A Personal Account of the Mountbattens During the Transfer of Power".

"... My father began soul-searching and decided to show Nehru the Mountbatten Plan to get his feedback. Nehru was incandescent and kept Krishna Menon up till dawn the night that he arrived, dictating the bombshell letter dated the 11th May (1947) to my father which rejected many points of the plan which he saw as the Balkanisation of his country. My father rethought and with the incredible and brilliant V P Menon, redrafted the whole plan...," writes Pamela, who travelled with her parents to India in 1947.

Following Nehru's rejection of the plan, Lord Mountbatten "rethought and...Resubmitted it (the plan) to London—much to the India Office and Attlee's confusion and perturbation", points out Pamela, who was 17 at the time.

Mountbatten then travelled to London and got the amendments to the plan—already agreed to by Nehru—"approved".

Mountbatten returned "...To India victorious and able to press ahead urgently with the moves that would lead to Dominion Status for both India and Pakistan. The first thing that was needed was to meet and get the Indian leaders' agreement (of course he already had that from Nehru), and secondly, it needed announcing to the country and the wider world," she writes. The Viceroy also saved Nehru—a Kashmiri

Brahmin—"who was emotional about the (Kashmir) problem" humiliation by convincing the Maharaja of Kashmir to accept the Mountbatten plan.

"Nehru being a Kashmiri was intent on travelling to Kashmir himself to see the Maharaja, but my father realised the dangers inherent in that plan and luckily we could take up a long-standing invitation to visit the Prince ourselves. There was therefore a political expedient to our trip to Kashmir—to convince the Maharaja to accept the plan—and save Nehru the humiliation," writes Pamela, who was coaxed by her daughter India to record her 15-month stay in India.

Edwina's "special relationship" with Pandit Nehru was very useful for the Viceroy too. "Pandit Nehru was a Kashmiri himself, so he was emotional about the problem. If things were particularly tricky my father would say to my mother, 'Do try to get Jawaharlal to see that this is terribly important...'" However, Lord Mountbatten's charm offensive—a tool he used before launching his pragmatic strategies—fell flat on Mohammed Ali Jinnah, who was intent on creating Pakistan.

The Mountbattens, who were very optimistic about the chance to mediate between Jawaharlal Nehru and Congress and Jinnah and the Muslim League, found it difficult to "crack" Jinnah. "My father could talk of nothing else because he could not crack Jinnah and this had never happened to him before. He later admitted that he didn't realise how impossible his task was going to be till he met Jinnah," writes Pamela.

In a letter to his elder daughter the last Viceroy signalled just how depressed he was with the situation. "'I have boobed', he wrote mournfully. It was the only time he admitted it," writes Pamela.

In a section titled "Operation Seduction" Pamela points out that Jinnah was intent on creating Pakistan ever since he had been introduced to the concept at the history-shaping meeting in Waldorf in London in 1933.

However, Mountbatten thought that Partition was an absurd idea but inevitable as the Indians wanted independence and couldn't agree.

Edwina also recorded her impressions of the Nehru-Jinnah meet: "Two very clever and queer people. I rather liked them but found them fanatical on this Pakistan and quite impractical." In another diary entry she calls Jinnah a "meglo-maniac (sic)" and says "god help Pakistan". Jinnah even put paid to Lord Mountbatten's plan who wanted to become Governor-General (G-G) of both India and Pakistan—by announcing that he (Jinnah) would become G-G of Pakistan.

"This left my father to decide whether to accept the offer to become G-G of India and therefore to go against every non-partisan plan he had stood for in his tenure. Indeed his later acceptance of the governor-generalship of India did tarnish his impartial reputation and kindled persistent rumours that he was anti-Muslim League," she writes.

The only time "Mr Jinnah"—as Lord Mountbatten called him—showed "emotion" was when he was seeing the Mountbattens off after the Independence Day function in Karachi.

"Jinnah was an icy man, but on this occasion he showed emotion. He leant over to my father, put his hand on his knee and said with evident feeling...'Your Excellency, I'm so glad to get you back safely.'"

9

Nehru on Others Perspective

The story of the end of the Raj is one of the greatest tales of 20th Century history and since the day the last Union Jack was pulled down in Delhi there has been a stream of books on one or other aspects of the subject. ALEX VON TUNZELMANN has now added to these a very racy account of the whole saga in her debut work, *INDIAN SUMMER: THE SECRET HISTORY OF THE END OF AN EMPIRE.*

This is a book which has already earned her a place amongst the growing band of popular historians now re-writing, and thankfully enlivening, history for the modern reader. Her account of the unraveling of the Raj and of the chief characters who unraveled it provides a very welcome and rivetingly lively summary of the lengthy and tortuous process that started in the late 19th Century and was concluded, at least formally, on two days in August 1947 (a day each for the two successor states, first Pakistan then India). Von Tunzelmann handles this massive story, and the huge amount of information that she has absorbed from the books and files that lie behind it, adeptly and without over-burdening the reader with her erudition.

Her writing is so fluid that it reads deceptively like a novel, though there is no make believe in it. She has the panache Edith Simon displayed in her *Luther Alive*. This is indeed a history that is alive. Her account of the horrors that engulfed India after partition is particularly vivid; I have not read a better account of the deaths, maimings, abductions, rapes and arson that accompanied the mass emigration of the fleeing millions seeking a home on the other side of the artificial line between the Muslim state of Pakistan and the secular state of India that was drawn by the departing British administration.

She is a terrific biographer; her characterisations are succinct and, for the most part, sympathetic. Her characters play their roles in this tragedy as realistic human beings, their failings balanced judiciously by their achievements, the weighty affairs of state they handle enlivened by the human touch, Gandhi's arm on the Vicereine, Edwina Mountbatten's, shoulder, Edwina's walks in the forest with Jawaharlal Nehru.

The book is not really a 'secret history' for there is not much of it that has not been penned elsewhere, as her excellent bibliography demonstrates, but it is what could be described as almost a multi-personality biography, for von Tunzelmann uses the life histories of the principal players (Gandhi, Nehru, the two Mounbattens and, to a much lesser, extent Jinnah and Churchill) to weave the story of the Indian national struggle from the late years of the 19th century to its denouement in the second half of the 20th.

Minor characters, if they can be called so, get similar treatment with lesser star billing; Edward VIII in his earlier, happier days as David, Prince of Wales; the many members of Gandhi's family; Jinnah's sister, Fatima; Nehru's daughter, Indira. This approach has the advantage of telling what is in reality a very winding story, with its countless sub-plots, dead ends, unexplained causes and confused outcomes, intelligibly.

It allows von Tunzelmann to show how that story made sense to each of these participants, and so gives it a form that we can grapple with. If you are to cover all of this, as she does, in only 318 pages, and not produce a dry-as-dust summary, this is a better way than most to do it.

This approach does, inevitably, have its drawbacks, for over such a huge period of time (the book ranges over more than one hundred years) much occurs that cannot be explained by, or attached to, a small number of lives, no matter how key they were. The Indian (by which I mean what became both the Indian and Pakistani) national struggles are therefore on occasion reduced rather to the activities of Gandhi, Nehru and Jinnah.

The complicated chicaneries that have for ever obfuscated a true understanding of the Kashmir problem are not easily dealt with in this fashion. This is less damaging than the concentration upon the Mountbattens for the British side of the story. Theirs is no doubt by far the most attractive part of the British participation; they were young, they were glamorous and, amazingly for who they were (Mountbatten was a minor Royal in his own right and his wife, Edwina, one of the richest women in the world in hers), they were politically radical. Amongst the rather moth eaten assemblage of British dignitaries who handled British Indian affairs at the end of the Raj, they sparkled as if they themselves were the jewels in the Imperial Crown that they were busily giving away.

And they genuinely liked and loved, the latter particularly in Edwina's case, Indians. But the dreary succession of British policy, of scheme after scheme, commission after council, that trudged on from the early years of the 20th Century as the British tried to deal with, then finally rid themselves of, their Indian problem was something in which the Mountbattens had no part, and to which they provided, only on very rare occasions, the odd scintillating noise off in the wings. To some extent, then, history here takes second place to biography.

There is another problem with the balance in this book, which is its denigration of Gandhi. This is deliberate, though it is not a new phenomenon. Others before von Tunzelmann have focused on Gandhi's horrible treatment of his family; his inflexibility, particularly when faced with an attack on anything he took to be a matter of principle (which was, in reality, most things); his, at the times when he wasn't being inflexible, impossible vacillation; his naive unrealism when suggesting courses affecting the life or death of millions; his incredibly selfish, immoral really, use of the naked bodies of his own teenage relatives to test his purity.

Von Tunzelmann clearly doesn't like him at all, and though she tries hard to give Gandhi credit, giving full space to a few of his major deeds, such as the salt march, the picture she paints of him is lacking and leaves one wondering why there was so much of an outpouring of grief across India when he died and why her hero, Nehru, was so totally devoted for all of his life to the Mahatma.

Her treatment of Churchill is, to a lesser degree, similar. Here are all Churchill's anti-Indian-isms paraded again, and none of them are deniable, most are reprehensible. But it is really not possible to maintain that the diehards would have died less hard without them or that they had much effect on the overall course of events. They were, no doubt, a disagreeable part of his character, but he was, as was Gandhi, a bigger figure than the one we see here in the margins of this story. Both men were symbols of many facets of their times and nationalities. Big men can have mud on their boots.

Big men and women can also fall in love, and von Tunzelmann's account ends as the story of a love affair, the unlikely and touching relationship between Edwina Mountbatten and Jawaharlal Nehru. She is right to give this such pride of place in her final pages. It was an affair directly touching on the survival and future of India and on the relations between India and Britain. The affair also proves, albeit circumstantially, her assessment of these two principal characters.

For one of the real virtues of this book is that von Tunzelmann will have none of the post-Strachian cynicism that leaves us with no one to admire. She recognises, nay trumpets, these facts: that individual human beings can rise above prejudice and background and find common ground; and that some human beings can, for at least part of their lives, be heroes and heroines. It is difficult to think of a man and a woman better fitted for those accolades than Nehru and Edwina, or whose relationship could more authoritatively have overturned the pessimistic final parting of Briton and Indian of Forster's *Passage to India.* For then the very stars were against Fielding and Aziz. Thirty years later, Britain and India parted in Edwina and Nehru's farewell kiss.

It is not sentiment to recognize greatness of character and bravery of conduct nor the effect of love on human affairs. Alex von Tunzelmann has this, as she has the major things in her book, absolutely right.

Gandhi Sent Word to Jinnah that he would not Object to Jinnah being the Leader of Free India Instead of Nehru

Nehru gets a lot of blame for going with Mountbatten's desire for not just partitioning the country hastily but also for agreeing to divide Punjab and Bengal.

Gandhi had refused for seven years, since Jinnah proposed a separate Muslim nation, to support a 'vivisection of the Mother,' arguing 'Muslims can never cut themselves away from their Hindu or Christian brethren. We are all children of the same Mother.'

He was so serious about saving India that he sent word, a few months before Partition, to Jinnah through Mountbatten that he would not object to Jinnah being the leader of free and united India instead of Nehru. But Jinnah—who always mistrusted the Mahatma, calling him 'wily Gandhi'—had no use for such overtures.

Nehru is also faulted for not listening to Gandhi in getting Jinnah to mediate in the escalating violence in undivided Kashmir. Gandhi even wondered if holding a plebiscite in Kashmir could end the looming violence there.

Why did Nehru listen so much to Mountbatten?

Those who forget history...

Nehru had talked about Mountbatten's fatal charm," Wolpert says. "Of course, he was flattering Mountbatten when he said that. But Nehru unfortunately came too much under the influence of Mountbatten, exacerbated by Nehru's education in England. Nehru was charmed by the English upper world, he thought he could trust and work with Mountbatten.

"Mountbatten's royal blood appealed as much to the rulers of princely states in India ," Wolpert continues, "as his radical views and social charms did to Nehru. His charm was so much Nehru was blinded by it."

Asked if Nehru's relationship with Mountbatten's wife Edwina played a role, the historian says, "It helped him cloud the danger of what Mountbatten was doing." Wolpert doesn't fight the idea that Partition looked inevitable by 1947, and he understands why Nehru, seeing the way Hindus had been killed in Bengal and Punjab, agreed to the partition of the two provinces.

"But the real solution to any massacre is not to make more violence by drawing a line blindly through a province," the historian points out.

Years later, Mountbatten would whisper now and then how he had botched up the Independence process.

Years after Partition, Mountbatten would whisper now and then how he had botched up the Independence process.

Nehru 'finally awakened,' and admitted in a letter to the Nawab of Bhopal, a friend, 'Partition came and we accepted it because we thought that perhaps that way, however painful it was, we might have some peace.

'And yet, the consequences of that Partition have been so terrible that one is inclined to think that anything else would have been preferable,' Nehru added.

At the end of his six-year research and writing, Wolpert was looking for a picture for the book's dust jacket. He had gone through hundreds of pictures of Partition. And he had also seen pictures offering glimpses of thousands of people who perished in the tragedy—some estimates believe over a million were killed.

"Suddenly, I came across an image that encapsulated the tragedy," he says. It is a picture by the well-known photographer Margaret Bourke-White, showing mostly bare-footed refugees going to places they felt would be safe from the communal carnage.

The image of a Sikh man in the same photograph carrying a woman on his shoulders also spoke volumes, Wolpert says. "The picture brought to our attention the fact that these poor, barefoot people with no possessions had to make the perilous journey because of the idiocy and arrogance of those who had a duty to protect them."

Partition – an event that even after so many years arouses multi-faceted responses, where long silences give way to sudden outbursts, where as much is buried as is revealed. The recent years particularly have seen a rich body of literature on Partition, which is as vast as it is diverse. More intriguing than the fictional recalling of the traumatic times has been the new excitement in portals of academe to combine a study of the whys and hows of Partition with an analysis of pain and the limits of violence epitomised by it.

One is often troubled by this new-found interest in Partition. Memory, after all, is not just about remembering, it is also about forgetting. At the same time, to look at Partition through memory has also to do with the general dissatisfaction with the way conventional history about it has been written. And in spite of the vast, extremely rich writings now available on Partition, particularly the works of Urvashi Butalia, Ritu Menon and Gyanendra Pandey, one is still not sure if we have managed to grasp it in its totality, and more important, to come to terms with it. The present book under review, put together in two volumes by the editors of the Indian Council of Historical Research, adds another chapter to the narratives on Partition. What is important here is that it covers a vast arena, in a total of 40 essays. However, I am not quite sure if it anywhere breaks new ground. Many of its writers have written more eloquently and extensively on the subjects covered elsewhere. While many of the essays are immensely readable, I think the main purpose that the volumes serve is to provide a peep into some of the work on the subject at one place.

Let me at the outset comment on the weakness of the two volumes. I think what they lack is a comprehensive introduction. It is the same for both the volumes, revealing that not much has gone into its writing. There is no attempt by the editors to weave together a narrative thread and build certain key theoretical arguments, broad themes and insights on the basis of the rich array and variety of essays. They fail to address crucial questions of politics of identity.

At one place in the introduction the editors remark, "In any case, the fear of the Muslims has proved unfounded in the end as a substantial section of this community found a secure home in India and are thriving as freely as any other community in independent India" (emphasis mine) (p 8). I think the statement is too sweeping, especially when the memories of recent pogrom in Gujarat are fresh, and fails to even acknowledge the increasing communalisation of politics in recent times, the mounting insecurity, and attacks on Muslims and other minorities, and a greater than ever need to acknowledge and combat communalism. The introduction also resorts to a simplified binary dualism between popular view and scholarly view, between historian's history and people's history, while actually the two deeply intersect, with no neat divisions between the two, as the essays themselves prove. In fact, there is a greater need for a space where the two commentaries are intermeshed.

Having said this, I must say that some of the essays in the volumes are a pleasure, especially in the second volume. Let me however begin with the first volume, which is more concerned with 'high' politics, of Congress and Gandhi, individuals like Mountbatten and the formation of the Constituent Assembly. The first chapter by V N Dutta attempts to figure out the role of Lord Mountbatten in the Radcliffe Award, and if he unduly influenced him to change the boundary award in favour of Indian Pakistan – a question which does not have a definite answer. Gandhi was the saddest and at his heroic best during the days of Partition, a well known fact, different facets of which are covered in two articles by B R Nanda and Chittabrata Palit.

The imperialist stand is reviewed and questioned by Bishwa Mohan Pandey. Lal Bahadur Verma writes on a subject, which I think is much more eloquently covered from a different angle by Krishna Kumar in the second volume and more so in his recent book, on the impact of different approaches to Partition in the writing of history books in India and Pakistan. The late Partha Sarathi Gupta highlights the importance of documents as a corrective to stereotyped accounts. Sucheta Mahajan analyses the role of Congress in failing to keep the country united, an issue covered in a much more detailed fashion by her elsewhere. Salil Mishra, in chronicling the coalition politics in UP during 1937, lucidly reveals a turning point in the history of Partition.

The papers by Jayanta Sengupta, K S Singh and Bir Good Gill respectively show the happenings in the Oriya princely states, the role of some prominent tribal leaders and tribal politics in central India and the north-east and the role of the Akalis in Punjab. Dwijendra Tripathi and Sri Prakash essentially explore the politics of economics, in relation to the event. While most essays are competent, I found them often dry reading, perhaps because they are often 'official', 'statist' narratives, dissatisfaction with which has been often expressed by those working on Partition, and avidly by Gyanendra Pandey in his latest book *Remembering Partition.* Incidentally, I am surprised that there is no essay by him in the volumes, since he has written in depth on the subject.

THE HUMAN DIMENSION

What has interested me more in the present work under review has been the second volume, which highlights the literary representations of Partition and the human dimension of the event. The essays here roughly cover personal reminiscences, recollections by contemporaries, impressions mirrored in creative literature and events and incidents which inspired the visual media, narratives and popular culture. Krishna Kumar's essay on the way Partition is written about in school textbooks across the divide provides us with a starting point to examine mentalities and attitudes.

However, since his book is recently out, it is much better to read that. The linguistic divide in northern India, particularly from the early twentieth century and the final triumph of sanskritised Khari Boli Hindi over Hindustani and Urdu has been covered widely in the writings of Christopher King, Suniti Chatterjee, and many others in a detailed fashion. R K Agnihotri writes on this well trodden field, but I am surprised that there is no reference to King's *One Language Two Script's* in it.

Literature dominates in this volume, and naturally so, since nowhere else has Partition been expressed more poignantly. A number of leading lights of literature have lent their pen to the volume, including Mrinal Pandey, Alok Bhalla and K S Duggal. Mrinal Pandey's short essay is actually almost a review of Urvashi Butalia's book *The Other Side of Silence.* Some essays are very short and almost read like literary notes, for example that of Duggal. Alok Bhalla has two essays and in the one where he undertakes a long and detailed interview with Bhisham Sahni, whose Tamas will rank among some of the best literature on Partition, is of great interest and relevance to us.

It is a delight to read Sahni, where there is almost a nostalgia for the syncretic culture of the past. His second essay talks of the problems in Khalid Hasan's English translation of Manto's Partition stories, simultaneously raising critical questions on the ethics of a translator. Alok Bhalla features yet again, this time through the essay of M Asaduddin, who finds in the stories on Partition collected by Alok Bhalla in three volumes multiple perspectives and visions of the event. Nandi Bhatia, Anindita Mukhopadhyay, Ameena K Ansari, Jayanti Chattopadhyay, M Asaduddin, Kamlesh Mohan, Shikoh Mohsin Mirza -- all cover various literary writers and diverse dimensions of literary representations of the Partition. The paradoxical question of why partition found only fleeting presence in Bengali literature is taken up by Tapati Chakravarty.

Perhaps the most readable paper in the two volumes is one by Satish Gujral, where he reveals that he is not only a sensitive painter but can also narrate his reminiscences of Partition in a moving personal manner, revealing fragments and moments of brutality and indignity. Combined with the essay by Kehsav Malik, on the paintings of Satish Gujral on Partition, we get an insight into a sensitive and creative mind and heart. The short but well written essay by Partha Chatterjee reveals how in Ritwik Ghatak's films, Partition never figures directly; rather it is a riveting memory image of a cataclysmic event. Some essays are very short, like that of Badri Narain Tiwari on the way Partition is perceived in the popular mind in the Bhojpuri region. Urvashi Butalia can be regarded as one of those who has shown deep sensitivity on Partition and particularly what it meant for women. In an essay, interspersed with thought provoking anecdotes, she reveals how silences speak and how oral histories deeply enrich conventional historical sources in understanding Partition. Combined with the essay by Monmayee Basu on the suffering of the Hindu women in Bengal directly affected by Partition, they make an effective case for oral evidence, especially to get women's side of the story.

Minus footnotes, many of the essays in this volume make for easy and touching reading. This volume is much more involving, since it touches a core, and brings forward the pain and tragedy in a sensitive manner. The two volumes together have so many essays that it is impossible for a reviewer to cover all of them, and thus I have just been able to provide a bird's-eye view on them.

Finally, I think that any work on Partition is incomplete if it is not plural. Suvir Kaul, in his recent edited book on the subject, *Partition of Memories,* has lucidly remarked that each time we teach the story of Partition in order to demonstrate Jinnah's guilt or the culpability of the Muslim League, and ignore the role played by religious chauvinists within the Congress or other political and social organisations, we tell a tale that deepens the divides signified by Partition.

Only a history which makes an attempt to underline the different and plural truths of what happened at the time, can help us to be more tolerant and better human beings. Literary narratives, oral accounts, constructs and interpretations as much as actual events, local happenings – all these acquire a critical importance for this very reason. The two volumes, in spite of their limitations and the fact that they break no new ground, are partially successful in bringing together these plural and multifaceted dimensions of Partition.

NEHRU, JINNAH OVER JUNAGADH ISSUE

In New Delhi the only issue was when and how to move in. The Governor-General, Mountbatten, reported to the King: "A Cabinet meeting to consider the Junagadh situation summoned for 5 p.m. on 17th September. I was informed that the members of the Cabinet had, prior to this meeting, decided among themselves that military action was the only answer." He sent for Nehru and Patel and persuaded them "to take no decision which the world could interpret as putting India in the wrong and Pakistan in the right, and that all the resources of negotiation should first be exhausted"

A second track was set afoot, however, with Patel's blessings. V.P. Menon, Secretary to the Ministry of States, and N.M. Buch, Government's Regional Commissioner at Rajkot, along with military officers, discussed the situation with local politicians. U.N. Dhebar, later Congress president, reported to Patel on September 21, setting out the agreed strategy-a proclamation denouncing the Nawab of Junagadh and appointing a provisional government. "The Manifesto or Proclamation will be drawn upon American lines." The headquarters of the government "will be on Indian soil. As we acquire Junagadh territories, Government will shift there. We shall receive moral and material support. We will hold the meeting in course of the next week in Bombay. We shall send draft proclamation tomorrow" .

Jinnah complained to Mountbatten about Indian troop movements in the region (September 18). Mountbatten's reply (September 22) reiterated India's position denying "information about large troop concentrations around Junagadh." He said: "Pakistan Government unilaterally proceeded to action which, it was made plain, Government of India could never and do not acquiesce in. Acceptance of accession to Pakistan cannot but be regarded by the Government of India as an encroachment on Indian sovereignty and inconsistent with friendly relations that should exist between the two Dominions.

This action of Pakistan is considered by the Government of India to be a clear attempt to cause disruption by extending the influence and boundaries of the Dominion of Pakistan in utter violation of the Principles on which partition was agreed upon and effected". None could doubt "the Principles" he was hinting at. He asked Pakistan to reconsider (that is, nullify) the accession or face "responsibility of consequences". He repeated Nehru's offer-"accept the verdict of the people of Junagadh in the matter of accession, the plebiscite being carried out under joint supervision of Indian and Junagadh governments"; effectively, under India's since the decrepit regime of Junagadh could hardly perform (page 608). It was a demand for surrender. Pakistan had no cards to play. India held them securely in its hands and decided to play them to a decisive conclusion.

September 25 was a fateful day. The Ministry of States issued a detailed press note complaining that Pakistan had accepted the accession "without any warning" (Sardar's Letters, page 80). In Bombay on that day, a Provisional Government of Free Junagadh was set up with Samaldas Gandhi as its president. Narendra P. Nathwani, later a High Court Judge, was one of its members. K.M. Munshi, who was close to Patel, drafted the "Declaration by the Subjects of Junadagh State" (vide K.M. Munshi; Somanatha: The Shrine Eternal; pages 68-9 for the text). Pakistan had accepted the accession "in disregard of such declared wishes and in defiance of all natural ties which bind the people of Junagadh (82 per cent of whom are non-Muslims) to the people of Kathiawar and to the Dominion of India and in breach of the understanding on the basis of which certain parts of India were allowed to secede and form into a separate State of Pakistan; namely that only contiguous areas predominantly inhabited by Muslims were to be included into the Dominion of Pakistan with the free and willing consent of the people inhabiting those areas."

Munshi recorded: "The Provisional Government of Junagadh moved to Saurashtra and took possession of the Junagadh House at Rajkot. Young men from all over Saurashtra flocked to its banner of freedom. Large sums of money flowed in, volunteers were armed and trained. On the Dessehra Day, the "Day of Victory"-October 24, 1947-the volunteers of the Provisional Government began their operations. People rose against the Nawab's rule in several parts of Junagadh."

Did Jinnah and Liaquat follow contradictory policies? For Liaquat asked Mountbatten's Chief of Staff Ismay in Karachi: "Why, if it was suggested that a referendum should be held in Junagadh one should not be held in Kashmir?" This was discussed by the Indian Cabinet on September 22. Ismay was of the opinion that "one of the main objects of the Pakistan

Government was to use Junagadh as a bargaining counter for Kashmir".

Liaquat and Nehru met in New Delhi on October 1 under Mountbatten's auspices. He reiterated the commitment to the democratic principle: "Nehru nodded his head sadly. Liaquat Ali Khan's eyes sparkled. There is no doubt that both of them were thinking of Kashmir." Nehru took Patel into confidence on September 25: "We are already considering the possibility of military action".

V.P. Menon records that on October 4, the Government of India considered the Junagadh situation: "It was decided to inform the Prime Minister of Pakistan that the only basis on which friendly negotiations could start and be fruitful was the reversion of Junagadh to the status quo preceding the accession of Junagadh to Pakistan and that the alternative to negotiations was a plebiscite." So much for the sanctity of the Instrument of Accession.

In a statement on October 5, 1947, the Government of India said: "Any decision involving the fate of large numbers of people must necessarily depend on the wishes of these people. This is the policy which the Government of India accept in its entirety and they are of the opinion that a dispute involving the fate of the people of any territory should be decided by a referendum or plebiscite of the people concerned. This is a method at once democratic, peaceful and just. They suggest, therefore, that the issues regarding Junagadh should be decided by a referendum or plebiscite of the people of the State. Such a referendum or plebiscite should be held under impartial auspices to be determined by the parties concerned."

Two days later, the Government of Pakistan issued a statement setting out its views on the accession of Junagadh. The statement suggested the withdrawal of troops by the Government of India from Sardargarh and Batva and by Junagadh from Babariawad: "The Pakistan Government have also informed the Government of India of their willingness to discuss the conditions and circumstances in which a plebiscite should be taken by any State or States." Why did Jinnah not affirm this on November 1?

Unable to bear the pressures, Shah Nawaz Bhutto pleaded with Jinnah, on October 27, urging that "you immediately arrange for a conference of the representatives of the two Dominions to decide the Junagadh issue." On November 5, the Junagadh State Council decided on "a complete reorientation of the State policy... even if it involves a reversal of the earlier decision to accede to Pakistan". The Dewan was authorised to negotiate.

Bhutto cashed the blank cheque by opening negotiations with Samaldas Gandhi on November 7 through Capt. Harvey Jones, Senior Member of the Junagadh State Council, asking him to take over the State's administration. It was decided, however, to hand over the State to the Government of India instead. On November 8, Bhutto wrote to Buch on these lines (V.P. Menon, Integration of Indian States; page 137).

On November 9, the Indian Army moved into Junagadh. Nehru formally informed Liaquat about the move. Admiral Satyindra Singh has recorded the Navy's plans "to land the Indian Army for the Junagadh operations-Exercise Peace as it was called" (The Statesman; September 21, 1997). On December 8, at a meeting with Liaquat in New Delhi, as Mountbatten recorded: "Pandit Nehru, while openly admitting that India had been in some ways in the wrong about Junagadh, claimed that the parallel with Kashmir was not tenable because of the vast differences in scale between the two".

Both Nehru and Mountbatten realised now what India was up against. "The fact is that Kashmir is of the utmost vital significance to India as well as to Pakistan. There lies the rub," Nehru wrote to Sri Prakasa, High Commissioner to Pakistan. Earlier he had dismissed Pakistan's interest in Kashmir and began doing just that later. New Delhi sticks to this stand even in 2001, rendering compromise impossible. Nehru admitted: "Kashmir is going to be a drain on our resources, but it is going to be a greater drain on Pakistan.

In a military sense we are stronger." India could not quit. "Kashmir gives us an example of communal unity and cooperation. This has had a healthy effect in India and any weakening in Kashmir by us would create a far more difficult communal situation in India" (SWJN; Vol. 4; pages 346-7). Nehru lived to see the situation in Kashmir deteriorate to a point where Jan Sangh leader S.P. Mookerjee could exploit it in 1952-53 to whip up communalism. Things have worsened since. The "drain" on resources continues.

Mountbatten told both Nehru and Liaquat on December 8 that "the whole future welfare of India depended on an agreement over Kashmir between the two Dominions. The effect that such an agreement would have on world opinion would also be very great" (ibid; p. 361). But, Sir Chimanlal Setalvad had foreseen it all even as the events had begun to unfold. In a letter to The Times of India (October 3, 1947) he wrote: "Many of those who are enthusing over the activities of the so-called 'Provisional Government' of Junagadh do not seem to realise the dangerous consequences that are likely to follow from what is happening.

The Junagadh Government has acted unwisely in acceding to Pakistan, ignoring geographical considerations and the wishes of its subjects, but that affords no justification for what is being done. The 'Provisional Government' was formed and functioned for some days in Bombay with the avowed object of overthrowing by force the established Government in Junagadh."

He renewed his plea after the Kashmir crisis erupted. "Pandit Nehru in his broadcast has rightly asked the Pakistan Government how and why the invaders of Kashmir came across the Frontier Province or West Punjab, and how they came to be fully armed. He charges the Pakistan Government with violation of international law and an unfriendly act towards India. He alleges that the Pakistan Government was either too weak to prevent the invaders of Kashmir from marching across its territory or that it was willing that this should happen. Exactly the same poser can be put to the Indian Dominion with regard to Junagadh".

The Government of India held a plebiscite in Junagadh as well as five of its erstwhile feudatories on February 20, 1948. It was conducted by an ICS officer C.B. Nagarkar. Out of an electorate of 2,01,457, 1,90,870 cast their votes. Only 91 voted for Pakistan. Of the 31,434 votes cast in the five princeling areas, only 39 voted for accession to Pakistan (Menon; page 142). The result would not have been different even if the U.N. had conducted this plebiscite.

But it puts paid to the debating ploys about "no self-determination for a part of the nation" and "the core of nationalism". Junagadh was quintessentially Indian. Negotiations on plebiscite in Kashmir came to a naught because for five years (1949-53) Nehru would not yield on the powers of the Abdullah government or on the strength of Indian forces in the State. Their presence was not in issue. He then proceeded to argue that efflux of time had rendered the accord on plebiscite obsolete.

Pakistan's aggression in 1965 extinguished the option of plebiscite. But its grievances of old persist. Thanks to India's policies, the alienation of Kashmiris has deepened. Time has not extinguished the "Kashmir dispute". None in the wide world believes it has.

Today, in 2001, India needs seriously to grapple with the problem of forging a sound and realistic foreign policy in a democracy so that it can craft a Kashmir solution which does not entail the State's secession-yet goes beyond the Line of Control. India cannot countenance the former; Pakistan cannot, the latter. Therein lies a challenge to diplomatic creativity.

The Volume gives glimpses of Jinnah's remarkable personality. A man of sterling integrity, courage and sharp and cold intelligence, he stumbled badly in the hour of triumph and left the State he had created a heritage it could have well done without. Nehru did likewise.

While respecting their memory, we need to learn from their mistakes in order to chart a new course. Recall the murky record, we must. For, as George F. Kennan wrote: "When the ambivalence of one's virtue is recognised, the total inequity of one's opponent is also irreparably impaired". This applies to both sides-and Junagadh remains a dark chapter which neither wishes to recall.

10

Nehru's Letters to Sardar Patel

Sardar Vallabhbhai Patel's letter to Jawaharlal Nehru on 7 November 1950 not only deploring Indian Ambassador KM Panikkar's action but also warning about dangers from China

My dear Jawaharlal,

Ever since my return from Ahmedabad and after the cabinet meeting the same day which I had to attend at practically fifteen minutes' notice and for which I regret I was not able to read all the papers, I have been anxiously thinking over the problem of Tibet and I thought I should share with you what is passing through my mind.

I have carefully gone through the correspondence between the External Affairs Ministry and our Ambassador in Peking and through him the Chinese Government. I have tried to peruse this correspondence as favourably to our Ambassador and the Chinese Government as possible, but I regret to say that neither of them comes out well as a result of this study. The Chinese Government has tried to delude us by professions of peaceful intention. My own feeling is that at a crucial period they managed to instill into our Ambassador a false sense of confidence in their so-called desire to settle the Tibetan problem by peaceful means.

There can be no doubt that during the period covered by this correspondence the Chinese must have been concentrating for an onslaught on Tibet. The final action of the Chinese, in my judgement, is little short of perfidy. The tragedy of it is that the Tibetans put faith in us; they chose to be guided by us; and we have been unable to get them out of the meshes of Chinese diplomacy or Chinese malevolence. From the latest position, it appears that we shall not be able to rescue the Dalai Lama. Our Ambassador has been at great pains to find an explanation or justification for Chinese policy and actions.

As the External Affairs Ministry remarked in one of their telegrams, there was a lack of firmness and unnecessary apology in one or two representations that he made to the Chinese Government on our behalf. It is impossible to imagine any sensible person believing in the so-called threat to China from Anglo-American machinations in Tibet. Therefore, if the Chinese put faith in this, they must have distrusted us so completely as to have taken us as tools or stooges of Anglo-American diplomacy or strategy. This feeling, if genuinely entertained by the Chinese in spite of your direct approaches to them, indicates that even though we regard ourselves as the friends of China, the Chinese do not regard us as their friends. With the Communist mentality of "whoever is not with them being against them", this is a significant pointer, of which we have to take due note.

During the last several months, outside the Russian camp, we have practically been alone in championing the cause of Chinese entry into UN and in securing from the Americans assurances on the question of Formosa. We have done everything we could to assuage Chinese feelings, to allay its apprehensions and to defend its legitimate claims in our discussions and correspondence with America and Britain and in the UN. Inspite of this, China is not convinced about our disinterestedness; it continues to regard us with suspicion and the whole psychology is one, at least outwardly, of scepticism perhaps mixed with a little hostility. I doubt if we can go any further than we have done already to convince China of our good intentions, friendliness and goodwill.

In Peking we have an Ambassador who is eminently suitable for putting across the friendly point of view. Even he seems to have failed to convert the Chinese. Their last telegram to us is an act of gross discourtesy not only in the summary way it disposes of our protest against the entry of Chinese forces into Tibet but also in the wild insinuation that our attitude is determined by foreign influences. It looks as though it is not a friend speaking in that language but a potential enemy.

In the background of this, we have to consider what new situation now faces us as a result of the disappearance of Tibet, as we knew it, and the expansion of China almost up to our gates. Throughout history we have seldom been worried about our north-east frontier. The Himalayas have been regarded as an impenetrable barrier against any threat from the north. We had a friendly Tibet which gave us no trouble. The Chinese were divided. They had their own domestic problems and never bothered us about frontiers. In 1914, we entered into a convention with Tibet which was not endorsed by the Chinese. We seem to have regarded Tibetan autonomy as extending to independent treaty relationship. Presumably, all that we required was Chinese counter-signature. The Chinese interpretation of suzerainty seems to be different. We can, therefore, safely assume that very soon they will disown all the stipulations which Tibet has entered into with us in the past. That throws into the melting pot all frontier and commercial settlements with Tibet on which we have been functioning and acting during the last half a century. China is no longer divided.

It is united and strong. All along the Himalayas in the north and north-east, we have on our side of the frontier a population ethnologically and culturally not different from Tibetans and Mongoloids. The undefined state of the frontier and the existence on our side of a population with its affinities to the Tibetans or Chinese have all the elements of the potential trouble between China and ourselves. Recent and bitter history also tells us that Communism is no shield against imperialism and that the communists are as good or as bad imperialists as any other. Chinese ambitions in this respect not only cover the Himalayan slopes on our side but also include the important part of Assam. They have their ambitions in Burma also. Burma has the added difficulty that it has no McMahon Line round which to build up even the semblance of an agreement. Chinese irredentism and communist imperialism are different from the expansionism or imperialism of the western powers. The former has a cloak of ideology which makes it ten times more dangerous. In the guise of ideological expansion lie concealed racial, national or historical claims.

The danger from the north and north-east, therefore, becomes both communist and imperialist. While our western and north-western threat to security is still as prominent as before, a new threat has developed from the north and north-east. Thus, for the first time, after centuries, India's defence has to concentrate itself on two fronts simultaneously. Our defence measures have so far been based on the calculations of superiority over Pakistan. In our calculations we shall now have to reckon with communist China in the north and in the north-east, a communist China which has definite ambitions and aims and which does not, in any way, seem friendly disposed towards us. Let us also consider the political conditions on this potentially troublesome frontier. Our northern and north-eastern approaches consist of Nepal, Bhutan, Sikkim, Darjeeling and the tribal areas in Assam. From the point of view of communication, there are weak spots. Continuous defensive lines do not exist. There is almost an unlimited scope for infiltration. Police protection is limited to a very small number of passes. There, too, our outposts do not seem to be fully manned. The contact of these areas with us is by no means close and intimate.

The people inhabiting these portions have no established loyalty or devotion to India. Even Darjeeling and Kalimpong areas are not free from pro-Mongoloid prejudices. During the last three years, we have not been able to make any appreciable approaches to the Nagas and other hill tribes in Assam. European missionaries and other visitors had been in touch with them, but their influence was in no way friendly to India or Indians. In Sikkim, there was political ferment some time ago. It is quite possible that discontent is smouldering there. Bhutan is comparatively quiet, but its affinity with Tibetans would be a handicap. Nepal has a weak oligarchic regime based almost entirely on force: it is in conflict with a turbulent element of the population as well as with enlightened ideas of the modern age.

In these circumstances, to make people alive to the new danger or to make them defensively strong is a very difficult task indeed and that difficulty can be got over only by enlightened firmness, strength and a clear line of policy. I am sure the Chinese and their source of inspiration, Soviet Union, would not miss any opportunity of exploiting these weak spots, partly in support of their ideology and partly in support of their ambitions. In my judgement the situation is one which we cannot afford either to be complacent or to be vacillating. We must have a clear idea of what we wish to achieve and also of the methods by which we should achieve it. Any faltering or lack of decisiveness in formulating our objectives or in pursuing our policies to attain those objectives is bound to weaken us and increase the threats which are so evident.

Side by side with these external dangers, we shall now have to face serious internal problems as well. I have already asked Iengar to send to the External Affairs Ministry a copy of the Intelligence Bureau's appreciation of these matters. Hitherto, the Communist Party of India has found some difficulty in contacting communists abroad, or in getting supplies of arms, literature, etc., from them. They had to contend with the difficult Burmese and Pakistan frontiers on the east or with the long seaboard. They shall now have a comparatively easy means of access to Chinese communists and through them to other foreign communists.

Infiltration of spies, fifth columnists and communists would now be easier. Instead of having to deal with isolated communist pockets in Telengana and Warrangal we may have to deal with communist threats to our security along our northern and north-eastern frontiers, where, for supplies of arms and ammunition, they can safely depend on communist arsenals in China. The whole situation thus raises a number of problems on which we must come to an early decision so that we can, as I said earlier, formulate the objectives of our policy and decide the method by which those objectives are to be attained. It is also clear that the action will have to be fairly comprehensive, involving not only our defence strategy and state of preparations but also problem of internal security to deal with which we have not a moment to lose. We shall also have to deal with administrative and political problems in the weak spots along the frontier to which I have already referred. It is of course, impossible to be exhaustive in setting out all these problems. I am, however, giving below some of the problems which, in my opinion, require early solution and round which we have to build our administrative or military policies and measures to implement them.

a) A military and intelligence appreciation of the Chinese threat to India both on the frontier and to internal security.

b) An examination of military position and such redisposition of our forces as might be necessary, particularly with the idea of guarding important routes or areas which are likely to be the subject of dispute.

c) An appraisement of the strength of our forces and, if necessary, reconsideration of our retrenchment plans for the Army in the light of the new threat.

d) A long-term consideration of our defence needs. My own feeling is that, unless we assure our supplies of arms, ammunition and armour, we would be making our defence perpetually weak and we would not be able to stand up to the double threat of difficulties both from the west and north-west and north and north-east.

e) The question of China's entry into the UN. In view of the rebuff which China has given us and the method which it has followed in dealing with Tibet, I am doubtful whether we can advocate its claim any longer. There would probably be a threat in the UN virtually to outlaw China, in view of its active participation in the Korean war. We must determine our attitude on this question also.

f) The political and administrative steps which we should take to strengthen our northern and north-eastern frontier. This would include the whole of the border, ie. Nepal, Bhutan, Sikkim, Darjeeling and the tribal territory in Assam.

g) Measures of internal security in the border areas as well as the states flanking those areas such as Uttar Pradesh, Bihar, Bengal and Assam.

h) Improvement of our communication, road, rail, air and wireless, in these areas and with the frontier outposts.

i) The future of our mission at Lhasa and the trade posts at Gyangtse and Yatung and the forces which we have in operation in Tibet to guard the trade routes.

j) The policy in regard to the McMahon Line.

These are some of the questions which occur to my mind. It is possible that a consideration of these matters may lead us into wider question of our relationship with China, Russia, America, Britain and Burma. This, however, would be of a general nature, though some might be basically very important, e.g., we might have to consider whether we should not enter into closer association with Burma in order to strengthen the latter in its dealings with China. I do not rule out the possibility that, before applying pressure on us, China might apply pressure on Burma. With Burma, the frontier is entirely undefined and the Chinese territorial claims are more substantial. In its present position, Burma might offer an easier problem to China, and therefore, might claim its first attention.

I suggest that we meet early to have a general discussion on these problems and decide on such steps as we might think to be immediately necessary and direct, quick examination of other problems with a view to taking early measures to deal with them.

Vallabhbhai Patel, The legacy of Nehru

THE first months of independence were anything but easy. Often emotional, Jawaharlal was caught up in the human drama of the times. He was seen weeping at the sight of a victim one day, and erupting in rage at a would-be assailant hours later. Friends thought his physical health would be in danger as he stormed from city to village, ordering his personal bodyguards to shoot any Hindu who might attack a Muslim, providing refuge in his own home in Delhi for Muslims terrified for their lives, giving employment to young refugees who had lost everything. In one typical incident of the period, Jawaharlal emerged from a visit to a fasting Mahatma Gandhi in mid-January 1948 and confronted a demonstration of refugees chanting "Let Gandhi die!" He leapt from his car and dashed towards the demonstrators shouting, "How dare you say these words! Come and kill me first!" The demonstrators immediately ran away.

Affairs of state were just as draining. The new Prime Minister of India had to deal with the consequences of the carnage sweeping the country; preside over the integration of the princely states into the Indian Union; settle disputes with Pakistan on issues involving the division of finances, of the army, and of territory; cope with massive internal displacement, as refugees thronged Delhi and other cities; keep a fractious and divided nation together; and define both a national and an international agenda. On all issues but that of foreign policy, he relied heavily on Patel, who welded the new country into one with formidable political and administrative skills and a will of iron. A more surprising ally was the former Viceroy, now Governor-General of India, Lord Mountbatten.

For all his culpability in rushing India to an independence drenched in blood, Mountbatten made Nehru partial amends by staying on in India for just under a year. As heir to a British government whose sympathy for the League had helped it carve out a country from the collapse of the Raj, Mountbatten enjoyed a level of credibility with the rulers of Pakistan that no Indian Governor-General could have had. This made him a viable and impartial interlocutor with both sides at a time of great tension. Equally, as a Governor-General above the political fray, he played a crucial role in persuading maharajahs and nawabs distrustful of the socialist Nehru to accept that they had no choice but to merge their domains into the Indian Union.

When fighting broke out over Kashmir between the two Dominions (whose armies were still each commanded by a British general), Mountbatten helped prevent a deeper engagement by the Pakistani Army and brought about an end to the war. And the Governor-General and his wife distinguished themselves by their personal interest in and leadership of the emergency relief measures that saved millions of desperate refugees from misery and worse. In 1950, when India became a Republic with its own Constitution, Jawaharlal arranged for it to remain within the British Commonwealth, acknowledging the British sovereign no longer as head of state but as the symbol of the free association of nations who wished to retain a British connection. Mountbatten's influence was decisive in prompting Jawaharlal to make this choice. Nehru's close relations with Edwina Mountbatten have been the stuff of much posthumous gossip, but his relationship with her husband was to have much more lasting impact on India's history.

As Prime Minister, Jawaharlal had ultimate responsibility for many of the decisions taken during the tense period 1947-49, but it is true to say he was still finding his feet as a governmental leader and that on many key issues he simply went along with what Patel and Mountbatten wanted. Nehru was the uncontested voice of Indian nationalism, the man who had "discovered" India in his own imagination, but he could not build the India of his vision without help. When the Muslim rulers of Hindu-majority Junagadh and Hyderabad, both principalities surrounded by Indian territory, flirted with independence (in Hyderabad's case) and accession to Pakistan (in Junagadh's), the Indian Army marched in and took over with scarcely a shot being fired. In both cases the decision was Patel's, with acquiescence from Nehru....

Apart from handling weighty matters of state, Jawaharlal had to deal with issues of domestic politics. He had surprised some of his most ardent supporters by his reluctance to embrace radical change, and his willingness to retain, and indeed rely on, the very civil servants and armed services personnel who had served the British Raj, the "steel frame" of which continued as the administrative superstructure of independent India. The Government proved its worth in handling the absorption of some seven million refugees from Pakistan, a colossal political and administrative feat. But the civil service continued in the traditions of colonial governance learned from their British masters; Nehru did little to instil in them a development orientation or a new ethic of service to the people. Continuity, not change, was the watchword. Many of the freedom fighters, who had gone to jail while these officials prospered under the British, were dismayed ...

Gandhi's assassination by a Hindu fanatic strengthened his hand on the communal issue. Even Patel agreed to the RSS being banned, though the ban was lifted after a year. On other questions, ranging from the grant of "privy purses" (or annual subventions to the erstwhile maharajahs to compensate for the loss of their princely states) to the clash between the right to property and the need for land reform, he found himself outmanoeuvered by the party's right wing. Patel ran his Home Ministry as firmly as he administered the country as a whole, and he brooked little interference from Nehru.

Lord Mountbatten left India for good on 21 June 1948, ten months after he had presided over its freedom—and its dismemberment. He was succeeded as Governor-General of the Dominion by the man who had once been thought more likely than Jawharlal to be Gandhi's heir, C. Rajagopalachari. Though temperamentally a conservative, "Rajaji" had no patience for the communal sympathies of the Congress right, and so in his own way complemented Jawaharlal as head of state. But when the time came for that position to be converted to that of President of the Republic (upon the adoption of independent India's new Constitution on the symbolic date of 26 January 1950, the old "Independence Day" becoming the new Republic Day), Patel engineered the election of his crony Rajendra Prasad as the Congress candidate.

Jawaharlal had been completely bypassed; he was so surprised that he actually asked Prasad to withdraw and propose Rajagopalachari's name himself. Prasad cleverly suggested that he would do whatever Nehru and Patel agreed upon, at which point Nehru understood and threw in the towel. One of Prasad's first acts upon election was to ask that 26 January be changed to a date deemed more auspicious by his astrologers. Jawaharlal flatly turned him down, declaring that India would not be run by astrologers if he had anything to do with it. This time, Nehru won.

Nehru and Patel came dangerously close to a public clash only once. In 1950, under pressure from the right to intervene militarily in East Pakistan where a massacre of Hindus had begun, Jawaharlal first tried to work with his Pakistani counterpart, Liaquat Ali Khan, on a joint approach to communal disturbances and then, when this had been ignored, offered President Prasad his resignation. (Stanley Wolpert has speculated that Jawaharlal, exhausted and heartsick, was contemplating eloping with Edwina Mountbatten, who had just been visiting him at the time.) But when Patel called a meeting of Congressmen at his home to criticize Jawaharlal's weakness on the issue, Nehru fought back, withdrawing his offer of resignation, challenging Patel to a public debate on Pakistan policy and even writing to express doubt as to whether the two of them could work together any more. The counter-assault was so ferocious that Patel backed off and affirmed his loyalty to Jawaharlal, supporting the pact Nehru signed with his Pakistani counterpart (which had even prompted the two Cabinet Ministers from Bengal to resign). The entire episode marked the closest the Congress would ever come to repudiating Nehru in his lifetime.

But in those early days Jawaharlal was not always a successful political infighter. His setback over Prasad's election was echoed in the elections to the Congress party presidency a few months later. Having withdrawn from the race himself on the grounds that it would not be proper for him as Prime Minister to also serve as party President, Jawaharlal supported his old rival Kripalani against the rightist Purushottamdas Tandon (the very man whose inability to win Muslim support for the chairmanship of the Allahabad municipality had given Jawaharlal his experience of mayoralty in 1923). But Tandon had Patel's backing, and despite Jawaharlal's open opposition, won handily, with over 50% of the votes in a three-man field. Nehru publicly grumbled that the result would only please communal and reactionary forces in the country, and refused to join Tandon's Working Committee.

When finally cajoled into doing so he made no secret of his reluctance. He spent the next year undermining Tandon much as his mentor Mahatma Gandhi had undermined Bose thirteen years earlier. In September 1951 Jawaharlal brought matters to a head by resigning his party positions and making it clear that he and Tandon could not co-exist: one of them had to go. Tandon did. Jawaharlal himself was elected Congress President, his earlier scruples about the Prime Minister serving in such a position completely forgotten.

There was another reason for the decisiveness of his victory. By this time Nehru's greatest rival, Sardar Patel, was dead. He had suffered a heart attack a few months after the Mahatma's assassination; then stomach cancer struck, and in December 1950, having fulfilled his historic role of consolidating India's fragile freedom, he passed away, aged 76. Patel and Nehru had also served as a check upon each other, and his passing away left Jawaharlal unchallenged. If ever there was a moment when he might have been tempted by the prospect of near-dictatorial authority, this might have been it, but Jawaharlal remained a convinced democrat. He was not, however, a native one. He realized that the Home Ministry, with its control over the institutions of law and order, was a valuable tool for a potential competitor. He was therefore careful after the Sardar's death to appoint only trusted associates—with no competing political ambitions or agendas of their own—to the Home Ministry.

Sardar Vallabhbhai Patel—Relations with Nehru

Sardar Patel's relationship with Nehru has always been a source of controversy and intense historical interest. But it's most important phase came between 1947 to 1950, India's first years as a free nation. Chakravarti Rajagopalachari, Nehru and Patel formed the *Triumvirate* which ruled India. Prime Minister Nehru was intensely popular with the masses, but did not enjoy the enormous loyalty and respect Patel had for his political judgment, leadership and integrity within the Congress Party and among most Indian nationalists. Even the British were forced to admit that Patel was the only leader capable of standing up to Gandhi, and the most dangerous as well. Patel was intensely loyal to Gandhi, and both he and Nehru looked to him to arbitrate disputes.

Nehru and Patel sparred intensely over national issues. Patel objected to Nehru overruling his Home Ministry's officials, such as sending his own representative to Ajmer, the scene of communal violence, despite a senior Ministry official having already gone there and Patel himself personally briefing Nehru. Nehru had not bothered to inform Patel of his intentions. Nehru felt offended by Patel making important decisions regarding the states integration without reference to him or the Cabinet. Beneath this lay core ideological differences. Patel was a Hindu who was proud of ancient traditions and Indian culture. He was from the sturdy peasantry of Gujarat, who proudly owned and worked their lands. Nehru was a socialist who despised rituals and religious dogma, who was rich and Westernized in thinking, attitude and mannerism.

An exasperated Patel did not want to battle Nehru, and asked Gandhi to relieve him. He did not have Nehru's youth and popularity, which would overtake him in time, and he knew that an open political battle would hurt India. After much personal deliberation and contrary to Patel's judgment, Gandhi on January 30, 1948 told Patel not to leave the Government, and to stay by Nehru's side. India, according to Gandhi, desperately needed the joint leadership, and Patel. He was assassinated just an hour afterwards. Patel was the last man to have had an intimate conversation with the Mahatma.

At Gandhi's wake, Nehru and Patel embraced each other, and addressed the nation together. However, criticism soon arose from the media and other politicians that Patel's Home Ministry had failed to protect Gandhi. An emotionally exhausted Patel wrote out a letter of resignation, offering to leave the Government despite Gandhi's word so that he may not embarrass Nehru's administration any further. Patel's secretary convinced him to withhold the letter, seeing it as fodder for Patel's enemies and political conflict in India.

Nehru sent Patel a personal letter dismissing any idea of personal differences and that he wanted Patel to leave. He reminded Patel of their 30 year partnership in the freedom struggle, and that after Gandhi's death, it was especially wrong for them to quarrel. Moved, Patel personally and publicly endorsed Nehru's leadership and refuted any suggestion of discord. Patel dispelled any notion that he would like to be India's Prime Minister. He recognized Nehru's importance, and his sacred word to Gandhi. The two committed themselves to joint leadership, and non-interference in Congress party affairs. However, the two would criticize each other in matters of policy. Nehru remained an opponent of Patel's plan to forcibly integrate Hyderabad, and against Patel's advice asked for the United Nations to arbitrate the Kashmir dispute. The former Nehru had to conceed in 1948, and the latter became a source of intense criticism in the years afterward.

Nehru also resisted Patel's counsel on sending assistance to Tibet, which had been invaded by China, and ejecting the Portuguese from Goa by military force. The former resulted in the 1962 Sino-Indian War and the latter was done by Nehru himself in 1961. Patel did not himself force the issue at the time. But Patel did not help Nehru when he had purposely bypassed him, only later to need his help. Nehru attempted to oppose the will of a majority of Congressmen by suggesting that Governor General Chakravarti Rajgopalachari become India's first President. Nehru's arbitrariness and imposition angered the party, which backed its favorite, Dr. Rajendra Prasad. Patel did not help Nehru to win his way, and Prasad became the President of India in 1950. Nehru also opposed the 1950 Congress presidential candidacy of Purushottam Das Tandon, a Hindu conservative leader. Endorsing Jivatram Kripalani himself, Nehru attempted to thwart Tandon's bid, threatening to resign if he were elected. The party voted for Tandon, and Patel endorsed Tandon in Gujarat, where Kripalani received not one vote despite hailing from that state himself. Patel also personally encouraged Nehru and assured him that he should continue as Prime Minister after Prasad's election to the Presidency, which had made Nehru feel that the party was revolting.

Nehru, Patel and Gandhi

The history of India would have been different had Sardar Patel not been the Deputy Prime Minister when India became independent in 1947. The triumvirate- Gandhiji, Nehru and

Sardar Patel were responsible for giving direction to the destiny of the country. Sardar Patel consolidated the country into one united whole in a unique manner.

Formative Years

Born on October 31, 1875 at Nadiad, in the Kaira district of Gujarat, Vallabh Bhai Patel was the son of Zaverbhai Galabhai Patel, a Leva Patidar. This class of cultivators was known for their simple character, industrious habits and straightforward dealings. Vallabh Bhai possessed an ingenous mind as a school boy. He was a rebel whose exceptional organisational abilities were recognised by his schoolmates and teachers. Patel passed the matriculation examination from the Nadiad High School in 1897.

Patel had two ambitions to fulfil, first to become a pleader and later a barrister. During those days a matriculate could become a lawyer by taking the pleaders examination. He became a pleader in 1900, and started practising in Godhra. In 1902 he shifted to Balsad, a taluka headquarter, where he practised as a criminal lawyer for nearly eight years, during which period he had built a name for himself as a most successful criminal lawyer. In 1910, he left for London and joined the Middle Temple, where he took an examination in Roman Law and stood first. He returned to India in 1913 and started practising as a barrister in Ahmedabad, fulfilling his second ambition.

Gandhiji's Disciple

The impact of Gandhiji's personality on Vallabhbhai was tremendous. It gave him a new mission in life. The Champaran struggle waged by Gandhiji had a sweeping effect on Patel's mind. In Gandhiji's Champaran victory Patel saw the beginning of a new agrarian revolution. His interest in politics had been kindled, as became abunduntly clear in the Provincial Political Conference organised by the Gujarat Sabha and presided by Gandhiji at Godhara. The conference appointed a permanent committee with Gandhiji as the President and Patel as one of the secretaries. He became a staunch follower of Gandhiji. From then on there was no looking back. Blessed with rare qualities of fortitude, integrity and an iron determination, Patel played an important role in the freedom movement.

Indomitable Personality

It was due to his sterling leadership and practical vision that the peasant movement in Gujarat became a success. It was in this struggle that the organisational capacity for which Sardar Patel was famous in the whole country became visible. He took over as the nascent nation's Home Minister at a very crucial juncture in history and devoted himself whole heartedly to ensure that the country which was already partitioned, remained intact and united.

Building a Union

On the eve of their departure, the British government announced that its paramountcy would lapse not only over the British territory but even over the native States. This meant that as many as 625 small and big native States would become independent like India and Pakistan. Consequently, the country would be divided into a number of small and big units.

Before embarking on this mammoth task, Sardar sought to ensure the stability of administration by forging a bridge of faith and confidence with the"Steel Frame". Most of the I.C.S. officers suspected that the Congress leaders, particularly Sardar in view of his past experiences with them, would have no faith in the I.C.S. But Sardar rose to the occasion and reposed total trust in their capability to serve the nation. He was, thus, able to win their unstinted support in the endeavour of nation building.

Attempts were afoot for finalising the standstill agreement with the States. It provided that the Central Government will be vested with powers of defence, foreign policy and communications even over the States. Travancore, Hyderabad and some other States declared themselves sovereign States and created hurdles in the agreement. On the other end, Jinnah with a view to tempt Jodhpur, Jaisalmer and other border States made them an unconditional offer to align with Pakistan on their terms.

POLITICAL SAGACITY

To find an amicable solution to this complicated situation, Sardar issued a statement to the princes wherein he appealed to their sense of patriotism and reiterated that the new States department in no way, desire to have supremacy over them. "If at all, any sense of supremacy is required, it would be with common understanding and for common good. We are at a momentous stage in the history of India. By common endeavour, we can raise the country to new greatness, while lack of unity will expose us to unexpected calamities. I hope the Indian States will realise fully that if we do not cooperate and work together in the general interest, anarchy and chaos will overwhelm us all great and small, and lead us to total ruin". The statement which amply reflected his statesmanship and political sagacity, removed whatever doubts lurked in the minds of the princes.

There was a popular agitation in Travancore and the State acceded to India. The Nawab of Bhopal could not take all this but when he realised that there was no alternative, he sent the instrument of accession duly signed to Sardar. A man of iron will and absolute fearlessness, Sardar Patel tackled the question of 550 and odd State territories and principalities in such a strategic manner which left even his wildest critics in complete amazement. Almost within a year he redrew the map of India with every princely State joining the Indian union and thus, forming part of the political stream of life that was endowed with cultural unity and harmony.

Intricate Situation

The intricacy of the situation can perhaps be gauged by the fact that there were 26 small States in Orissa and 15 in the Chattisgarh area of present Madhya Pradesh. It required skilful diplomacy on the part of Sardar Patel to persuade them to merge into bigger, more viable units. Even more ticklish was the case of Saurashtra where there were 14 big States, 119 small States and other units under different administrations totalling 860. The herculean task of merging all of them into the Saurashtra union was also accomplished by Sardar Patel.

Soon, State after State started acceding to the Indian Union. One after the other, Gwalior, Indore, Dhar, Dewas all accepted the advice of Sardar. Rajputana States followed the same. The Sikhs of Punjab also cooperated with the merger.

Even by August 15, Hyderabad kept aloof. Hence, Lord Mountbatten himself started negotiations. At one stage, it appeared that there was a settlement but Nizam found himself helpless against the pressures of Razakars. The Razakars started harassing the local public. Thus, when the situation went out of control, Sardar with the consent of the Governor General initiated police action. In 108 hours, the Nizam surrendered and Hyderabad acceded and merged with India. The Nawab of Junagadh accepted an accession with Pakistan. Sardar solved this complex problem in his own inimitable way and the Nawab and his Diwan left Junagadh for Pakistan.

Thus, the 'Yagna' for establishment of a united India undertaken by Sardar was completed with the merger of Hyderabad. Politically, India became one and united. In the history of India stretched over ages, India became one and united for the first time and that too without shedding a drop of blood. That was the marvel of the personality of Sardar. The sterling qualities of leadership he had shown as leader of Satyagraha, flowered in greater way in the administration of the country, maintenance of law and order and ensuring stability of the country and making it invulnerable.

11

Nehru Views on Indian Foreign Policy

India's Foreign Relations reflect a traditional policy of nonalignment , the exigencies of domestic economic reform and development, and the changing post-Cold War international environment. India's relations with the world have evolved considerably since the British colonial period (1757-1947), when a foreign power monopolized external relations and defense relations. On independence in 1947, few Indians had experience in making or conducting foreign policy.

However, the country's oldest political party, the Indian National Congress (the Congress—see Glossary), had established a small foreign department in 1925 to make overseas contacts and to publicize its freedom struggle. From the late 1920s on, Jawaharlal Nehru, who had the most long-standing interest in world affairs among independence leaders, formulated the Congress stance on international issues. As a member of the interim government in 1946, Nehru articulated India's approach to the world.

During Nehru's tenure as prime minister (1947-64), he achieved a domestic consensus on the definition of Indian national interests and foreign policy goals—building a unified and integrated nation-state based on secular, democratic principles; defending Indian territory and protecting its security interests; guaranteeing India's independence internationally through nonalignment; and promoting national economic development unencumbered by overreliance on any country or group of countries. These objectives were closely related to the determinants of India's foreign relations: the historical legacy of South Asia; India's geopolitical position and security requirements; and India's economic needs as a large developing nation. From 1947 until the late 1980s, New Delhi's foreign policy goals enabled it to achieve some successes in carving out an independent international role. Regionally, India was the predominant power because of its size, its population (the world's second-largest after China), and its growing military strength. However, relations with its neighbors, Pakistan in particular, were often tense and fraught with conflict. In addition, globally India's nonaligned stance was not a viable substitute for the political and economic role it wished to play.

India's international influence varied over the years after independence. Indian prestige and moral authority were high in the 1950s and facilitated the acquisition of developmental assistance from both East and West. Although the prestige stemmed from India's nonaligned stance, the nation was unable to prevent Cold War politics from becoming intertwined with interstate relations in South Asia. In the 1960s and 1970s, New Delhi's international position among developed and developing countries faded in the course of wars with China and Pakistan, disputes with other countries in South Asia, and India's attempt to balance Pakistan's support from the United States and China by signing the Treaty of Peace, Friendship, and Cooperation with the Soviet Union in August 1971.

Although India obtained substantial Soviet military and economic aid, which helped to strengthen the nation, India's influence was undercut regionally and internationally by the perception that its friendship with the Soviet Union prevented a more forthright condemnation of the Soviet presence in Afghanistan. In the 1980s, New Delhi improved relations with the United States, other developed countries, and China while continuing close ties with the Soviet Union. Relations with its South Asian neighbors, especially Pakistan, Sri Lanka, and Nepal, occupied much of the energies of the Ministry of External Affairs.

In the 1990s, India's economic problems and the demise of the bipolar world political system have forced New Delhi to reassess its foreign policy and to adjust its foreign relations. Previous policies proved inadequate to cope with the serious domestic and international problems facing India. The end of the Cold War gutted the core meaning of nonalignment and left Indian foreign policy without significant direction. The hard, pragmatic considerations of the early 1990s were still viewed within the nonaligned framework of the past, but the disintegration of the Soviet Union removed much of India's international leverage, for which relations with Russia and the other post-Soviet states could not compensate.

Pragmatic security, economic considerations, and domestic political influences have reinforced New Delhi's reliance on the United States and other developed countries; caused New Delhi to abandon its anti-Israeli policy in the Middle East; and resulted in the courtship of the Central Asian republics and the newly industrializing economies of East and Southeast Asia. Although India shares the concerns of Russia, China, and many members of the Nonaligned Movement about the preeminent position of the United States and other developed countries, different national interests and perceptions make it improbable that India can turn cooperation with these countries to its advantage on most international issues. Furthermore, although Cold War politics have ceased to be a factor in South Asia, the most intractable problems in India's relations with Pakistan—conflict over Kashmir, support for separatists, and nuclear and ballistic missile programs—still face the two countries.

Role of the Prime Minister

Nehru set the pattern for the formation of Indian foreign policy: a strong personal role for the prime minister but a weak institutional structure. Nehru served concurrently as prime minister and minister of external affairs; he made all major foreign policy decisions himself after consulting with his advisers and then entrusted the conduct of international affairs to senior members of the Indian Foreign Service. His successors continued to exercise considerable control over India's international dealings, although they generally appointed separate ministers of external affairs.

India's second prime minister, Lal Bahadur Shastri (1964-66), expanded the Office of Prime Minister (sometimes called the Prime Minister's Secretariat) and enlarged its powers (see The Executive, ch. 8). By the 1970s, the Office of the Prime Minister had become the de facto coordinator and supraministry of the Indian government. The enhanced role of the office strengthened the prime minister's control over foreign policy making at the expense of the Ministry of External Affairs. Advisers in the office provided channels of information and policy recommendations in addition to those offered by the Ministry of External Affairs. A subordinate part of the office—the Research and Analysis Wing—functioned in ways that significantly expanded the information available to the prime minister and his advisers. The Research and Analysis Wing gathered intelligence, provided intelligence analysis to the Office of the Prime Minister, and conducted covert operations abroad.

The prime minister's control and reliance on personal advisers in the Office of the Prime Minister was particularly strong under the tenures of Indira Gandhi (1966-77 and 1980-84) and her son, Rajiv (1984-89), who succeeded her, and weaker during the periods of coalition governments under Morarji Desai (1977-79), Viswanath Pratap (V.P.) Singh (1989-90), Chandra Shekhar (1990-91), and P.V. Narasimha Rao (starting in June 1991). Although observers find it difficult to determine whether the locus of decision-making authority on any particular issue lies with the Ministry of External Affairs, the Council of Ministers, the Office of the Prime Minister, or the prime minister himself, nevertheless in the 1990s India's prime ministers retain their dominance in the conduct of foreign relations.

MINISTRY OF EXTERNAL AFFAIRS

The Ministry of External Affairs is the governmental body most concerned with foreign affairs, with responsibility for some aspects of foreign policy making, actual implementation of policy, and daily conduct of international relations. The ministry's duties include providing timely information and analysis to the prime minister and minister of external affairs, recommending specific measures when necessary, planning policy for the future, and maintaining communications with foreign missions in New Delhi. In 1994 the ministry administered 149 diplomatic missions abroad, which were staffed largely by members of the Indian Foreign Service. The ministry is headed by the minister of external affairs, who holds cabinet rank and is assisted by a deputy minister and a foreign secretary, and secretaries of state from the Indian Foreign Service.

In 1994 the total cadre strength of the Indian Foreign Service numbered 3,490, of which some 1,890 held posts abroad and 1,600 served at the Ministry of External Affairs headquarters in New Delhi. Members of the Indian Foreign Service are recruited through annual written and oral competitive examinations and come from a great variety of regional, economic, and social backgrounds. The Foreign Service Training Institute provides a wide range of courses for foreign service officers, including a basic professional course, a comprehensive course in diplomacy and international relations for foreign service recruits, a refresher course for commercial representatives, and foreign language training.

The Ministry of External Affairs has thirteen territorial divisions, each covering a large area of the world, such as Eastern Europe and the post-Soviet states, or smaller areas on India's periphery, such as Afghanistan, Iran, and Pakistan. The ministry also has functional divisions dealing with external publicity, protocol, consular affairs, Indians abroad, the United Nations (UN) and other international organizations, and international conferences. Two of the eighteen specialized divisions and units of the ministry are of special note. The Policy Planning and Research Division conducts research and prepares briefs and background papers for top policy makers and ministry officials. The briefs cover wide-ranging issues relating to India's foreign policy and role in the changing international environment, and background papers provide information on issues concerning international developments. The Economic Division has the important task of handling foreign economic relations. This division augments its activities to reflect changes in the government's economic policy and the international economic environment (see Liberalization in the

Early 1990s, ch. 6). In 1990 the division established the Economic Coordination Unit to assess the impact on India of the Persian Gulf crisis arising from Iraq's invasion of Kuwait, changes in Eastern Europe and the Soviet Union, and formation of a single market in the European Economic Community (after 1993 the European Union), as well as to promote foreign investment. The Economic Division also runs India's foreign aid programs, including the Indian Technical and Economic Cooperation Programme, the Special Commonwealth African Assistance Programme, and aid to individual developing countries in South Asia and elsewhere. The ministry runs the Indian Council for Cultural Relations, which arranges exhibits, visits, and cultural exchanges with other countries and oversees the activities of foreign cultural centers in India.

The Ministry of External Affairs had a budget of Rs8.8 billion (for value of the rupee—see Glossary) for fiscal year (FY—see Glossary) 1994. The largest single expense was the maintenance of missions abroad: Rs3.8 billion, or close to 44 percent of the ministry's expenditures. Foreign aid totaled Rs1.3 billion, or 15.1 percent of the ministry's expenditures. The single largest recipient—as in most previous years—was Bhutan (Rs690 million), whose government operations and development are heavily subsidized by India.

OTHER GOVERNMENT ORGANIZATIONS

Besides the Office of the Prime Minister and the Ministry of External Affairs, there are other government agencies that have foreign policy-making roles. In theory, the ministers of defence, commerce, and finance provide input to foreign policy decisions discussed in cabinet meetings, but their influence in practical terms is overshadowed by the predominant position of the prime minister and his advisers. The armed forces are removed from policy making and have influence only through the minister of defence, to whom they are subordinate (see Organization and Equipment of the Armed Forces, ch. 10).

Only a limited role in foreign policy making is provided for India's bicameral Parliament (see The Legislature, ch. 8). Negotiated treaties and international agreements become legally binding on the state but are not part of domestic law unless passed by an act of Parliament, which also has no say in the appointment of diplomats and other government representatives dealing with foreign affairs. For the most part, because of the widespread domestic support for India's foreign policy, Parliament has endorsed government actions or sought information. The most important official link between Parliament and the executive in the mid-1990s is the Committee on External Affairs of the Lok Sabha (House of the People), the lower chamber of Parliament. The committee meets regularly and draws its membership from many parties. Usually it has served either as a forum for government briefings or as a deliberative body.

THE ROLE OF POLITICAL AND INTEREST GROUPS

Institutional connections between public opinion and foreign policy making are tenuous in the mid-1990s, as they have been since independence. Although international issues receive considerable attention in the media and in academic circles, the views expressed by journalists and scholars in these publications have little impact on foreign policy making. Interest groups concerned with foreign relations exist inside and outside Parliament but are less organized or articulate than in most other democracies. These organizations include such business groups as the Federation of Indian Chambers of Commerce International; religious groups, especially among Muslims; and various friendship or cultural societies promoting closer ties with specific countries. Among the latter are informal groups known as the "Russian" and "American" lobbies.

Opposition political parties often have more effectively articulated differing views regarding foreign policy, but even these views had little impact on policy making until the 1990s. Other than the Congress (I)—(I for Indira), only the communist parties, the Janata Party, and the Jana Sangh and one of its successors, the Bharatiya Janata Party (BJP—Indian People's Party), developed coherent platforms on foreign policy (see Political Parties, ch. 8). After the mid-1950s, the communist parties were broadly supportive of Indian foreign policy. At the beginning of Janata Party rule (1977-79), Prime Minister Desai promised to return to "genuine nonalignment." However, security considerations forced Desai and his minister of external affairs, Jana Sangh stalwart Atal Behari Vajpayee, to adhere to the foreign policy path carved out by the Congress (I)—nonalignment with a pro-Soviet orientation. BJP foreign policy positions differed most strongly from those of the Congress (I). The BJP criticized nonalignment and advocated a more vigorous use of India's power to defend national interests from erosion at the hands of Pakistan and China. The BJP also favored the overt acquisition of nuclear weapons. By the early 1990s, the rising political fortunes of the BJP had an impact on the conduct of foreign policy, forcing the coalition government of V.P. Singh, which depended on BJP support, to take a hard line in the Kashmir crisis in 1990. Pressure from the Congress (I) also had an impact on India's response to the Persian Gulf crisis.

Jawaharlal Nehru, the first Prime Minister of India, has been under criticism from different quarters all through. The reasons of this have been diverse for different political streams. Currently a section of intellectuals is blaming him for forcing India into Socialist Russia's camp. Their argument comes in the backdrop of Left's pressure not to sign the nuclear deal with U.S. One of the inherent arguments of critics of left and others is that not signing it will keep us away from the deeper friendship of U.S., the land of wealth and prosperity, whose alliance will benefit us a lot. In the complex scenario, which our world is, to support or oppose a political line is not easy enough. Also the left while opposing the nuclear deal has an attitude towards nuclear power, energy itself, which is not acceptable to most peace workers. While one will like that the left takes a stand which is totally against the nuclear energy and weapons, this is not the case. The major built in argument in their current stance in opposing the nuclear deal with U.S., is that this will push us in the camp of America, as its satellite ally and that will be the doom of India's foreign policy, which has been that of non alignment. There is a criticism that in the name of non-alignment India was tilted towards the Soviet block of yesteryears. Some also pose the question, is it possible in today's post 'Soviet regime' era to remain non-aligned, not to toe the singular pole of global power, America? Critics of Nehru's foreign policy undermine the fact that India's foreign policy was aimed at minimizing the domination of imperial powers in the World in general and India in particular. Though U.S. and USSR both were the superpowers, there was some difference in their attitude. While opposing the concept of global poles, one also recognizes that most of the countries which were coming out from the slavery of colonial powers needed to develop their industrial infrastructure. U.S. and U.K. were not for helping these countries with the technological support for this infrastructure while USSR partly helped India in building the foundation of industries, which in turn laid the base for the major industrial growth in times to come.

The contrast is most visible, when India is compared to its major neighbor Pakistan, which allied with America, and the difference in the in the trajectory of two nations is there for all to see. Pakistan, happy with the short cut of supply of industrial goods, as a US ally, free market, no license permit raj, a free economy to begin with landed up as a puppet economy in due course. India seeing that the industrialists here cannot set up the base of industrial growth on their own opted for the mixed economy, public sector, many of which were supported by the USSR, for heavy industries and private sector for the rest. The public sector was labeled as Socialist by all and sundry, without givingmuch thought to the concept of socialism, and was strongly opposed by the right wing economists, communalists and western imperialist powers. U.S. pursued its policies of supporting its minor allies by giving them weapons and ready made goods in return for various things including their loyalty to its global designs.

This struggle between capitalist and socialist model was in turn also a shadow boxing between the upcoming economies in the third world countries and the domination of western ex-colonial powers. U.S. and its allies, with their economic interests being jeopardized by the independent attitude and policies of the third world nations, the success of Soviet block in various fields, stepped up their ideological campaign against socialist ideology. What the Western powers wanted was that the third world should not set up their own industrial base and shouldremain dependent on the U.S. and its allies. The socialist policies in India meant essentially a public sector which will provide the base for growth of theindustries in general and lift up India's level from an economically dominated colony towards the possibility of an strong economy with own say. Interestingly as India began to chart its course after getting independence, the thinking of the big industrialists, which got reflected in the Bombay plan, and Nehru's fascination for growth model of the countries like USSR, which helped them come out fromthe clutches of feudal economic system, matched wellat this point of time. Industrialists did want the state to set up infrastructure industries. Here centralized planning and its accompaniments, which later became frozen and were unable to change with times and led to the demise of Soviet socialist economies.

India's charting independent path with the help of others, more particularly with USSR, in setting up theinfrastructure, helped it stand on its feet, while most of the countries which became independent at that time and opted for pro U.S. policies eventually marched towards banana republics, without the core, the base for their social and economic systems. Parallel to this economic path, India took the road of non alignment. The major opposition to the nonalignment policy came from the BJP and its predecessor Bharatiya Jansangh, who have always advocated thick relations with U.S. Politically their ideologueGolwalkar had listed communists as a threat to Hindu nation. So far the policies of RSS-BJP had always been in parallel to those of US. In late 1940s America was following MaCarthism and hunting communists. Around that time in the aftermath of Gandhi murder, Golwalkar was writing to the Sardar Patel that RSS workers should be released from jails and in turn they will help the government to contain communists. And today when U.S. is leading the global anti Muslim tirade, RSS is the lead organization spreading anti Muslim venom here in India.

USSR had no problems with the this non alignment course in foreign policy so it not only endorsed it but also kept giving core support to India for its indigenous growth. US annoyed with India's not accepting US patronage branded India's policies andnon alignment in general as the decoy for being proUSSR. India did keep supporting the national liberation struggles in Vietnam and many other nations to the annoyance of US. Today with the changed of World scenario, US is keen that India does not formanother block away from U.S., that's why its tilt towards India, away from its nurturing of Pakistan till date.

The basic dilemma which countries like India faced was weather to have 'ready made goods' or to produce the same the hard way. US wanted India to go on this readymade path, while India defied it and pursued independent path. The same got reflected in the foreign policy and attempt to stay clear of US-USSRblocks. It's another matter that USSR for its own strategic reasons was supportive of the non alignment. This had reflection in India's policy vis a vis Israel-Palestine. Israel, the hub of US interests, hand in glove with Western powers, dominated theregion, led to the exile of lakhs of Palestinians and installed an authoritarian state. Palestinians has been struggling for years to get back their own land. Here the aggressor-victim duel was clear and India did opt to keep away from Israel and kept supporting the cause of Palestine. US designs in the region wereprompted by the lust for oil, its policy is hegemonic, it theme, 'Oil is too important to be left to the Arabs'.

In this direction it overthrew the Government of Mossadeq in 1953, installed Raza Shah Pehlvi who in turn brought in superficial westernization notbothering to develop the country's infrastructure. The political rebellion against him was given a religious turn and so came in Ayatollah Khomeini. And with this began another chapter in World history. US projected it as signaling the rise of Islam as the 'new threat'to freedom and democracy and this slogan has been serving it in all its aggressions in the Middle East.

While condemning the foreign policy charted out by the builder of Modern India, Nehru, these ideologuesconveniently forget that it is important for the Worldas a whole to promote democratization amongst nationsand democratization within nations. The attempt tokeep India out of the stifling patronage of US is of paramount importance to ensure the building of democracy amongst nations, away from the hegemony of global bully. The current hegemonic, bullying policies of US, which are the major cause of violence in theworld, aggression on Afghanistan and Iraq was preceded by promotion of terrorist outfits, Al Qaeda and its clones, to fight Soviet occupation of Afghanistan. These need to be understood in their proper perspective. We do have to keep the goal that the world marches towards peace and harmony amongstnations and amongst people.

In the contemporary scenario it is easy and also fashionable enough to criticize Nehru's economic-foreign policy. It is difficult to see todaythat it is precisely these policies of public sectorand non alignment which resulted in India charting the course of democracy and economic growth. One is not saying that what has been achieved is satisfactory. The point is this was the comparatively better option, which did help us go some distance in the direction of industrialization-education in the givencircumstances. World is essentially global, how westrike a balance between external support and internal growth is a million rupee question. Blindly submittingto the wishes of super power number one, may land us up in the direction of many a banana republics or leadto the fate which our neighbor is seeing due toembracing the Uncle Sam.

Time that we build the non aligned movement again, time that we promote regional alliances, time that we see the vision of Nehru in its perspective of indigenous growth and global democracy away from thedomination of one or the other superpower. *India Foreign Relations*

India's Foreign Relations reflect a traditional poiicy of nonalignment, the exigencies of domestic economic reform and development, and the changing post-Cold War international environment. India's relations with the world have evolved considerably since the British colonial period (1757-1947), when a foreign power monopolized external relations and defense relations. On independence in 1947, few Indians had experience in making or conducting foreign policy. However, the country's oldest political party, the Indian National Congress (the

Congress—see Glossary), had established a small foreign department in 1925 to make overseas contacts and to publicize its freedom struggle. From the late 1920s on, Jawaharlal Nehru, who had the most long-standing interest in world affairs among independence leaders, formulated the Congress stance on international issues. As a member of the interim government in 1946, Nehru articulated India's approach to the world.

During Nehru's tenure as prime minister of India (1947-64), he achieved a domestic consensus on the definition of Indian national interests and foreign policy goals—building a unified and integrated nation-state based on secular, democratic principles; defending Indian territory and protecting its security interests; guaranteeing India's independence internationally through nonalignment; and promoting national economic development unencumbered by overreliance on any country or group of countries. These objectives were closely related to the determinants of India's foreign relations: the historical legacy of South Asia; India's geopolitical position and security requirements; and India's economic needs as a large developing nation. From 1947 until the late 1980s, New Delhi's foreign policy goals enabled it to achieve some successes in carving out an independent international role. Regionally, India was the predominant power because of its size, its population (the world's second-largest after China), and its growing military strength. However, relations with its neighbors, Pakistan in particular, were often tense and fraught with conflict. In addition, globally India's nonaligned stance was not a viable substitute for the political and economic role it wished to play.

India's international influence varied over the years after independence. Indian prestige and moral authority were high in the 1950s and facilitated the acquisition of developmental assistance from both East and West. Although the prestige stemmed from India's nonaligned stance, the nation was unable to prevent Cold War politics from becoming intertwined with interstate relations in South Asia. In the 1960s and 1970s, New Delhi's international position among developed and developing countries faded in the course of wars with China and Pakistan, disputes with other countries in South Asia, and India's attempt to balance Pakistan's support from the United States and China by signing the Treaty of Peace, Friendship, and Cooperation with the Soviet Union in August 1971. Although India obtained substantial Soviet military and economic aid, which helped to strengthen the nation, India's influence was undercut regionally and internationally by the perception that its friendship with the Soviet Union prevented a more forthright condemnation of the Soviet presence in Afghanistan. In the 1980s, New Delhi improved relations with the United States, other developed countries, and China while continuing close ties with the Soviet Union. Relations with its South Asian neighbors, especially Pakistan, Sri Lanka, and Nepal, occupied much of the energies of the Ministry of External Affairs.

In the 1990s, India's economic problems and the demise of the bipolar world political system have forced New Delhi to reassess its foreign policy and to adjust its foreign relations. Previous policies proved inadequate to cope with the serious domestic and international problems facing India. The end of the Cold War gutted the core meaning of nonalignment and left Indian foreign policy without significant direction. The hard, pragmatic considerations of the early 1990s were still viewed within the nonaligned framework of the past, but the disintegration of the Soviet Union removed much of India's international leverage, for which relations with Russia and the other post-Soviet states could not compensate.

Pragmatic security, economic considerations, and domestic political influences have reinforced New Delhi's reliance on the United States and other developed countries; caused New Delhi to abandon its anti-Israeli policy in the Middle East; and resulted in the courtship of the Central Asian republics and the newly industrializing economies of East and Southeast Asia. Although India shares the concerns of Russia, China, and many members of the Nonaligned Movement about the preeminent position of the United States and other developed countries, different national interests and perceptions make it improbable that India can turn cooperation with these countries to its advantage on most international issues. Furthermore, although Cold War politics have ceased to be a factor in South Asia, the most intractable problems in India's relations with Pakistan—conflict over Kashmir, support for separatists, and nuclear and ballistic missile programs—still face the two countries. India foreign relations-1995 loc data

Nehru's Bungling Foreign Policy

In one of the most incisive books written about the Tibetan situation, "The Fate of Tibet: When big insects eat small insects" by Claude Arpi, Mr. Arpi shows that not only did the Nehru government betray Tibet, but it also severely destabilized India's national security. In 1947, India had special rights in Tibet, a legacy of the British Raj. In 1949, though clearly aware of China's strategic interests in Tibet, Nehru failed to get any assurance from China that it would not invade the region. However, what is worse is the fact that he did nothing to prevent China from committing blatant aggression against a weak and peace loving Tibet, in 1950. Mr. Arpi provides proof in his book that argument that India was not in a position to halt Chinese aggression in Tibet in 1950 is erroneous and misleading. India had three trade agencies with military escorts within Tibet and with the support and help of the democratic world could have checked the communist aggression. Paying more attention to the Korean War than the happenings in Tibet, Nehru gave an open and clear invitation to China that she could unhesitatingly conquer the poor and helpless nation. In one stroke, Nehru's government was single-handedly responsible for converting the Indo-Tibet border into the Indo-China border. Nehru's reaction was expressed merely in words saying that the "Indian government was perplexed and disappointed by the Chinese Government's action".

Once Tibet was occupied, China undertook a gigantic road-building program between 1951-52. In 1959, Nehru said that it had taken his government over 2 years to notice that the Chinese had been building a road on the barren heights of Aksai-Chin plateau in Ladhak. In his book Mr. Arpi shows that Nehru and his associate Krishna Menon were fully aware of the Chinese encroachment in Aksai-Chin. In 1955, an English Mountaineer named Sydney Wignall deputed by General

Thimayya verified reports that the Chinese were building a road through Aksai-Chin. This basically shows that government did know about the encroachment but did nothing about it.

After the Chinese invasion, the Indian government was expected to spring to its feet and make an attempt to consolidate its borders with China. Instead Pandit Nehru started an era of false and pretentious friendship with the Chinese, which culminated in the famous Hindi-Chini-Bhai-Bhai campaign. The Chinese for one, never considered India as any friend, instead cleverly used Nehru's stupidity to further their interests. After having "gifted" Tibet to China, the fictitious fraternization concluded in the so-called "Panch-Sheel" Treaty. Prime Minister Nehru and the Chinese counter part, Chou-En-Lai, signed this treaty on April 29, 1954. "Panch Sheel" literally meant five norms of good conduct, viz. mutual respect for each other's territorial integrity and sovereignty, mutual non- aggression, mutual non-interference in each other's internal affairs, equality and mutual benefit and peaceful co-existence. China very diplomatically signed the treaty but was never intent on following its norms. The treaty was aptly described in the Indian Parliament by the Late Acharaya J.B. Kripalani, a former President of the ruling Congress Party, as "born in sin".

Bibliography

Anthony, J. Parel : *Hind Swaraj or Indian Home Rule*, Cambridge University Press, 1925.

Atri, Ajit : *Gandhi's View of Legal Justice*, New Delhi, Deep and Deep Pub., 2007.

Bakshi, S.R. : *Gandhi and the Congress*, New Delhi, Sarup & Sons, 1996.

Balan, K. : *Mahatma Gandhi and Jawaharlal Nehru : The Two Stalwarts Who Shaped India*, Delhi, Authorspress, 2002.

Chavan, Sheshrao : *Gandhi and Ambedkar : Saviours of Untouchables*, Delhi, Authors Press for Bharatiya Vidya Bhavan, 2001.

Dalton, Dennis : *Gandhi's Power : Nonviolence in Action*, New Delhi, OUP, 2001.

Das, Dipty Moyee : *Gandhi's Doctrine of Truth and Non-Violence : A Critical Study*, New Delhi, Dominant Pub., 2008.

Dash, Nibedita : *Life and Thoughts of Gandhi and Nehru*, New Delhi, Dominant, 2004.

Gandhi, Gopalkrishna : *Gandhi is Gone, Who Will Guide Us Now? : Nehru, Prasad, Azad, Vinoba, Kripalani, JP and Others Introspect: Svagram, March 1948*, New Delhi, Permanent Black, 2007.

Guha, Ramachandra : *India After Gandhi : The History of the World's Largest Democracy*, New Delhi, Picador, 2007.

Kapoor, A.N., V.P. Gupta and Mohini Gupta : *Cross-Currents of Indian History and Culture : The Gandhian Era*, New Delhi, Radha, 2007.

Kaushik, Asha : *Globalization, Democracy and Culture : Situating Gandhian Alternatives,* Jaipur, Pointer, 2002.

Kripalani, Krishna : *All Men are Brothers,* Navjivan Publishing House, 1937.

Kumarappa, Bharatan : *Nature Cure,* Navjivan Publishing House, 1944.

Mathur, J.S. : *Gandhi : In the Mirror of Foreign Scholars,* New Delhi, Gyan Pub., 2007.

Mishra, Anil Dutta : *Challenges of 21 Century : Gandhian Alternatives,* New Delhi, Mittal Pub., 2003.

Nanda, B.R. : *Gandhi : A Pictorial Biography,* New Delhi, Publications Division, 2005.

Ramesh S. Betai : *Gita and Gandhiji,* New Delhi, National Gandhi Museum, 2002.

Saxena, Sushil Kumar : *Ever Unto God : Essays on Gandhi and Religion,* New Delhi, Pragati for Indian Council of Philosophical Research, 1995.

Yadav, K.C. : *Gandhi : The Spirit of India,* Gurgaon, Hope India Publications, 2003.

Index

□□□